LOADS OF MONEY:
GUIDE TO INTELLIGENT STOCK MARKET INVESTING

COMMON SENSE STRATEGIES
FOR WEALTH CREATION

DR TEJINDER SINGH RAWAL

PARTRIDGE

Copyright © 2019 by Dr Tejinder Singh Rawal.

ISBN:	Hardcover	978-1-5437-0456-3
	Softcover	978-1-5437-0455-6
	eBook	978-1-5437-0457-0

All rights reserved. No part of this book may be used or reproduced by any means, graphic, electronic, or mechanical, including photocopying, recording, taping or by any information storage retrieval system without the written permission of the author except in the case of brief quotations embodied in critical articles and reviews.

Because of the dynamic nature of the Internet, any web addresses or links contained in this book may have changed since publication and may no longer be valid. The views expressed in this work are solely those of the author and do not necessarily reflect the views of the publisher, and the publisher hereby disclaims any responsibility for them.

Print information available on the last page.

To order additional copies of this book, contact
Partridge India
000 800 10062 62
orders.india@partridgepublishing.com

www.partridgepublishing.com/india

This book is dedicated to all the wise men and women:

    who investigate before they invest
    who wait before they criticise
    who listen before they speak
    who save before they retire
    who think before they write
    who earn before they spend
    who try before they quit
    who give before they die.

CONTENTS

Introduction ix

1   Money Matters 1
2   Start Early 9
3   Investment Strategy for Different Phases of Your Life 15
4   Rule Number 1: Never Lose Money 23
5   Why My Mutual Fund Investment Is Not Giving a Good Return 29
6   Thank You, Mr Speculator 37
7   Your Time Starts Now! 53
8   The Mindset of an Investor 65
9   Look for the Economic Moat in the Company You Buy 73
10 Cryptocurrencies, Gold, Diamonds, and Other Fads 85
11 Efficient Market Hypothesis 99
12 Some Investment Follies 107
13 Irrational Exuberance and Stock Market Bubbles 121
14 Value Investing 137
15 The Margin of Safety 159
16 Don't Trust Your Broker for Investment Advice 175
17 Why Dividends Matter 181
18 Stock Splits, Bonus Shares, and Buy-backs 189
19 What to Look for in Companies You Buy 199
20 Buying a Share Is Like Buying a Business 207
21 Understanding Financial Statements 213

22	The Financial Ratios. 233
23	Know Your Taxes 257
24	Market Timing Does Not Work. 265
25	Assessing Quality of Management 271
26	How Much to Diversify Your Portfolio? 281
27	Financial Crisis Equals Opportunities 287
28	Top Stock Market Myths 297
29	Putting It All Together 309

Afterword 321
Select Bibliography 323

INTRODUCTION

> Every day, self-proclaimed stock market "experts" tell us why the market just went up or down, as if they really knew. So where were they yesterday?
>
> **Author unknown**

Congratulations on picking this book. I will mentor you to a path of investment success, where lie riches beyond imagination. However, moneymaking is not easy, nor is it quick. If you picked up this book to find a get-rich-quick formula, you are in for a big disappointment. Let me warn you in the beginning: I have not written this book with the aim of changing your fortune overnight. I intend to instil in you the fundamental philosophy required to make money with high certainty and with the least risk. It is the same philosophy that has made Warren Buffett the most successful investor and one of the richest men in the world. I am here to help you with the wisdom of the best investors of all time, distilled and presented in a format that anyone with no previous experience in investment can master and profit from it. I guarantee you success; the techniques are simple, but I must warn you that this approach to investing requires considerable discipline.

Trying to get rich quick is dangerous. To make a fast buck, you need to speculate and gamble. You must play on leverage, either by borrowing money or by speculating intraday or by trading in derivatives. The price of derivatives is subject to violent fluctuations. A price surge results in quick, handsome gains, but a fall may wipe off your whole capital.

Investing is all about taming your emotions, and this book teaches you that. During my career in finance spanning over three decades, I have mentored hundreds of people, and I found that the best results are achieved not by people with a postgraduate degree in finance but by people who stay unperturbed in the face of noise in the market. I made my first investment at age of 16; that was 37 years back. Since then I have seen people come to market, make money, lose money, and vanish from the market, never to be seen again. You seldom come across old investors. Most of them have burnt their fingers when young and have decided that stock market was not their cup of tea. Or the stress took its toll, and they died young.

Over the years, I have seen the stock market mature from being an old world institution. Trading was done by open outcry on the floor of the Bombay Stock Exchange (BSE). The brokers gathered at a 'counter' where particular scrips were traded, and the buying and selling prices were cried out loud. When the deal was struck, the dealing clerks wrote the contract details with a pencil in a *kaccha sauda* book, which he later transferred to a *pukka sauda* book. Trading was the privilege of select South Bombay brokers.

After the trading session was over, BSE released a *bhav* copy, the quotes of trade done. To most of the investors, the rates became available the next day when the *Economic Times* published it. *Economic Times* would dedicate four pages to the share price of the earlier day, and the reason many people bought the paper was for that section.

Your broker gave you a contract note of the transactions executed on your behalf. There was no means of identifying the correctness of price quote: the broker often put the peak price shown in the *bhav* copy when you purchased it and the lowest price when you sold it. So you always ended buying at the highest rate and selling at the lowest; the difference was the 'gala' picked by the broker.

Then followed the long and complicated procedure of delivery of physical shares. Failed deliveries, signatures difference, forged share certificates, frivolous litigations—it used to be an ordeal completing the transactions. The market was inefficient: high transaction cost, a wide gap between the buying price and selling price, frequent disputes and litigations, a long settlement period. It was tough going through the process.

Come the 1990s, and things have changed 360°! Shares are in *demat* format now. Trading is terminal based and is no longer a prerogative of a select club. No failed deliveries. Transaction costs are low. Settlement is quick (and money can be credited into your account). The risk management system is robust. We can boast of a state-of-the-art trading platform now. You can open an online trading account and can trade from your laptop or even from your mobile phone. There is no better time to invest.

Has it helped investors make more money? No! Cost per transaction has come down, but total transaction cost has increased because of frequency of trading. Since you can trade at the click of a mouse (or on your mobile app even while travelling), impulsive buying and selling has increased. You buy at the speed of thought, and you sell at the speed of thought. You watch TV news and get panicky when you see the value of rupee sinking to a new low, and you sell off your holdings. In the earlier regime, it was the inefficiencies in the market and the tedious process of completing a transaction that prevented your impulsive and bad decisions. The technology has amplified it. Now you can make mistakes faster and lose money faster.

I have watched the developments for over thirty years. With every boom, new money enters the market. Kids with pockets full of money ride the momentum, make a quick buck, and invest more money. They even believe they have found the laws of success. Every share they buy keeps rising. They throw caution out the window. The most repeated quote echoing in the market over the years is "This time, it's different'.

Once they become more confident, they want to make money faster. The broker tells them to go for derivatives. Futures and options (F & O) are great for making more money with less capital. F & O are leveraged; you can buy larger quantities when buying F & O and thus make money many times over. They are great instruments for losing money. When the prices go down, it can wipe off every penny from your bank account. Sooner or later, the tide turns, and the worst happens. In the next trade cycle, another set of kids with money enter the market. Those who cannot learn from history are doomed to repeat it.

I wish for Indian investors to mature with the maturing of the market. They have not. That brings me to why I wrote this book.

Why I Wrote This Book

One of my missions in life is to take people to the road of personal riches and growth. If done following the approach outlined in this book, the success rate is 100%. The following pages contain a tested approach that the best investors in the world follow to make a fortune for themselves.

Successful investing requires a thorough understanding of investment philosophy. It requires discipline not to waver from the course when things are not happening the way you want them. This mental make-up is missing from most investors in the Indian market. Successful investors like Benjamin Graham, Philip Fisher, and Peter Lynch wrote great books on investments; but the Indian investor finds many of the principles enumerated there difficult to apply into the Indian context. Our stage of development is different, our business models are different, and applying the same principles to the Indian scenario is fraught with perils. We need to change them to make them work in our environment. This book fills that big void.

I am saddened to look at the status of retail investors in India. The Indian household savings rate, which is at 30%, is perhaps the highest in the world. I wish a large part of this savings went into equity. If they did, it would translate into higher corporate growth and could contribute to the growth of GDP. Most of the savings go to either low-income-yielding government bonds, bank deposits, real estate, or worse, gold and silver. Invested in equity, this money could grow, helping one meet life goals and retire comfortably. Few do that; the participation of retail investors in Indian equity is ridiculously low. Indian indices have performed well over the years, yet the fruits of development have not accrued to retail investors. Indian markets have benefited institutional investors, domestic and international.

In a population of 130 crore people, there are only 2 crore investors. Less than 2% of the population. How can one expect the people of a country to reap the fruits of progress if they don't take part? Compare this to USA, where 60% of the households own stocks. Of the 2 crore investors, 80% are in 10 cities, which means that except for a few people in top cities in the country, no one else is buying stocks. Painful statistics.

If you probe further, you'll find the picture grimmer. The real long-term investors are just a fraction of this 2 crore. Most of the 'investors' are not investors in the true sense of the term; they are speculators and day traders, out in the market for making a quick buck.

India is a success story of inclusive growth in many areas. The best example is the telecom sector. Indians own 750 million mobile phones. Almost every family, however poor it may be, has access to telecommunication. I wish the same revolution takes place in investment. India, with its high domestic savings, has a potential to rise to the top of the chart, if the savings get channelled the right way and the fruits of development become available to every person in the country. It is a mission, and it is heartening that you are partnering with me in the realisation of this dream. I promise you step-by-step mentoring in every aspect of investment. You need not repeat the mistakes that others did in the past. If life is trial and error, let the errors of others be your trial. You have got only one life to grow rich, to earn loads of money. I guarantee you that you can and you will, if you imbibe the principles enumerated here.

Let Us Know the Rules of the Game before We Start

We will use the term *value investing* often in this book. Value investing is a simple investment strategy that does not need an extensive background in finance (though knowledge of finance will help). The concept is simple, and you are already using it for buying stuff other than investments. It assumes that shares have intrinsic value, and if they are being sold at a discount to the intrinsic value, you may buy them. This is same as buying a refrigerator when available on a discount.

We will also use the term *intelligent investor* sometimes. The choice of the word *intelligent* is deliberate. To distinguish it from pure Graham-style value investing, we use the term *intelligent investor* to mean an investor who follows variants (for example, *growth investing*) of value investing. You may use the two terms synonymously.

A value investor is an intelligent bargain hunter. After reading the book, you may pick up the shade of value investing, which is in sync with your personality traits.

Value investing requires diligence and patience. It is a long-term strategy. You cannot expect your investment to rise overnight (it may sometimes, but that is not the idea behind investing). You may need to sit on your investment for a long time before the market recognises its intrinsic value and accords it the fair valuation.

Value investing is more like an art form. There is no mechanical formula to use, though you will use basic mathematics to filter out stocks and you need a great deal of patience. A stock may be an exciting investment, but unless available at a discount, you will not buy it.

I know that the Indian market has its own peculiarities; this book has taken care to discuss them. I use examples from the Indian market, though the readers in other countries should profit from it too.

The numbering system. India has its peculiar numbering system: 1 lakh means a hundred thousand, and you write it not as 100,000 but as 1,00,000; 1 crore means 10 million, and you write it not as 10,000,000 but as 1,00,00,000. Since the primary readers of this book are likely to be Indians, I use the Indian numbering system. This is also to pay respect to the country that gave the modern number system to the world. Readers in other countries may please ignore the placement of commas in the numbers to make them look meaningful.

Gender-specific terms. In this book, I use gender-specific terms to ease the text flow. Whenever a gender-specific term is used, it should be understood as referring to both genders. This is done for the purpose of making the text easier to read, and no offence or sexism is intended.

Stocks versus shares. There is a subtle difference between a stock and a share, so subtle that we can ignore it. In this book, I use both terms interchangeably. I also use the term *scrip* (another synonym) sometimes.

Personal Goals

Personal goals are often ignored while discussing investing strategies. Few of us are investing for the sake of investing. We invest because we have certain personal goals: to retire rich, to lead a more comfortable life, for our children's education, to travel the world, and so on. Investment is a vehicle to take you to your dream path. Before you plan your investment, you should know yourself well: what your present station in life is, where you want to be 10 or 20 years from now. If your day-to-day life depends upon the money you are investing, equity is not the right investment for you. Equity investment must be nurtured to grow. You should understand several points.

1. Have a firm belief in your investment philosophy

Your shares may decline 50% after you buy them. The hedge fund investor Ray Dalio, who had predicted the 2008 recession, cautions you to prepare yourself for big corrections. In a recent interview, he said there is a 70% chance that USA will get into a severe recession before the 2020 elections. If your current lifestyle depends upon your investments, you may find yourself in a soup if it comes true. If you are dependent on the investment, you will be under considerable stress and may not make a logical decision and may end up doing the worst: selling in panic when the market is low.

This also explains why you need to understand the principles contained in this book. Many a time, you need to be a contrarian in approach. One should see the intelligent investor at the buy counter rather than the sell counter when the prices see a sharp fall. This does not happen unless he has a full conviction of his investment strategy.

Investment needs time to mature, and only after you have invested for a long period will you generate sufficient reserves to depend upon your investments for your lifestyle requirements. A rule of thumb: if you might need the money in less than five years, it would be unwise to invest in stocks. Stock market success comes after you have invested for 10, 15, or 20 years or beyond.

2. In a bull market, people may think you are a fool

Frenzy and irrational exuberance drive the bull market. The price rise has nothing to do with fundamentals and is a pure demand–supply situation, a voting machine rather than a weighing machine. The *panwallah* who overhears the conversation between traders becomes an expert, and people seek his tips, because they work. In a bull market, the value investor doubts his own competence because the rise in his shares is lower than the surge in some shares with doubtful credentials. In the peak of the 2007–08 boom, newspapers carried the articles that value investing was dead, that the old medicine worked no longer. After the bubble burst, the value investors had the last laugh.

3. Be fearful when others are greedy, and be greedy when others are fearful

This principle should be at the back of the mind of every investor at every stage of his investing career. Though I have no interest (or competence) in predicting the market, I can often see the fall coming. When I see experts on TV debating if the Sensex at the end of next year would be 1,00,000 or 1,50,000 and there are no dissenting voices, I know too much air has filled the bubble.

We do not recommend market timing since our approach to investing is bottom up. Yet with sufficient experience in the market, you will gain insight into exuberances and excesses built into the system, and it may be unwise to buy at those levels. We also know some prudent investors can find great value buys at all market conditions.

Learn to swim against the current. The crowd behaviour is often illogical. In the book *The Art of Contrary Thinking*, author Humphrey B. Neill states: 'The crowd is most enthusiastic and optimistic when it should be cautious and prudent; and is most fearful when it should be bold.' Money is made by following your own investment creed and sticking to it in the face of adverse weather. Those who develop that discipline alone succeed.

4. If you are looking for a lot of actions, this book will disappoint you

The purpose of this book is to teach you tried and tested methods of investing which works in all situations. We are not here to provide you the thrill. Value investing is unglamorous. It requires a lot of hard work, reading, understanding, and analysing the financial statements and other information. Then you buy your shares and hold them for a long time. You don't have to sit on the computer screen every day nine o'clock in the morning. If the stock markets closed for three years after you bought your shares, you will stay contented, because you are not looking for day-to-day price fluctuations and have no intention of selling your investment soon. Nobel laureate Paul Samuelson puts it aptly: 'Investing should be like watching paint dry or grass grow. If you want excitement, take $800 and go to Las Vegas.'

If you find this boring, intelligent investing is not for you. But this is the surest way of making money in the long run, minimising risk at the same time.

5. Speculation and investment cannot go together

If you are a speculator, you cannot be an investor and vice versa. There are notable exceptions to this, but let me caution you against such a tendency. Either you speculate or you invest. Period.

6. The most important trait of an intelligent investor is the mindset

The investor remains unperturbed in the face of adversities. He remains unemotional even when he is 'in the money'.

Detachment is the key; an investor who can control his emotions in all situations rises up the ladder faster than someone with a high IQ who cannot control his emotions.

7. Knowing what you don't know is more useful than being brilliant

We should know what we don't know and either learn it or stay away from things beyond our circle of competence. The greatest investment folly is to get into an area of which you have no knowledge. It surprises me to see many people plunge in deeper water without learning to swim.

It Is Simple but Not Easy

These principles are simple to understand but requires discipline to put in practice. If you follow the investment principles outlined here, your investment is likely to beat all other asset classes, and it may be the safest investment choice. But it is not for everyone. Not many have the patience and the mindset of an intelligent investor.

Theoretically, it may be easy to detach emotions from your investment, yet when real money is at stake and when market behaves irrationally, few can control their emotions. It is difficult to stay unruffled in a falling market. It is difficult not to get tempted when the market rises every day and you can make money by buying anything and selling it the next day. Few people can distinguish between erratic price fluctuations and underlying fundamentals of the stock.

Value investors continue to be a thin minority the world over; the most successful investors in the world follow a version of value investing philosophy. There is not much guidance available to Indian investors. There are a few comprehensive books to take the investors to an advanced level, but there aren't enough number of seasoned investors willing to mentor others.

This book will change the course of life for many investors in India and put them on to the road to successful value investing. I wish it sets off a domino effect to create many successful investors who teach and guide others. We need enough trainers in the discipline of value investing. We need SEBI(The Securities and Exchange Board of India) to go beyond the basic investors' training and conduct programmes in value investing all over the country. Till they do that, let you readers be the mentors and educators guiding others to the path of success. Good money in the hands of good people does great things.

Value investing is difficult because you do things in ways different from the crowd. You ignore the latest investment fad. You swim against the current. You cannot do this unless you are in command of what you are doing.

My investment method is based on the fact that men seldom take rational decisions. The principles of economics do not deliver unless we combine them with behaviour finance.

Behavioural finance is a recent discipline which explains how investors can find anomalies in securities market and profit from it. Unlike what economics (since the times of Adam Smith) made us believe, people in the marketplace do not behave rationally. They base their investment decision on emotions and perceptions, which make no logical sense. Behavioural finance tries to find out the rationale behind irrational decisions.

In a perfect market, there is an unlimited number of buyers, an unlimited number of sellers, and both buyers and sellers have access to all the information. The equilibrium between the demand curve and the supply curve leads to price determination. However, markets are far from being perfect, the human being far from being rational. Every buyer has his own perception about the assets he is buying or selling, and his perception may differ from the way another buyer or seller perceives them. Classical economists believe that even if individual buyers or sellers behave irrationally, the aggregate cancels out the compensating errors and gives a rational price.

This seems ridiculous. How can the total of irrational behaviour become rational? What if instead of cancelling the errors, it amplifies it? The possibility of the latter is greater than that of the former. Just as two wrongs cannot make one right, many irrational transactions cannot create a logical behaviour.

Consider a particular fund being sold by two consultants. The first one tells his client that the fund has been returning 12% per annum for the past three years; what he does not tell his client is that the return is progressively reducing. The second consultant tells the client that the return has been going down. Obviously, the former consultant can make better sales than the latter, though both have presented the same statistics. This just proves that perfect information and rational decision-making are just a myth.

The groundbreaking work of psychologists Daniel Kahneman and Amos Tversky in the 1970s and the 1980s and the follow-up psychological research over the last three decades show striking insights on the complex ways in which the human mind operates. This research identified pervasive, deep-seated, subconscious biases and heuristics that occur in human decision-making and revealed a new perspective on why we behave as we do. While these revelations have their origins in psychology, they hold such important implications for the world of finance that Kahneman received the Nobel Prize in Economics.

The importance of behaviour in the marketplace is such a significant factor that, so far, six economists have been awarded the Nobel Prize on this subject. It surprises me to see how experts ignore the behavioural aspect when predicting the prospects of a company.

The prospect theory, propounded by Kahneman and Tversky, states that gains and losses are perceived differently by investors, as investors base their decisions on perceived gains and not on perceived losses. The joy of earning a rupee does not equal the pain of losing a rupee. The pain of losing money weighs twice as much in our mind as the happiness from gaining the same amount. This explains why people often get panicky and sell low in a falling market; they are not able to reconcile the fact that they are losing, and they feel that they must sell off and cut their losses. In contrast, when the market is rising, the investors feel that the higher the price goes in relation to their purchase price, the smaller the later gain. The whole concept of risk and reward is skewed. For the proof, you don't have to look beyond people around you who show panic in a falling market and sell when there is blood in the market instead of buying it.

Only those who can train their minds not to succumb will gain. You must train your minds to exploit this anomaly to your advantage. Armed with this unwavering investment philosophy, go shopping and bargain hunting when the panicky average investor is selling.

CHAPTER 1
Money Matters

"There are three faithful friends—an old wife, an old dog, and ready money."

Benjamin Franklin

I made a quick search for 'make money fast' on Amazon.com. It returned over 2,00,000 results. Go through any of those 2,00,000 books; you'll see each one will give a magic formula that may make you a millionaire with little efforts. Just follow the formula, and money will keep pouring in. I wish life were that simple.

If you are looking to make money fast, this book is not for you. This book is not for people in a hurry. It is for people willing to learn the principles they can apply and make their investment grow, taking advantage of market idiosyncrasies and the power of compounding. This book is for those who will understand that investing as a lifetime pursuit which will help them realise their dreams and create a stable source of income and wealth.

I did not search that on Google, for I could imagine, if over 2,00,000 books talked about making money fast, how many websites and blogs must talk about them. In the world of big data analytics and information overload, so much information is available to us by the click of the mouse or touch of the screen (or sometimes 'Hey, Siri, can you tell me ... ?') that it has become impossible to sift the usable knowledge out of the heap of incongruous data. One thing that has not improved in the online real-time era is common sense. It continues to be uncommon and, in some ways, has diminished. It seems to be losing out as people gain more and more technical skills but do not understand and appreciate the larger picture.

There are some equipped with common sense, the insight to think, and that trait is common to all successful investors. Contrary to what many of us would believe, you need not be an Ivy League graduate with a degree in finance and economics to make it big in the stock market. As we shall see later, such degrees may sometimes be a deterrent to you becoming a successful investor. As someone said, 'Two kinds of people seldom make money in the market—those who know nothing and those who know everything.' The market is the total of millions of random variables; the hubris that you know everything is a recipe for disaster.

Warren Buffett has always maintained that IQ is not the single defining factor in investment success. 'You don't need to be a rocket scientist. Investing is not a game where the guy with the 160 IQ beats the guy with a 130 IQ. Rationality is essential,' says Buffett. Even if you have an IQ of 160, Buffett says you should just 'give away 30 points to somebody else' because 'you don't need a lot of brains to be in this business'. He adds, 'What you do need is emotional stability. You have to be able to think independently.'

Charlie Munger says, 'It is remarkable how much long-term advantage people like us have gotten by trying to be consistently not stupid instead of trying to be very intelligent. There must be some wisdom in the folk saying "It's the strong swimmers who drown."'

Strong swimmers often get into trouble by swimming into deeper waters. Weak swimmers stay close to the shore. We are not interested in complicated mathematical equations that are designed to exploit short-term windows in the market to make quick money.

That strategy is stressful and bad for your heart and health. We are interested in simple strategies that have their foundation in avoiding stupidity. Being stupid would mean buying an asset without a margin of safety.

Pursuit of wealth without the right tools and temperament makes many first-time investors vulnerable. The other extreme is more than unwarranted caution, the quest for security. While the younger investors fall for the former, the older ones are often seen obsessed with the latter. Mindless pursuit of wealth is risky as throwing a die; the outcome may or may not be favourable. And if one round of throwing a die wins the game for you, it does not mean that, in the next round, you will win again.

Extreme caution makes you so risk-averse that you invest in government bonds, not realising that while your capital is guaranteed in government bonds, the return is sometimes lower than the rate of inflation. So while you take back your ₹1,00,000 after 10 years, you realise that inflation has eroded the value of your money, and the ₹1,00,000 that you received with a smile on your face is much less than the ₹1,00,000 that you invested.

Most of the newbies on the stock market think more activity means more return. They swing at every ball thrown to them, and the more they miss the balls, the more fervently they play. The more they play, the more it hurts. They find penny stocks attractive, because a stock selling at ₹3 yesterday might rise to ₹5 today, giving unbelievable returns, which seems too good to be true. In the long run, that return is too good to be true because it does not exist. The net consequences of buying penny stocks at the end of the year is unpredictable, it is akin to a lottery, with the probability of loss higher than the gain. By trading frequently, you end up making more money for your broker than for yourself.

Brokers are happy to have clients who are impulsive and who buy and sell at every noise that happens on CNBC. My broker tells me that he makes 10 times more money in commission from someone who has invested 1/5 of my investment (a difference of 50 times) because that investor trades every day and every churn of your capital must put a smile on the face of your broker.

The government is also happy with the guy who trades frequently: the profits from short-term gains are taxed at a higher rate. Long-term investors pay a reduced rate of tax, which they pay when they exit a particular investment. In effect, they are reinvesting the money saved from brokerage and the tax money, resulting in a higher return when compounded over a long period. Some of them, like I do, defer the tax payment almost indefinitely, as my favourite investment period is forever.

This is not to say all stock brokers and investment advisers are bad or ill-intentioned people. The problem is with the basic characteristic of the market: frequent trading is the norm rather than an exception. It is the investor who has to decide on his investment method. Buying and holding seem unglamorous in a world where information is delivered in a nanosecond from one part of the globe to another. In a supposedly efficient market, every piece of information is said to be factored in real time into the price quotation, so the temptation is to buy and sell at the point where a new piece of information is getting factored into the price quote. These frequent transactions are good for the market: more buyers and sellers, frequent trading, and a transparent trading platform all lead to Adam Smith's model of the 'perfect market'.

However, one must understand that being 'perfect' does not make the market efficient. Irrationality is the key feature of the market, and it is this feature that makes the market attractive to a long-term investor.

You need to have certain traits to be a successful investor. Your character, traits, and behaviour will be put to the severest test in the market. You need to have patience, common sense, perseverance, humility, foresight, desire to succeed, detachment, mindfulness, thirst for knowledge, and ability to admit your mistakes and learn from them. Most importantly, you must have a belief in yourself and in this investment method. Don't think I am asking for too much. I am not.

Most people already have these traits; they lie dormant in some of us. If I am your first mentor in investing through this book, nobody has told you before that it pays to sit cool on your investment instead of engaging in frantic activities. But if you know you are impulsive and short-sighted and short-term happenings make you lose your long-term focus, then I may not be able to help. Gut feeling is the worst feeling to have in the stock market. If you feel the stock market will be up based on your gut feeling, you will soon prove yourself wrong.

Even if you prove yourself right sometimes, it is not the way to invest. Research has proved that you often go wrong when you go by perception. By the time you form your opinion, the situation has already changed. We are bad in timing the market. In a bull market, whatever you predict comes true. Because everything is rising, what you predict rises. The bull market leads to overconfidence. You believe your gut feeling always proves right, a case of mistaking correlation for causation. One day the market refuses to follow your gut, and the whole edifice of paper profits you were building falls like a pack of cards.

Professional investors make the same mistake. It is interesting to find that when you talk to people about their investment philosophy, they say they are long-term investors. They are long-term investors only as long as the market is trending up. The day it falls, they panic and become short-term investors again, selling when the market is low.

We are advocating a scientific approach to discovering mispricing here and exploiting that to your advantage. The method is foolproof and works in all situations in the long run.

The good thing is that having these traits will make you successful not only in investing but in other areas of life and career too. It will enhance your personality, and you will rise above the mediocre. Good investors are great human beings too.

Money Is Abstract and Indifferent

You cannot touch money. It is abstract. You can touch a gold coin or a ₹100 note. A gold coin is metal, and the currency note a piece of paper—a piece of paper that gives you the right to meet ₹100 worth of obligation.

Money is neither good nor bad. It is the craving for money that could be good or bad. Money is indifferent to what or who you are. It doesn't care for your race, ethnicity, sex, or colour of your skin. It makes no difference to money if you are a criminal or a sage. Money treats us all equally. It is not biased. Whether you are a billionaire or a poor person, money does not pass any value judgment. It does not care if you are worthy of owning it or not.

Money Is Important

Whoever said money can't buy happiness didn't know where to go shopping. To quote W. Somerset Maugham: 'Perhaps the most important use of money—it saves time. Life is so short, and there's so much to do, one can't afford to waste a minute; and just think how much you waste, for instance, in walking from place to place instead of going by bus and in going by bus instead of by taxi.'

Creation of Wealth Is Easier than You Think

Every year thousands of people join the millionaires' and the billionaires' club. If you look into their background, few of them were born with a silver spoon. Some of them were lucky: their rich uncle kicked the bucket, leaving no other legal heir, or some won a lottery. But a large majority of them worked their way up.

The subjects of this book are the people who used proven ways to create wealth and reap success. This book picks up the distilled information from the lives of successful investors and presents it in a ready-to-use format.

We offer no abracadabra. The book is not about shortcuts; it is not about speculation and gambling. It does not promise to teach something that the author has discovered buried in a pot under the sea. It teaches the principles of success in wealth maximisation. The principles are there in public domain, principles which people like Warren Buffett have put into practice and made it big. Though not magic, they work with 'magical' precision if applied faithfully.

CHAPTER 2

Start Early

The best time to plant a tree was 20 years ago.
The second best time is now.

Chinese Proverb

As an adviser and mentor to many people, I am often asked to say in simple terms how to create great wealth. There is no secret formula involved here. It is no rocket science and is one of the easiest things to understand and learn. However, it is strange that not many do it. The formula is: start early. Start investing your money at the earliest; let the magic of compound interest create a sizeable wealth for you.

Though the price of real estate has come down considerably in recent times, for most Indians, buying a house remains a difficult financial decision. It may mean committing substantial part of your future earnings also, especially if you are considering buying a property in one of the metro cities. Children's education is an expensive affair these days, and depending on the stream chosen, it may leave you poorer by ₹50 lakhs or even more. Marriages continue to be expensive affairs in India, and people usually end up spending way beyond the justifiable limits. Add to this the contingencies, the medical emergencies, the lifestyle-related expenditure (tours abroad, phones, cars), and it looks like a big gap between saving and the required amount.

While it is a daunting task, it is achievable. Invest early—the earlier, the better—so that the multiplier of compound interest can multiply your capital many times over. Once it gets going, the magic is unstoppable: ₹1 becomes ₹2, ₹2 becomes ₹4, ₹4 become ₹8 . . . And soon your money grows at an astonishing rate of growth even when invested in securities that grow at a low annual rate of growth.

A young professional who has just started his career will find low investible surplus, and he would think it is better to spend that small sum instead of investing it, as a small savings might not contribute much to his long-term corpus requirement. This is the biggest mistake he could make. Sow the seed early, water it regularly, and I assure you, the crop you reap will be stupendous. It will be higher than the return of his friend who starts later even if the latter invests more money.

Most people procrastinate. Some are inspired by the 'eat, drink, and be merry' philosophy, while many others remain ignorant. People don't know what they could have done with their money. They don't realise their investment options until it is too late and until it spirals into a crisis.

A typical procrastinator may be seen discussing the macroeconomic situation which is 'grim', 'recessionary', 'bleak', or 'terrible' and is waiting for the situation to improve so he can invest. If he is not concerned about the macroparameters, he is not able to decide on which stock to invest in. He sits on cash which earns zero return in absolute terms (and negative return when inflation is considered) or burns cash since there is no worthwhile investment vehicle available.

Investing early has interesting consequences for you. You may retire early while your colleagues are still struggling to make ends meet. Even if you reduce the contribution at a later stage of your life, it may not make a significant difference to your corpus, which will have grown to an impressive figure by then. Your twenty-year-old tree will have developed enough roots and branches to stand on its own by then.

Some readers may realise their folly but will have already lost the precious time. The lost time cannot be regained. What then is the optimum solution for you? To make up for the lost time, you will now need to invest a larger quantum. You may have to curtail certain expenditures or increase your sources of income to match up the pace of the tortoise that started slow and steady twenty or thirty years back and is now way ahead of you in the race.

Einstein is said to have called compound interest the eighth wonder of the world and said, 'Those who understand it earn it, and those who don't pay it.' For the magic of compound interest to work, the baseline needs to reach a certain scale. Compounding is parabolic. The longer the time you give for the base to build, the higher it will take you. Few people have enough patience or foresight to realise this. If you want the magic of compound interest to work for you, you must start at the earliest and build the base early so that the ball gets rolling on its own. If you have understood the importance of compounding in the early stage of your career, nothing can stop you from becoming rich. Even a modest income, if invested and stays invested for a long period, can make you wealthy beyond imagination.

Warren Buffett gives the example of the *Mona Lisa* to explain the power of compounding. King Francis I of France had asked Leonardo da Vinci to paint the *Mona Lisa* at a cost of $20,000. It holds the Guinness world record for the highest known insurance valuation in history at $100 million in 1962. This figure looks astounding until you consider that if $20,000 had been invested at 6% per annum, it would have grown to $1 quadrillion by 1962; that's 3,000 times the national debt. He says, 'If Francis had kept his feet on the ground and he (and his trustees) had been able to find a 6% after-tax investment, the estate now would be worth something over $1,000,000,000,000,000. That's $1 quadrillion or over 3,000 times the present national debt, all from 6%. I trust this will end all discussion in our household about any purchase or paintings qualifying as an investment. However, as I pointed out last year, there are other morals to be drawn here. One is the wisdom of living a long time. The other impressive factor is the swing produced by relatively small changes in the rate of compound.'

In 1987 when I started my practice, I had purchased two computers with MS-DOS operating system from Wipro for ₹45,000. (For those who are curious to know, one of them had two floppy drives and no hard disk. You put the operating system floppy in drive A, and the data and application floppy in drive B. The other one had a floppy drive and, thankfully, a 10 MB hard disk. The computers had a 128 KB RAM.) If instead of buying the computers, I had bought Wipro shares for ₹45,000, they would have been worth more than ₹400 crores now, after considering bonus, splits, dividends, and price rise! That is loss of profit!

CHAPTER 3

Investment Strategy for Different Phases of Your Life

A butterfly does not return to a caterpillar after it is mature. We must learn to grow and evolve into a stronger, wiser and better version of ourselves. Life occurs in stages and taking a step at a time is key to learning and growing.

Kemi Sogunle

Financial analysts like to divide your life into different phases and suggest the right mix of assets at different stages. Your capacity to take risks and the requirement of funds would be different at different stages of your career, but the advice given is often too simplistic and kind of a one-size-fits-all model, ignoring your individual situation, and often the advice is the exact opposite of what you should do in that phase of your life.

By now you have understood that equity as an asset class beats all other assets if you have invested for a long time. Equity is a risky asset class for a 3-year time frame, and the return may be erratic and unpredictable. If you stay invested for 5 years, fluctuations even out, making your return more predictable than before. If you remain invested for 10 years, equity is likely to overtake any other asset class, with a low standard deviation, making it perhaps less risky than other asset class. Hold it for 20 years and more, and equity now becomes a powerful weapon, the lowest-risk compounding machine that magically keeps multiplying itself every few years, beating all other investments in terms of risk and reward. So your asset allocation at various stages of your career will also be impacted by how long you have been investing and what quality of equity assets you have created in your portfolio.

Based on this, let us consider the investment options in various phases of your life and also understand why conventional wisdom is wrong. The *you* in the ensuing discussion is someone who has read this book and is an informed investor.

When You Start Your Career

When you start your career, you are perhaps living off all your income. The excitement of starting your career is great, and you are no longer dependent on your parents for money. This is the stage of instilling discipline that will stand by you for the rest of your life. Understand that every rupee you invest during this stage of your career will multiply manifold. There is a big difference between the money compounded for forty years and the money compounded for, say, fifteen years at the latter part of your career.

You Are Building Your Wealth

Money you earn can be saved or spent. If spent, it is gone forever; if invested, you are curtailing present consumption so that the amount is set aside for future gratification. It is time to learn the balance between the present and the future. Learn to make a budget, understand your sources of income, and understand the nature of your expenses. Make sure that in no case will your expenses exceed your income.

Track your expenses. Learn to record your transactions. You can avoid a lot of wasteful expenditure if you budget and record your transactions.

Plan Your Retirement

Yes, this is not a misprint, and I mean it in all seriousness. It is time to contribute to your corpus, which you will build brick by brick into a mighty edifice. Learn to create a surplus out of your budget every month, and however small that may be, it must be invested. The best place to invest your money at this stage of your career is equity. Invest and let the power of compounding take care of the rest.

Buy a House

If you don't own a house, the first asset you should think of acquiring should be a house. Taking a loan is not a good idea, but I would like to make an exception for the purchase of a house. Though property prices have cooled off during the last decade, in India, houses are still disproportionately priced in terms of a multiple of the annual income of an average middle-class person. The interest on property loan is less than any other loan, as it is secured against the mortgage, and the interest paid is tax deductible. So if you do not already own a house, one priority at this stage of your career should be to buy one.

Your Children's Education

Your children's education, from early education to college, can be the next goal. Conventional wisdom suggests less-aggressive asset allocation, meaning adding debt components (bonds, fixed deposits, or any other interest-bearing securities), and analysts give a ballpark allocation of 60 : 40 or similar. This generalisation may not help in your individual case, and my suggestion here does not differ from the earlier: keep investing as much in equity as possible.

Equity market is cyclical, and it may be at the bottom of a trade cycle when you need the money. Still, staying invested in equity makes a better deal for many reasons. First, while cycles occur, predicting the trend is near impossible. For two or three years in the down cycle, your shares may be down by as much as 20% to 30% or in a black swan situation even more from the previous peak. However, if you are invested for a long time, the low may still be higher that your purchase price, and more likely, you may still be 'in the money'. Second, historically equity has been generating a higher return than bonds. The cumulative higher return is likely to accumulate more money in your investment kitty. You may be wiser to see off a part of the equity to finance an event (your daughter's college education, for example) than by making a targeted investment in low-interest debt.

Your asset allocation, if skewed towards equity, is likely to give better returns than any other mix.

Retirement Planning

Retirement planning has to continue to be important all your working life. You need to keep adjusting your goal in light of changing circumstances so that your investment remains worthwhile. One important, though often ignored, factor to be considered here is that life expectancy is on the rise. Average life expectancy in India is around 70. If you are an educated urban dweller with good hygiene standards and access to good medical facilities, you are likely to live much longer. Those who allocate a higher portion of their assets to bonds in their forties and fifties often face a situation where inflation eats into their principal. Being risk-averse, they move away from 'risky' equities into the 'safe haven' of fixed-income securities, only to find that the capital may not last their lifetime. The conventional wisdom fails here too. The best solution is to invest early, invest in an inflation-beating asset class like equity, and stay invested as long as possible. I will keep reiterating at the cost of repetition that equity as an asset class, if invested following the principles enunciated in this book, will not fail. Equity in the long run is safer than bonds.

If you are at a stage of your life where the mortgage has been paid off and all your major liabilities (in Indian context, it may also include children's marriage) have been taken care of, it is time to review your retirement corpus. If there has been a drain or some shortfall, it is time to top it up. The best strategy is to invest early so you don't have to provide top-up allocation later, yet it makes sense to review the situation at the availability of additional funds and add to it when you need to.

Succession Planning

Succession planning should go hand in hand with wealth creation. Draw a will and define how your estate will be distributed after you. This process should start at an early stage of your life and should be reviewed every few years.

When to Sell Your Investments

While this topic has been covered elsewhere in this book, here is a one-line answer: when you need the money. Nothing can be simpler than this.

To sum up, we started with rejecting the one-size-fits-all solution. The typical life cycle depicted here is not likely to apply to you in toto. It may not apply at all. Your situation may differ from the one depicted here. Your risk appetite may be different. This discussion forms the philosophical basis; you must design your own product mix tailored to meet your unique requirements.

CHAPTER 4

Rule Number 1: Never Lose Money

Rule No. 1: Never lose money. Rule No. 2: Never forget rule No. 1.

Warren Buffett

Safety of Investment

The two extreme ends of the spectrum are, first, the people who take reckless risks and consider the stock market to be a get-rich-quick machine and, second, the people whose only aim in life is to protect their capital, to keep it safe and secure even if that means lower return on investment.

It is the latter category we discuss here. Ironically, the former category are people who take an unwarranted risk, burn their fingers, and become so defensive they often shift to the other extreme of the spectrum.

₹100 invested in government bonds for 20 years at a compounding rate of 6% per annum will grow to ₹320 before adjusting for taxes. Reduce taxes, and the amount will be much lower. Take into consideration the rate of inflation, and you'll soon realise you have been taken for a ride. Your money has grown only marginally if the rate of inflation has been low; if the inflation rate is higher, perhaps inflation has eaten into your capital, and what is left is less than what you have invested.

Equity has been growing historically in India at 13—14% per annum over a 20-year window. The amount of ₹100 invested in equity over the same period will have grown to ₹1,150 (taking 13% compounding). With the tax incidence on equity being much lower and applicable only at the point of exit, you can appreciate the difference between the two kinds of investment.

Chasing wealth recklessly may lead you to disaster; chasing safety is no less precarious. In fact, disaster in chasing safety is quantifiable and is certain. *The biggest risk is not taking any risk.* The intelligent investor understands that when he invests in profitable companies and stays invested for a long period, the longer he stays invested, the more he can mitigate the risk. For him, risk and return cease to be two contradictory terms. He can defy the conventional wisdom that the higher the risk, the lower is the return. He can now operate in an environment of low risk and high return.

It's not that prudence is bad. Certainly not. Safety is your goal, but know that safety does not mean parking your money in securities, which promise the return of capital but do not grow. The equity market is volatile in the short run, and your investments may fall by 20% in just a few days, it is also true that you cannot time the market and may buy at the peak where the prices may not hold for long and may head south after you buy it. There are years when the market continues to be low. Worse, there are years when the market continues to fall. You should invest more, not less, during such periods of uncertainty. Warren Buffett says the best time to buy is when there is blood in the market. Buy when everybody else is selling, and sell when everybody else is buying. You will stand out as an intelligent investor.

When there was a bloodbath in the market in the aftermath of the 2008 crisis, these words of wisdom came from Warren Buffett:

> A simple rule dictates my buying: Be fearful when others are greedy, and be greedy when others are fearful. And most certainly, fear is now widespread, gripping even seasoned investors. To be sure, investors are right to be wary of highly leveraged entities or businesses in weak competitive positions. But fears regarding the long-term prosperity of the nation's many sound companies make no sense. These businesses will indeed suffer earnings hiccups, as they always have. But most major companies will be setting new profit records 5, 10, and 20 years from now.

This is how great minds think, and this is how you create wealth. Applied in an Indian context, India is a robust economy, growing faster than most other economies in the world and is likely to grow at a steady pace over the next 10, 20, or 30 years. Short-term hiccups will occur, and they might prove to be a setback to the market. But know that the long-term trend is positive and the country will continue to grow stronger. Those short-term hiccups are not to be looked upon as impediments to wealth creation. They are an opportunity for greater wealth creation.

People will continue to panic at every bad news; the intelligent investor must use that panic as an opportunity. Every intelligent investor should remember these words as the gospel truth: 'Be fearful when others are greedy, and be greedy when others are fearful.'

Holding shares for a long period evens out fluctuations, and the low years are likely to be an advantage to you. And if you extend the holding period of your investment to a period beyond 10 years, stocks become as safe as bonds; if you extend it beyond 20 years, stocks become safer than any other investment.

This is the reason you should be investing early on. Stay invested with a long-term perspective, and since you will invest with a long-time horizon, your investment should be in businesses which continue to grow over a long period. This eliminates penny stocks and companies with uncertain business models or businesses with poor quality management.

Remember, you are not buying tickers. You are not buying 'tips'. You are buying a thin slice of ownership in a great business. If you are to hold on to an investment for a long term, you will need to test the business the same way a potential owner of a business does. You will examine the cash flow, return on capital employed, ratio of debt to equity, and a few more ratios, much like the owner of a business does. We will discuss the key financial analysis in another chapter, and rest assured that it is easy and requires nothing more than basic arithmetical skills. Here, suffice it to say that you need to have an owner's mindset when you buy your shares, amount to be invested notwithstanding. The criteria remain the same for a ₹1,000 investment and for a ₹1 million investment.

To sum up, with low risk comes low return, sometimes so low that after adjusting for inflation, you are left with nothing. High risk is associated with a high return; however, following the principles explained in this book, you can attain something which defies conventional logic: you can mitigate risk and still get higher returns.

CHAPTER 5

Why My Mutual Fund Investment Is Not Giving a Good Return

If you don't like the idea that most of the money spent on lottery tickets supports government programs, you should know that most of the earnings from mutual funds support investment advisors' and mutual fund managers' retirement.

Robert Kiyosaki

The mutual funds industry in India has had a chequered history. Unit Trust of India (UTI) was established in 1963 by an act of parliament. It was set up by the Reserve Bank of India and functioned under the regulatory and administrative control of the Reserve Bank of India. In 1978 UTI was delinked from the RBI and the Industrial Development Bank of India (IDBI) took over the regulatory and administrative control in place of RBI. The first scheme launched by UTI was Unit Scheme 1964 (US-64).

UTI, with what looked like a big amount in those days, collapsed in 2001. Investors felt betrayed. Between 1994 and 1995, UTI invested in 285 companies that ceased to exist in a few years. Between 1991 and 1996, UTI had invested ₹6,222 crore in shares of PSUs. The US-64 scheme alone had put in ₹4,722 crore in PSU shares. The market value of these investments was less than half 5–10 years later.

UTI kept flouting all the rules in the rule book. For example, dividends should always be paid out of earnings. For three years, during 1994–97, it took ₹2,221 crore out of its reserves just to maintain a high dividend of 20–26%. (Can you see the folly here? That's 20–26% dividends in an economy which was growing at a sluggish rate of growth!) This way, the UTI created an artificial perception of its financial health (aka window dressing). The consequence: on 30 June 1998, UTI had eaten into all its reserves, and now the balance sheet showed a reserve of −₹1,098 crore. UTI's largest ever investment in one company was in Reliance Industries (RIL). In 1994 it invested ₹1,073 crore in RIL through a 'negotiated off-the-market deal' at ₹385 a share.

The value tumbled to a low of ₹77.50 in January 1996. ₹32 crores (a big sum in those days) were invested in a company that had changed its name three times (no prize for guessing, the latest name had to do with cyberspace) to encash on the dot-com boom. All investments made by UTI went into companies with powerful promoters who could influence UTI management to invest with them. As many as 50 private placements were made in companies belonging to dubious but politically powerful promoters, most of them in media, dot-com, or technology. None of those companies exist now.

To cut a long story short, India's first rendezvous with mutual funds was that of cheating, political scam, creative accounting, window dressing, nepotism, and corruption. The government-run fund was soon dead. UTI is better remembered by what the acronym means in medical parlance: the urinary tract infection.

Post liberalisation, LIC and banks were allowed to float mutual funds in the first phase, and in the second, in 1993, private funds were allowed to operate. Now there are over 11,000 mutual fund schemes in India. Since most of these schemes (where focus is equity or a mix of equity and debt) invest in companies listed on NSE, it will be interesting statistics to know there are 2,000 companies listed on NSE. Some companies out of these may not be worthy of investment or may not meet the legal or policy criteria of many funds, and this makes the domain too small.

Mutual funds are proxy vehicles. Since you do not have the time or resources to research stocks and to keep track of your investments on a day-to-day basis, you trust a third party, which is regulated by the government (SEBI) and which employs managers with professional qualifications. This gives you confidence, and you believe the judgement of a pinstripe-coat-wearing professional from a top B-school with an excellent ability to manipulate the spreadsheet will be superior to that of yours. Mutual funds also save you from the stress associated with the stock market, the anxiety of watching daily price movements.

Unfortunately, all this does not result in higher returns to the investor because:

1. Most mutual funds underperform in the market. Track the stock market index and track the average mutual fund; you'll find that mutual funds do not keep pace. Put in simple words, if you buy the index (either directly putting all index shares in the basket or buying an index fund which invests only in index), you will make more money than the money that comes from the intervention of professional money managers with a high IQ.

2. Few fund managers can afford to swim against the current. If a sector is languishing and is considered a bad investment by most

brokers, it may be a great investment idea for you but not for the fund manager. Even if he knows it is a tempting idea, if he buys it and it shows no growth in the next quarter or the quarter after that, his credibility as an analyst will be at stake. A stock which is out of favour may remain out of favour for many quarters and years. He must buy a share that does not show contrary trends in the short term, else he faces the music.

If he discovers a stock that is a true hidden gem lying in the dust of small-caps or mid-caps, barely noticed by the market, can he lap it and wait for it to turn into a multi-bagger? In all probabilities, he cannot. Many of such investments may take a long time to fructify; some of them may not grow at all, but if one out of ten becomes a ten-bagger, it takes care of ten that did not grow. Since the timeline for the maturation of these investments is obscure, no fund manager can take the risk of facing the music when his investment drags the fund value down. So what does he do? He'll buy the likes of Tata Steel or Asian Paints or ACC. This won't raise the eyebrows, and if ACC falls, he does not lose his job. Nobody will question the buy decision; they may even ask, 'What is wrong with ACC?'

The greatest tribute to the amateur investors is paid by the manager of one of the largest funds, Peter Lynch, when he says he continues to think like an amateur as frequently as possible.

3. Some funds may impress you with the track record of a particular scheme; know that the statistics are deceptive. There are 11,000 schemes in the market, and the annual return on these schemes vary from −20% to +50%. (This is randomised. One year with +50% does not mean that next year it will be same scheme with 50%; it might be another scheme.) It is easy for any fund manager to pick a few good schemes that have delivered a great return for a couple of years. This is called 'survivorship bias' (i.e. the logical error of concentrating on the people or things that

made it past some selection process and overlooking those that did not because of their lack of visibility). It is easier to showcase your best ware, keeping the ugly ones wrapped under the carpet.

4. Some people try to avoid this survivorship bias by diversifying among mutual funds, which is buying 10 different schemes instead of 1. Know that with 11,000 schemes in existence, all chasing a few scrips, this diversification is an exercise in futility.

5. Mutual funds can't beat the market because with assets of ₹10,52,757 crores (as of March 2015, that's the latest figure the Association of Mutual Funds in India has on its website). They are the market.

6. The high cost of running the funds is the main factor why funds cannot beat the market. As explained above, funds are managed by people of high calibre. However, the administrative cost of running the funds often drags the revenue down. An investor in equity can directly invest 100% of his investible money.

7. There is always the fear of redemption, and funds need to provide for that. Most people get panicky when the market falls, and when they should up their holding, they withdraw. In contrast, most of the money that becomes available to fund managers is when the markets are in a state of euphoria. They are forced to buy high and sell low.

8. Some funds indulge in dubious practices. UTI is the extreme example; things have improved since then but not completely corrected. Performance of fund managers is traced quarter on quarter and year on year. He must deliver at every reporting period. If the performance remains depressed, the fund manager often resorts to unethical practices, like selling loss-making investments at the end of a quarter so that it does not show as

a blot in the statements. Window dressing is also common in order to show financial information that's better than the actual.

9. We do not have long-term statistics from India, so I will draw this conclusion from USA data, and I presume the conclusion does not change. US$10,000 invested for 40 years in Treasury bills (government bonds) returned $48,000. The same amount invested in bonds during the same period gave a return of $102,800; in average mutual funds, $212,000; and in S & P 50 (the stock market index), $650,000.

10. Most money managers get paid as a percentage of assets under management. They must expand the asset base to earn more incentives. The objectives of the money managers are not aligned to that of the retail clients.

11. Since the client is likely to shift away from the worst performing funds, fund managers try to remain within the average, underperform the average, and the client moves away. There is no incentive to beat the average. By its very nature, fund business entails perfunctory performance.

The verdict is clear, mutual funds underperform. If you can stay invested in equity for a long term, following the long-term investing principles, you are likely to get a market-beating return; if you are not confident of your abilities to handle it, go for index funds. Go for mutual funds only if you want to stay just above the government bonds' rate of return.

Index fund is good for an average passive investor but not for the readers of this book. Indexing has a fundamental flaw: it is self-defeating. Index is the vehicle of choice for the efficient market hypothesis followers, who believe that the index is more efficient than individual shares. If more and more people buy index, the market should move towards a higher level of efficiency. Less and less people will now resort to fundamental and technical analysis. If every investor buys index, the price of the share prices will never change in relation to each other because nobody will be left out to offer a different price, eliminating all mispricing. This will kill the stock market.

'Mimicking the herd invites regression to the mean,' as Charlie Munger would say. He means that if we buy index funds, we are content with the average. However good the index will do, you remain with the index, because you have chosen your investment vehicle to drive at an average speed. If you want to beat the average, drive a different vehicle.

CHAPTER 6

Thank You, Mr Speculator

There are two times in a man's life when he should not speculate: when he can't afford it and when he can.

Mark Twain

In an experiment, scientists placed a shoal of fish in an aquarium. The aquarium had a glass partition in the middle, through which the fish could see to the other side of the aquarium. On the other side, they kept a wide variety of tempting food, which the fish could see, but the glass partition prevented them from going there. They would flock around the partition and would keep hitting the glass. They learnt that the territory beyond the glass was not meant for them, however tempting the food was, and they stopped waiting by the glass to see the world on the other side. Now they will swim close to the glass and turn back.

One night, the scientists removed the glass partition. The fish have by now learnt the distance they have to swim and then turn back, and that is what they continue to do. They swim to the now-imaginary glass partition and turn back to the other side. The manna from heaven lies right in front; they can see it, but they cannot now swim to it and are content within their self-defined boundaries.

What is true of fish is true of man too. Many of us found the stock market a great place to make money. We invested, and the money grew manifold. Then in 1992, the Harshad Mehta scam rattled the market, and the market came crashing down to its knees. The money just vanished in thin air. The investors swore not to invest in the market again; it created the glass partition equivalent.

The public memory is short, and as the market rose again, a new breed of investors now entered the market. 'This time, it's different' is the mantra now. The market was rising again, and you had to put money in any stock to see it grow. The music stopped when the CRB scam came to light in 1996. C. R. Bhansali had been raising money using fictitious companies and pumping that money in penny stocks, causing frenzy in the market. Stocks came tumbling down again. Now another set of investors swore never to invest again.

The story repeats itself in the Ketan Parekh scam (in 2001), the Satyam scam (in 2009), and the Sahara Housing scam (in 2010). Every time a scam breaks out, the market loses a herd of investors who's burnt their fingers and swears never to come back to the market again. The mental glass partition works forever for them. They tell their friends and children and grandchildren never to invest in the stock market as it is risky.

Is the Stock Market Risky?

The stock market has been risky and will forever continue to be risky for gullible investors who do not understand the intricacies. If you buy a stock worth ₹10 for ₹50 and are waiting for it to rise and make money for you, you are only waiting for a greater fool to bail you out. You are hoping to find someone willing to pay ₹70 for something that is worth ₹10 just because you bought it at ₹50 and must make profits. The stock market has no compassion, and while you may find someone willing to pay ₹70, it is not because you must get a profit but because he is a greater fool than you. He finds it attractive to buy it at ₹70. As long as the sellers can find greater fools, the price will continue to rise and fill the bubble with more gas. It reaches a point when the bubble is ready to burst and there is no greater fool left, and then it bursts in the hands of the one holding it last.

Any person who has been through this turmoil would say that:

1. equity is risky
2. debt is safe.

They are right; after all, they have learnt it the hard way. Equity will continue to be risky for people who invest the way many of us invest our money. History will continue to repeat itself, and every stock market crash creates a fresh herd of battered investors whom the market has lost forever.

Truth be told, equity is safer than debt, provided you understand the principles spelt out in this book. Debt is a safe way of losing your money to inflation.

It is time to understand the difference between an investor and a speculator.

Investor versus Speculator

There is a fundamental difference between an investor and a speculator. The examples cited above pertain to speculation and not investment. An investor is one who buys a stock after a careful study of its fundamentals and pays a price which gives him a margin of safety. He buys the stocks well below its intrinsic value. He studies the fundamentals of the company and arrives at the intrinsic value and does not buy unless he understands what he is getting and what he is paying for. He buys a stock as if he is buying a business. It may be a thin invisible slice in the business, yet the criterion remains the same. He likes to think of himself as part owner of the business.

The speculator is least interested in fundamentals; he wants to ride the momentum. 'Trend is a trader's best friend' is the maxim he swears by, and he buys a rising stock or (short) sells a falling stock, hoping to make profits in the momentum. He tries to extrapolate the trend and uses various techniques, many of them dubious, to find the point of trend reversal, before which he must exit the stock.

If only life were that simple! Most speculators, however articulate they may be, hit the dust when a black swan event strikes. Black swan events do occur, wiping off all the gains of the past. To quote Warren Buffett, 'Only when the tide goes out do you discover who's been swimming naked.'

Equity Is Not Risky in the Long Run

1. Equity is risky in the short run, but as you increase the time frame of investment, it becomes less risky. Over a long period, equity becomes safe.
2. Debt may look safe in the short run, but it becomes risky over a long period.

The credit for distinguishing between investment and speculation must go to Benjamin Graham. In the first chapter of his book *Intelligent*

Investor, Graham attempts to define *investment* thus: 'An investment operation is one which, upon a thorough analysis promises safety of the principal and an adequate return. Operations not meeting these requirements are speculative.'

Graham is clear. Unless you have applied your mind based on a careful study of the fundamentals of the company, which assures an adequate margin of safety and an adequate return, you are only speculating. Note that Graham is interested in 'adequate return' as the aim of the investment and not an exorbitant return. Aiming for an extraordinary return is likely to make your decision speculative. Not that extraordinary return does not accrue for an intelligent investor; in fact, it accrues more for him than to a speculator. Yet aiming for that is to live in a fool's paradise.

Another keyword to note here is the *safety of principle*. Any investment decision where you risk losing your principal is speculative. Graham and investors belonging to his school of investment defend their capital, and the first rule they keep in mind is 'not to lose money'.

This is important. An investment decision where you risk losing your capital, however attractive the return may look like, does not fall in the category of investment by conservative investors. A point that often causes confusion here needs clarification. Note the word *promise*. If an investor has ensured absolute safety of his capital and adequacy of return, it will be a situation too good to be true. What an investor ensures, through a careful study of intrinsic value and the margin of safety, is the increased probability of success. The higher the margin of safety at which he buys his investments, the lower the probability of him losing money. The intention is not to speculate but to take a considered decision.

People who live by the screen (and die by the screen) are speculators. They yell 'Buy! The market is on fire!' when the market is on fire and yell "Sell! The market is bleeding!" when the market is bleeding. They are on cloud nine when the market is peaking and are panicky when the market goes bust.

The investor takes an opposite stand. He understands that the market is high, way beyond the intrinsic value, and he waits and waits till the market reaches a point where enough margin of safety is created. He has all the patience in the world. Since he does not base his decision on momentum but on a careful analysis of the fundamentals, he will wait till the price becomes rational. And if a particular stock does not come within his valuations, he does not buy it even if it is a good stock, because he knows a stock is good only when it is cheap compared to its valuation.

The only way to beat the market is by making investment based on a systematic study and logic that is not popular in the market at that point. The contrarian who understands the difference between value and price is the most successful investor.

The biggest danger an investor carries is when he thinks he is investing while he is speculating. Buying on 'tips' or on impulse without proper research is what most investors do. Some rely on their trusted brokers, who, though honest to the client, pass on the tips that he got from his principal, who got it from the grapevine. You can visualise how dangerous such methods can be.

Understanding the difference between investment and speculation is the most important step that makes you a successful investor. When an investor buys a share, he buys a piece of ownership in the company. He bases his decision to buy on the current perception about the stock in the market and its divergence from what he thinks to be the fair price. He knows something that the combined wisdom of the market does not know because he has taken efforts to study the investment. (It is rare to find speculators sitting down with annual reports to understand the financial statements.)

A speculator does not know what the investor knows, nor does he crave for that knowledge. He is happy riding the trend. He believes if the price of a stock is rising, it will keep rising until some force changes its course. So he buys when it rises and keeps buying till it keeps rising. He sells what is falling and keeps selling it till the market shows a change in direction. As long as the majority will behave this way, there is nothing to suggest that this behaviour will change. The small minority of value investors will keep finding the mismatch between value and price and will keep exploiting that gap.

Martin Zweig, the author of *Martin Zweig's Winning on Wall Street*, makes a very valid point: 'If they beat the market over any period, no matter how dangerous or dumb their tactics, people boasted that they were "right." But the intelligent investor has no interest in being temporarily right.'

Remember, in a bull market, everyone becomes an expert, and however dumb his technique may be, he still makes money. Astrology, palmistry, technical analysis—everything seems to work. Every such phase creates a band of super experts, who never go wrong and have a Midas touch. The divine communications gets distorted when the market becomes erratic, and the experts find no place to hide.

Every bull phase creates investing fads, which are characterised by excessive enthusiasm about a particular investment style. It does not sustain beyond one season. Wealth is not created overnight and needs to be nurtured like a seed sown which, over a period, grows into a mighty fruit-bearing tree. There is no shortcut to wealth creation. Knowing where you are investing in is crucial to investment success.

An investor expects to gain in one of the following three ways:

1. He expects the growth of the company to be reflected in the increased share price in the future.
2. He expects the company to share the growth with him through distribution of dividends.
3. He expects the market to realise the gap between the price and the underlying value and the future investors to fill that gap by pulling the price up.

For speculators, a stock is not a fractional ownership of a company. He is least interested in the company he is buying. He is buying a ticker, a name on his screen that keeps going green and red. The faster the price changes, the more excited he is. He does not even care about the reason behind the price of a stock going up or down. He is least interested in that. The more the prices fluctuate, the happier he seems to be. He is trying to analyse what others must think about it and what the market is thinking, and he designs his strategy to make money by analysing the market behaviour.

A dull market does not fascinate him nor do the shares with low beta value (i.e. shares whose price does not fluctuate much). He is interested in fluctuations, and he is interested in trends. If the trend is up, which means there are more buyers than sellers, he takes the plunge, and as the price keeps rising, he keeps buying as if the price rise is confirming the trend. It is a dangerous game because he is not weighing the fundamentals. It does not bother him if the price goes beyond fundamental value.

In fact, he does not even know the fundamental value, nor is he interested in knowing it. To him, it is enough to know there is a buyer in the market willing to pay a higher price for his stocks. He lets the momentum drive the market as long as it does so. The moment he realises that the balloon is losing gas, he exits. He buys because it rises, and he sells because it no longer rises (or it falls). Seth Klarman says, 'They buy securities because they "act" well and sell when they don't. Indeed, even if it were certain that the world would end tomorrow, it is likely that some speculators would continue to trade securities based on what they thought the market would do today.'

Speculators have an obsession for predicting the price movement, and they will use many correlations (often pseudo correlations) to predict the price movement. Many of them resort to technical analysis to predict where the price is going. Technical analysis carries the mistaken belief that the price on a particular time (t) depends upon the price on the time $t-1$. It believes the price depends upon the previous price and not on the fundamentals and that a trend line, once established, will continue to trend unless some factor causes the reversal. The 'technicians' are always busy predicting the trend and the trend reversal. Pseudosciences wear intelligent looks in the world of economics and finance.

In the stock market, investors do not wear a different dress, nor do they use a different login process. You cannot make out from external appearances if someone is an investor or a speculator. You ask people if they are speculators or investors. More likely than not, they will say that they don't speculate, they invest.

Someone pretending to be an investor is often a speculator. (This includes big names in the world of investing.) In the Indian scenario, there are a few investors, and the market has a preponderance of speculators. Sometimes, in times of irrational exuberance, less-disciplined investors turn into speculators. When the market falls, panic drives many to speculation.

Finding out if someone is an investor or a speculator requires a keen observation about the investment philosophy of that person over a long period. There are no set criteria to put a transaction into the category of investment or speculation. When I invested 37 years back, good-intentioned well-wishers warned me that the stock market was nothing but speculation. My father also considered the share market to be a place for speculation. Every year, people with half-baked knowledge enter the market and get disillusioned soon. They join the tribe that calls stock investment speculative.

We understand that it is the skill, dedication, and intention that determines if the activity of buying stocks is speculation or investment. Some transactions are, per se, speculative. For example, day trading can be nothing but speculation. But shares can be a speculation or an investment (though I find *speculative investment* to be an oxymoron). Derivatives, by their very nature, look speculative, though they can be an investment in specific situations (for example, as a hedge).

For those of you who want to speculate, my advice is to play in the casino or buy lottery tickets. If you choose the former, you can have a great time in offshore Goa or Kathmandu or Macau or Las Vegas, with the best of wine being served free of cost. (Who said there is no such thing as a free lunch? Go to a casino; they dole out lots of freebies. They can see a wad of currency in your pockets.) If you choose the latter, it is all official, run by governments of each state. Why should you get exploited by some sucker when you can trust your government to do that?

Every investor is a gambler unless he understands the rationale behind his investment, studies the stock he is investing in, does his homework before committing his money to a stock, and has the intention of making profits out of market mispricing and not out of some game of chance.

As said before, the Indian market is marked by the overwhelming presence of speculators. This is so in more advanced markets also, but those markets have matured to the next level of maturity and have a small yet formidable group of successful investors. These are the people who have written success stories of those markets. Does this leave you in an undesirable situation? No, an investor is more likely to be successful amid all the noise and irrationality that prevail in the market. Chaos is an opportunity for a systematic investor.

Seth Klarman shares an interesting story to explain how speculators work. When sardines disappeared from their traditional waters in Monterey, California, there was a craze in the market for sardines. The speculators took the price of sardines to fizzy heights. One day after making great money trading sardines, a trader tasted the fruit of his labour. He treated himself to an expensive lunch. He opened a can of sardines and ate it. He became ill and expressed his anguish to the seller, saying that the sardines were no good. The seller replied that they were not eating sardines, they were trading sardines.

I had a similar experience in Varanasi, where I bought a kilo of laddus from a shop opposite the most famous temple. The sweet-seller asked me if I wanted to buy the laddus as offering to the Lord or for eating. I discovered that the laddus meant for offerings were hard as stone and would get recycled at the shop by the pujaris, to be sold again and again.

Speculators are like the sardine traders in Monterey or the sweet-sellers in Varanasi. They never bother to taste the sardines they are trading. As long as there are buyers, they are happy. Taste and quality are no concern for them.

Fundamentals have no meaning for the speculators. Why wait for the wealth to grow slow when you can grow it overnight? Why get rich slowly when you can get rich quickly? Moreover, there is comfort in being with the crowd. A speculator seldom bucks the trend. He moves with the crowd, never going against the current. Being in the majority gives him confidence.

With the invention of synthetic instruments like derivatives, the temptation to speculate is more than ever before. Investment is boring and slow; speculation is bold and fast. Using leverage and synthetic instruments, you can win big. However, you lose big too. When the leveraged spiral unwinds, it takes away the last piece of cloth from your person.

Thank You, Mr Speculator

Speculation is easy. It requires no hard work. It is exciting; you can buy and sell at every refresh of your screen. It is not unusual for speculators to sit with four computer screens in front, each showing the live price quotes of different segments or different markets. (Rakesh Jhunjhunwala, one of the most successful investors, handles five screens. Jhunjhunwala has a Jekyll-and-Hyde personality. One personality is a speculator; the other is a long-term investor. But that story is for another day.)

Speculation is as thrilling as the casino and, if the market is trending, lucrative too. But it is a lottery, some days you win, some days you lose. Speculators believe there is a greater fool sitting at another terminal. You buy at ₹100, and he will buy at ₹110 from you. When you don't find the greater fool, well, the market has found the greatest fool: *you*.

Is Speculation Bad for the Market?

I am often asked this question by people who do not understand the intricacies of the market. Whenever people lose money, they echo these sentiments. On 11 October 2018, Sensex fell by over 1,000 points, and the *Economic Times* reported that investors lost a wealth of ₹4 lakh crore in 5 minutes. The blood on the street belongs to the speculators and not the investors. And when they spilled blood, often you heard that speculation should be 'banned'.

Such sentiments are often expressed in the commodities market too. When the oil prices rises, all fingers point at speculation, and people blame the government for creating infrastructure for speculators to indulge in excessive speculation.

It looks so obvious. If something is so bad, should the government not declare it illegal? Well, the simple answer is, speculation is not at all bad for the market. Speculation may make the speculator an overnight king or a pauper since he wins big and loses big, yet it performs important economic functions for the market. The presence of speculators helps, not hinders, the attainment of perfection in the market. Let us try to understand what at first sight looks like a paradox.

As discussed earlier, speculation is the practice of engaging in risky financial transactions to profit from short-term fluctuations in the market price of a security rather than attempting to profit from the underlying financial attributes embodied in instruments such as capital gains, dividends, or interest.

Speculators pay little attention to the fundamental value of a security and instead focus on price movements. In doing so, they perform a host of economic functions.

1. Price Stabilisation Function

While this applies to commodities and securities, it will be easier to understand it as it applies to commodities. The economist Nicholas Kaldor has long recognised the price-stabilising role of speculators, who even out 'price fluctuations due to changes in the conditions of demand or supply'.

The speculator and hedge fund manager Victor Niederhoffer has beautifully explained it thus:

> Let's consider some principles that explain the causes of shortages and surpluses and the role of speculators. When a harvest is too small to satisfy consumption at its normal rate, speculators come in, hoping to profit from the scarcity by buying. Their purchases raise the price, thereby checking consumption so that the smaller supply will last longer. Producers encouraged by the high price further lessen the shortage by growing or importing to reduce the shortage. On the other side, when the price is higher than the speculators think the facts warrant, they sell. This reduces prices, encouraging consumption and exports and helping to reduce the surplus.

The speculator is an opportunist. He makes hay while the sun shines. He makes money by filling the gap. Speculators, along with arbitrageurs and hedgers, keep exploiting the price gap. This leads to a more perfect market with a more logical pricing. Contrary to what we believe, speculation helps price stabilisation in the long run. In the short run, speculation may cause hiccups in the market, but that is a part of the long-term stabilisation process.

2. Providing Liquidity to the Market

Another important service that a speculator provides to the market is, in risking his capital, he creates liquidity. Let us understand why this is so important.

We shall again use the example of a commodity since it is easier to understand. We consider a thinly traded commodity on NCDEX (which is the commodities market in India), say guar gum. Guar gum is an extract derived from guar seeds and is used as a natural thickener, emulsifier, stabiliser, bonding agent, etc. A chemical manufacturer who wants to buy guar gum goes to the market, but he may find no seller since the trades are not frequent. When a seller of guar gum wants to sell, there may not be enough buyers. In the former case, the buyer will have to pay a premium over the normal price since there is not as much quantity up for sale as the demand. In the latter case, the seller is likely to get a lower price. This price difference, known as the spread, occurs because there are not enough numbers of buyers and sellers at the same point in time. The speculator (an opportunist) will buy or sell any commodity where he finds the spread is large. He is risking his capital and filling the gap. Since a speculator often works with leveraged money, he can buy as much as ten times the actual buyer and can sell as much without owning a piece (thanks to the futures market).

With the market filled with a mix of investors (or actual users in the commodities market), hedgers, arbitrageurs, and speculators, you can imagine how much the volume will increase. It may be as high as 100 times the actual trade. (In the stock market and in the commodities market, you can find out how many of the deals are being settled for 'delivery' and how many are being 'rolled over'.) The presence of numerous players leads to a greater market efficiency. The greater quantity being traded lowers the spread, thus helping both buyers and sellers. It may sound ridiculous, but in tiny commodities like guar gum, the daily traded volume may sometimes be more than the annual production of the commodity!

3. **Bearing Risks**

A speculator loves risk; he earns his bread by taking risks. Sometimes he gets a cake to eat. Sometimes he sleeps on an empty stomach. He takes upon himself the risk that the seller or buyer of the commodity (or the investor in securities) would have been required to assume. A farmer can agree to sell his produce to a speculator in a forward market and can sleep knowing his produce has been pre-sold.

So much in praise of the hero of the market. And I am sure now you understand why you need speculators to help you succeed as an investor. Consider a hypothetical situation where every investor in the market is a clone of Warren Buffett. If everyone buys the mismatch between price and value, there will be no gap left soon, and once you reach the stage of equilibrium between value and price, there are no further profits to be made, except the profit arising out of the growth of the company. The equity market will have to be closed down since the uncertainty is gone. When all become Warren Buffett, Warren Buffett will be reduced to a purchaser of what looks like an equivalent of the government bond. Of course, this would never happen. Thank you, Mr Speculator.

CHAPTER 7

Your Time Starts Now!

If you want to have a better performance than the crowd, you must do things differently from the crowd.

John Templeton

Read this before you begin your journey to riches. This is the first step in the journey of a thousand miles.

Think Big

Most of the people who have made it big could do so because they knew they could do it; they believed they could do it. Many of us refuse to tune to the right channel. We don't dream ourselves wealthy; the obvious result is that we never grow rich because we never planned for it. You need to condition your mind into believing you are wealthy and successful. This is the precondition: unless you believe you can do it, you can't do it.

If you are waiting for a lottery or a windfall, you are wasting your energies. Lottery creates riches sometimes, but it would be folly to wait for the heavens to select you from out of billions. And even if you are the lucky one, historical evidence proves that few who became rich by winning a lottery sustained the riches. It's an unviable proposition: the probability of winning is bleak, and if you win, you may not keep that wealth for long since you have not trained your mind in the art of making and keeping wealth.

Set Your Goals

A fool and his money are soon parted because a fool does not define his goals. Unless you define where you want to go, you will never reach it. This is very important. Set your goals. You need to create your own mission statement and then, based on such a statement, define your goals, both long term and short term. Your goals should be quantifiable. 'I want to be rich' is not a defined goal. (Doesn't everyone want to be rich?) 'I want to have a net worth of ₹1 million by the age of 30' is a goal.

While the former is just a wish, the latter puts a quantified value to it, and you can measure your performance as you move towards achieving your goal. The best way to define and quantify your goal is to write it down. Write it down clearly and unambiguously as if you are writing work specifications.

Set the goal that will make you exert yourself. If you set your target too low, it will fail to be an effective motivation. Your goal should cause a little discomfort, a little stress, which produces positive results. It should be realistic, though it must be set a notch higher than your present capability. Setting a goal that is far too unrealistic will defeat the purpose. If you are setting an impossible goal, you are likely to throw it out the window sooner than later.

Read and Reread Your Goals Periodically

Compare the actual results with the projected. See how you are faring. If you are performing better than expected, is it time to revise your targets upwards? If you are performing poorly, are things going fundamentally wrong, or do you need to lower your expectations?

Do Not Have Too Many Goals

Setting too many goals may confuse you, and you may lose focus. Goals may often contradict each other and may lead to dilemma situations. Keep them simple, keep them short, and keep them limited to the things you want.

Your Goal Should Be Measurable

You should be able to track and measure your progress. They should be tangible. You should be able to visualise them. If you can visualise something, the chances of success are higher. Abstract goals get lost in oblivion.

Find a Mentor

It is very important for you to associate yourself with people who are rich and successful. Being in the company of successful people will give you positive energy and the motivation to succeed. Surround yourself with people who are failures, and you are also likely to become one. Mix with successful people; it will provide you the micronutrients that will build your inner strength to succeed. 'It's better to hang out with people better than you. Pick out associates whose behaviour is better than yours, and you'll drift in that direction,' says Warren Buffett.

Why will someone agree to be your mentor? It is a lot easier than you imagine. You may find a mentor, and you may ask him you want to succeed and you want to emulate his ways. Many will oblige. In fact, you will be surprised to find how many people are eager to help. Few people come forward to ask for genuine guidance, so if asked, you are likely to get it with pleasure. I have mentored many, and I know mentoring gives as much satisfaction to the mentor as it gives to the mentee.

If you cannot find an 'active mentor', you can find a 'passive mentor', a successful person you follow without that person knowing or caring about it. This way you can get the free mentoring from some of the most successful people in the world.

In the Hindu epic *Mahabharata*, Ekalavya is a young prince of the Nishadha tribes and a member of a low caste. He aspires to study archery in the *gurukul* of Dronacharya. After being rejected by Dronacharya, Ekalavya embarks upon a programme of self-study in the presence of a clay image of Dronacharya. He becomes the best archer in the world, with his skill far superior that of Arjuna, Dronacharya's favourite and most accomplished pupil.

Read biographies of successful people like Buffett and Gates. Read everything about them; find out the principles from their lives you can emulate. How about writing an email to a successful person, appreciating his work? Genuine admiration is bound to be appreciated.

Do not despise rich and wealthy men. Some people hold strong negative notions about wealth and find fault with the man who has made it big. The successful man is considered a product of luck, fortune, or ill-gotten wealth. It need not be so in a majority of cases. Stop fretting and fuming about wealth and appreciate the success of people who have made it. Take pleasure in the success of others, appreciate it, and tell them you like it. Genuine approbations never go waste.

Surround yourself with successful people. Remember, you are the average of five people who spend most time with you. Join clubs, associations, chambers of commerce, and other bodies where you are likely to come across successful people.

Don't let people around you divert you from your goals. Stay away from negative influences. There will be many people around you who will discourage you, laugh at you, and try to convince you that what you are up to is impossible to achieve. They will try to drag you down to their own level of perfunctory performance. Please stay away from naysayers and doubting Thomases.

Know How to Manage Your Money

The skill of managing your money is equally important, if not more important, than earning it. 'The art is not in making money but in keeping it' (Chinese proverb). Create wealth consciousness. Fortunes have been withered away because people failed to manage their money well. Rich people don't have a higher IQ than poor people; they are just good in the art of managing money.

You may argue, how could you manage your money when you don't have any? Don't put the cart before the horse. The money management skills must be learnt before you earn big money, not after that. When you have less money, you can experiment more, or you can try different rules—not so when the kitty is big. It is like learning to swim in the toddlers' pool before you try your swimming skills in the ocean. The ocean is unforgiving; the little pool is forgiving and friendly. Managing your money is more important than the amount of money being managed.

Record Your Transactions

If you want to be a successful investor, it is imperative that you keep a meticulous record of your transactions. You don't have to be an accountant to know how to maintain accounts. You can create a simple spreadsheet with receipts in one column and payments in another. You can find software like QuickBooks or Peachtree to do it for you. Those who hate the electronic world might maintain a simple diary to record their financial transactions. A crash course in basic accounting is desirable, though not a precondition, to maintaining your accounts. If Warren Buffett, with billions of dollars of wealth that he manages, still handles his own accounts, can't we take the lead?

Double-entry bookkeeping is a wonderful system of keeping accounts; it was invented in the fifteenth century by Luca Pacioli. A double-entry bookkeeping system is a set of rules for recording financial information in a financial accounting system in which every transaction or event changes at least two different nominal ledger accounts.

Financial information used to be recorded in books (hence *bookkeeping*), whereas now it's recorded mainly in computer systems. These books were called ledgers, and each transaction was recorded twice (hence, *double-entry*), with the two transactions being called a debit and a credit.

The accounting equation serves as an error detection system: if at any point, the sum of debits does not equal the corresponding sum of credits, an error has occurred. It follows that the sum of debits and credits must be zero. The system is self-balancing and is like a modern management information system in that the 'trial balance' is thrown out of balance if you do not record the double effects of a transaction.

While accounting is seemingly a mundane task, knowledge of accounting will stand you in good stead in your pursuit of wealth.

Pay Yourself First

Many people know this simple trick, but few practise it. You earn and you pay others until nothing is left for yourself. And you postpone your share to the next cycle. In the next cycle, there are more dues to be paid. This goes on and on. The stage when you have enough surpluses to pay yourself first will seldom arise. Parkinson's second law, 'Expenditures rise to meet income', keeps operating against you.

The best solution is to pay a 'salary' to yourself every month. This has to be set aside first before you pay others. You may think this may not work for you since your spending always exceeds your inflows. Prioritisation of resources is a matter of attitude and habit. You must start learning to prioritise when the resources are less, not when you have an abundance of resources. You can make money, or you can make excuses, but you cannot make both.

"Never Spend Your Money before You Have It" (Thomas Jefferson)

Generation Z, so appropriately called digital natives, takes pride in living on borrowed money. Plastic money has created havoc. Credit card companies will make the spending power available at your doorstep even if you don't need it. It will entice you to spend, spend, spend, spend without even owning money. We are a part of a massive consumption-oriented economy, where success is measured in terms of how much you spend rather than how much you earn. The result is obvious: we recently saw unprecedented sub-prime crisis in the West, which threatened to kill the financial system of the entire world.

Spending money before earning is like counting your chickens before they hatch. What if they don't hatch? You start creating a bubble, thinking that the future is rosy and bright. But things seldom work out the way you think they will. The bubble grows bigger and bigger, and you start borrowing in order to service the past debts. The situation worsens when your borrowing is spent in paying off the interest of earlier loans. You cannot afford to do so for long unless you are a government! Charles Dickens puts it so effectively in *David Copperfield*: 'Annual income twenty pounds, annual expenditure nineteen six, result happiness. Annual income twenty pounds, annual expenditure twenty pound ought and six, result misery.'

The only reason a great many people don't own an elephant is that they have never been offered an elephant for ₹1,000 down and easy weekly payments.

If you want to be rich, take a vow: 'Thou shall live within thy means.' Come what may. This is a sine qua non. Ignore the future. A more conservative and desirable stand is to keep in mind all future expenditure but not to consider future income unless it comes into your bank account. Do not borrow. Not that rich people don't borrow. Borrowed money does give leverage, but you will be better off not borrowing. This book is about getting rich the safe and sure way. Borrowing in any form is ruled out. No overdrafts, no credit card borrowings, no leveraged trading, no futures and options, no intraday trading.

Be Fully Committed to Creating Wealth

Everyone wants to be rich, but very few make it. There is a big difference between wish and commitment. Being rich requires a definite commitment, a pledge, a vow, a promise to yourself that you shall be rich, that you shall remain focused to your goal of creating wealth, and that no matter what your present station in life is, you shall attain a comfortable position. This dedication is necessary. Wealth is created in your mind first, and the material wealth follows.

Use Your Internal GPS System

Define your goals, lay down the road map, and keep driving towards your destination, mile after mile, never losing focus. If you have a clearly defined plan imprinted in your mind and a strong commitment to the fulfilment of the plan, the internal GPS system takes over and drives you to the destination, undeterred by diversions and speed breakers. If you keep reminding yourself of your goals constantly and develop a habit of not deviating from it, you set in motion the internal autopilot. You just watch things happen on their own, with no efforts on your part!

Let Your Money Work Hard for You

Most people work hard for money. Smart people make money work hard for them. If you work hard for money, there is a limit to which you can go. The limit is defined by your intellectual ability, your courage, your competence, and a host of other factors. But when you let your money work for you, you make your money make more money for you. And more money makes still more money. And so on. It breeds like rabbits and keeps breeding at a fast pace. Set aside as much money as you can so that it can be your rabbit farm—a small rabbit farm initially and will eventually grow exponentially. You can sit, relax, and enjoy the fruits of success. This game is better than *FarmVille* since you breed actual rabbits and not the 'e-rabbits' that *FarmVille* produces.

If you invest your money wisely in the stock market, you are actually participating in the dynamic economy. You are part owner of a business that works 24/7, creating wealth for all owners like you. The money works when you are sleeping or playing golf or are on a long vacation to the Far East. Its work is not related to your mood, nor does it stop working for you when you are sick. Compare this to the money that you earn by expending your own labour. The quantum of money you can earn is limited by many obvious factors.

Do Not Panic

Have courage and belief in your own self and in your investment methodology. Things are likely to go wrong. That should not deter you. If you do your homework well, an adverse situation can be turned into an opportunity. When investing in the market, things do go crazy. Mr Market behaves irrationally quite frequently, and irrational exuberance is often a rule rather than an exception. It requires wisdom to understand the market and courage to face the adversity. Be greedy when others are fearful and fearful when others are greedy. Remember this success mantra; it will always help you when you face the rough weather.

The strategy explained in this book is defensive. The author knows well that if things can go wrong, they will. The book comes with enough shock-abs to let you handle such situations.

Just Do It!

The time to act is now. Buckle up and get going. Money has a time value. If you start earning, saving, and investing early, you have already doubled your money before your friend even started investing. Procrastination is the thief of time, and time is money.

CHAPTER 8

The Mindset of an Investor

"No matter how great the talent or effort, some things just take time: you can't produce a baby in one month by getting nine women pregnant."

Warren Buffett

'The investor's chief problem—and even his worst enemy—is likely to be himself,' says Warren Buffett. Investment is as much about psychology as it is about economics. People often fail in the former. World-class economists don't make world-class investors. Many of them are the worst performers. Investment success depends on the mental make-up of the investor combined with technical competence.

Few know Albert Einstein invested much of his 1921 Nobel Prize money in stock markets. However, he lost a bulk in the stock market crash in 1929. Einstein was awarded 121,572.54 in Swedish kronor for his Nobel Prize in Physics, which was equivalent to over twelve years' income for Albert Einstein back then. He lost almost all of it and realised that his Nobel Prize–winning wisdom was not suitable for winning in the stock market. The stock market requires a different temperament. (Later, Einstein remarked that the power of compound interest is the most powerful force on earth.)

You are your worst enemy. Frenzy, exuberance and excesses in the market, dubious companies with window-dressed balance sheets, a sudden change in domestic and international macros may not harm you as much as your own temperament.

Patience

The most important trait that an investor ought to have is patience. No matter how technically sound you are, you are likely to face rough weather. The market will go down, your investment will underperform for quite some time, and unless you have inculcated the virtue of patience, you are likely to sell at the wrong time. Lack of patience makes people do dumb things with their money.

Greed and fear are two dominating forces in the market, and unless you have trained your senses to stay disciplined in the face of such extreme market behaviours, you are likely to succumb. Factors that distinguishes Warren Buffett, Charlie Munger, and Peter Lynch from other investors are the tremendous patience and discipline they have.

Buffett says he would be happy if the stock markets closed for ten years after he bought his investments so he would have no means to track his investments while they continued to grow. It requires nothing less than Job's patience to hold on to your investment when the market forces are against it—and a great deal of conviction in your investment philosophy.

Munger says, 'You have to be patient, wait until something comes along, which, at the price you're paying, is easy. That's contrary to human nature, just to sit there all day long doing nothing, waiting. It's easy for us, we have a lot of other things to do. But for an ordinary person, can you imagine just sitting for five years doing nothing? You don't feel active, you don't feel useful, so you do something stupid.' We are not out in the market, looking for investments; we are just waiting for the right investments which we have identified as having become available to us at the right price. Till the price comes to the level that gives enough margin of safety, we wait, with our ears and eyes wide open. We keep reading everything about the potential investment. The day the right investment becomes available to us at the price we wanted to buy it, we buy like crazy.

Investing Is Not Cricket

In cricket, the batsman must hit every ball that is bowled to him. If he does not, either the ball hits the stumps, or if he obstructs the stumps with his body, it will be an LBW. He has to decide at every ball how to play so he remains at the crease for a longer time and can score well when he can hit the sweet spot. The player remains under tremendous pressure, the cheering and shouting of spectators adding to the confusion.

The intelligent investor does not invest like the intelligent cricketer plays cricket. He has an advantage over the cricketer. He need not play every ball. He can decide not to play a ball he does not understand, and it has no penalty point. He can wait for a favourable ball to come, and he can hit that ball with full force.

Warren Buffett used the baseball analogy to explain this point. He says, 'The trick in investing is just to sit there and watch pitch after pitch go by and wait for the one right in your sweet spot. And if people are yelling "Swing, you bum!" ignore them.' Buffett only invests in companies that are within his 'circle of competence', a concept he first described in his 1996 shareholder letter. 'You don't have to be an expert on every company, or even many,' he says. 'You only have to be able to evaluate companies within your circle of competence. The size of that circle is not very important; knowing its boundaries, however, is vital.'

If you stick to what you know, you would never go wrong. You don't have to buy every stock that looks interesting to you. You should have the ability to filter out the noise and focus on the companies you can understand. Because of your education, experience, interest, research, and passion, you might have developed expertise in certain industries. Sticking to those industries would make your investment safe. You may ignore the Infosyses and Wipros if you do not understand the technology. They may be great investment ideas, but they are not for you.

Buffet says the size of your circle of competence is also not very important. Even a narrow circle is big enough to filter out the required portfolio size for you. However, an intelligent investor is a lifetime student. He keeps widening his circle of competence.

When students asked Buffett's advice on how to get rich, he would say, 'I could improve your ultimate financial welfare by giving you a ticket with only twenty slots in it so that you had twenty punches—representing all the investments that you got to make in a lifetime. And once you'd punched through the card, you couldn't make any more investments at all.'

If you decide that you have to hit only 20 balls during your entire investing career and there is no penalty for not playing a ball, you will be as careful as you can. You will buy only those companies you can understand well, else you will not hold it for a day.

If you look at the Indian market scene, it is opposite to this. People are burning off their energies and monies buying and selling stocks they don't understand at the drop of a hat. They perhaps bought them on tips and would sell them when they need money for buying another tip. At the end of the year, when they draw the accounts for the year, they find that while they have been moving at a frantic pace, they've travelled no distance. They end up making more money for intermediaries through commission than for themselves. We need a disciplined, systematised approach towards stock market investing.

The market is dominated by untrained traders who do not know how to control their emotions. Alternating bouts of greed and fear decide a trader's investment patterns. When buying a mobile phone, he carries out a vast amount of research about the megapixels of the camera and the GB in the RAM and the battery life. When investing, he leaves it on Mr Market to decide for him. If he were to spend half as time on his lakhs of rupees worth of investment as he spends on buying a ₹20,000 mobile phone, he would be much better off. He fails to see stock as a share in the business and looks at it as a money-making proposition. I hope every investor reads this book to train his mind to the right way to invest.

Insulation

The investor needs to inculcate the talent to turn out noise. Tune in to CNBC, and you'll see tickers moving up and down, trying to capture every news and every piece of rumour. More often than not, the 'information' is mere noise, with no effect on the fundamentals of the stock. The recent failure of IL&FS created panic waves in the market, and all NBFC shares went tumbling down. When the market reacts, it overreacts. Shutting down noise will make you rise much above the average investor whose buy and sell decisions are impacted by short-term noises in the market. Some people don't want to miss a single piece of chatter and stay glued to the screen all day long. In the connected world, information travels fast, and misinformation travels faster. A single WhatsApp message can bring a company down. (A recent example is Infibeam; one message caused a 70% fall in price.) And a single Tweet may make the stock soar. (A recent example is Elon Musk tweeting about Tesla getting international funding.) The reaction is often disproportionate to the financial implication of the news. (efficient market hypothesis proponents would frown.)

Focus

The ability to stay on course in the face of conflicting signals is an important winning trait. Staying on course is a close cousin of patience, and intelligent investors are known not to deviate. The average investor digresses from the course because he doesn't even know what path he has chosen. He does not define his investment goals. If you do not know where you want to go, you can never reach it. Hundreds of distractions coming his way every day are likely to make him sell when he should buy and vice versa.

The ability to stay calm in the face of a storm makes you a successful investor. When there is blood in the market, most people are seen running for cover. The intelligent investor stays calm and unperturbed and tries to find value in the market. During a frenzy, people who stay calm are likely to discover great investments, while others seem to be feeling the heat.

Do Your Homework

The intelligent investor remains patient and calm and does not succumb to noise and stays on course because of an important trait he possesses: he does his homework well. He knows why he has made a particular investment. He studies every quarterly result, half-yearly result, and annual results of the company he has invested in to know the original premise he based his decisions on is still valid; and if it is no longer valid, does it call for a change in decision? Experience suggests that if you have done your homework well and are satisfied about the fundamentals of the company, in a majority of cases, you are likely to find a reinforcement of your belief in subsequent events.

In a few cases, you are likely to see the fundamentals deteriorate. However, if fundamentals of one company you have invested in deteriorate beyond repair, you might consider exiting it. Selling at this point also requires a calm mind: if fundamentals have gone off the mark, the intelligent investor would exit the scrip, while the frenzy investor would wait for the share to come back to a particular price so he recovers his losses, which may prove to be a futile exercise.

The intelligent investor rarely sells his investment unless he needs money or unless he finds that fundamental assumptions are no longer valid. And when he sells it, he remains indifferent to the profit or loss made in the transaction. To him, the latter situation is nothing more than plucking out the weeds so that the rest of the farm may grow better.

CHAPTER 9

Look for the Economic Moat in the Company You Buy

The ability to learn faster than your competitors may be only sustainable competitive advantage.

Arie de Geus

The term *economic moat*, popularised by Warren Buffett, refers to a business's ability to maintain competitive advantages over its competitors in order to protect its long-term profits and market share from competing firms. Just like a medieval castle, the moat serves to protect those inside the fortress and their riches from outsiders.

In business, a competitive advantage is the attribute that allows an organisation to outperform its competitors. A competitive advantage may include access to natural resources, such as high-grade ores or a low-cost power source, highly skilled labour, geographic location, high-entry barriers, and access to new technology.

Buffett, an ardent follower of Benjamin Graham's *Security Analysis* and *The Intelligent Investor*, adopted Graham's value investing methodology with certain refinements so that he could stay invested in his stock for a fairly long time and could see his money grow for almost an indefinite period. Graham's tools provided means to find out the intrinsic value; Graham would sell his holdings when the market price went beyond the intrinsic value. With a little tweak, Buffett factored in the ability of the company to sustain itself and grow in the future. He knew well that you cannot predict the future. The best way out is to find the characteristics of a company that will give it durable competitive advantage; the probability of a company with economic moat succeeding is higher than that of a company not enjoying such a competitive advantage.

The economic moat is the leverage that a company has over its competitors. It provides a company either the ability to sell the same products and services cheaper to its competitors or the ability to provide better-quality goods or services at the same input cost. Control over cheap source of raw material is an example of such competitive advantage. De Beers, the largest diamond company in the world, was at one time controlling 90% of the raw diamonds. A company in situations like this can enjoy an unrestricted pricing power. There are various ways in which a company may create a competitive advantage for itself.

Not all competitive advantages provide an economic moat in the long run. Some competitive advantages wither away soon, and the super profits earned by a business do not continue in the long run. It is the nature of modern free market with perfect competition that when a firm makes superprofits due to a competitive advantage, other firms will move in soon and start producing the same goods or services, using the same factors that gave an edge to the former, and in the long term, the competitive advantage does not stay. This is so because there aren't enough entry barriers in the modern laissez-faire world.

Uber was a paradigm shift from the hailing-taxi business model. By becoming an aggregator, it became a seamless link between passengers and taxi owners. Economies of scale and real-time information enabled them to reduce the cost of travel substantially and pass on the benefits to customers. This in turn helped increase the customer base. People who drove their own car found it more convenient to ride an Uber. People who used to ride autorickshaws or even buses found it economical to ride an Uber. The tracking feature and centralised control over the driver and the ride created an environment of trust, and single women travellers also started preferring Uber over any other mode of transport. This is an excellent example of how innovations can help everyone and be a win-win thing in a capitalistic business model. (For example, before Uber came in, many cities had a taxi union, creating an entry barrier; it was not possible for a new operator to add to the fleet unless the union approved it, creating a virtual monopoly of old operators.) Uber was destined to become an overnight success.

However, unless a company learns to protect its competitive advantage using innovation, it is likely to be lost. Before Uber had even made an entry into the Indian market, home-grown Ola had already studied the business model of its future competitor and had already replicated 90% of the same model. So while Uber continues to have its competitive advantage over the traditional taxi service, it may not have any in comparison with Ola. What if a new player decides to enter the market now that Ola and Uber has almost killed the competition from the conventional sectors? In the era of technology, replicating the business methodology of a successful firm is easy; it is easier to reverse-engineer a software than to make a new one. Even patents and intellectual property rights can be bypassed by doing a workaround. The economic moat is more durable than this. It is a competitive advantage that the company will continue to enjoy during the time you remain invested in the company. The corollary is that you would like to stay invested in the company so long as the company continues to have a strong moat around itself.

Economic moat is the main pillar of Buffett's investment strategy. He describes it like this: 'The key to investing is not assessing how much an industry is going to affect society, or how much it will grow, but rather determining the competitive advantage of any given company and, above all, the durability of that advantage. The products or services that have wide, sustainable moats around them are the ones that deliver rewards to investors.'

In his 2007 letter to the shareholders of Berkshire Hathaway, Buffett came out with great insight on the concept of the economic moat:

> A truly great business must have an enduring "moat" that protects excellent returns on invested capital. The dynamics of capitalism guarantee that competitors will repeatedly assault any business "castle" that is earning high returns. Therefore a formidable barrier such as a company's being the low cost producer (Costco) or possessing a powerful world-wide brand (Coca-Cola, Gillette, and American Express) is essential for sustained success. Business history is filled with "Roman Candles," companies whose moats proved illusory and were soon crossed.
>
> Our criterion of "enduring" causes us to rule out companies in industries prone to rapid and continuous change. Though capitalism's "creative destruction" is highly beneficial for society, it precludes investment certainty. A moat that must be continuously rebuilt will eventually be no moat at all.

The moat should not be illusionary but a real solid moat. It should be able to protect the castle against competitors who will continuously attack it to gain entry and destroy the competitive advantage. The moat should sustain itself for many years. If the moat needs to be rebuilt and fortified continuously, it will cease to be a moat.

What Buffett hinted here was that the technology moat is often no moat at all. You build it; the next day, the competitors destroy it, and you need to rebuild it. This was one of the reasons Buffett preferred 'old economy' companies over new companies. Old economy companies have built their moat in the form of customer loyalty and goodwill over generations, and such moats are not easy to destroy. People will keep brushing their teeth in a foreseeable future; the moat that Colgate built over its 145 years of existence is strong enough to protect it for quite some time.

It also brings us back to the topic of the circle of competence. You cannot determine the strength of a moat if you are not staying within your circle of competence. The apparent moat outside of your circle of competence may be illusory.

Let us consider the example of a *pav bhaji* stall that a young entrepreneur sets up at, let us say, MG Road. (This could be any city. All cities in India have a road called MG Road). He finds that all others are selling pav bhaji at ₹60 a plate. He decides to offer exactly same quality pao bhaji at ₹45, which is below the cost of production of the other stalls. Soon customers queue up at his stall, ditching other stalls that they've been patronising all their lives. Many others close shop because they cannot compete with this new operator. He now has ten times more customers than the average stall. Since he has a greater bargaining power now because of the size of his firm, he can now source his pav, butter, and other raw materials directly from the manufacturer, eliminating a series of middlemen. He now has a cost advantage over other stall owners. However, this advantage is likely to be short-lived. Soon, another stall owner will discover his strategy and will replicate it, and the competitive advantage will vanish.

Let us take the example further. This young stall owner has managed to create a short-term competitive advantage. Now that he has a large customer base, he comes out with a different type of pav, which he has invented, and he gets his pao patented. This makes his competitive advantage durable as other stall owners cannot replicate his product now.

If the new pav is well-received by the market, now he is able to raise the price of his pao bhaji without worrying about the competition, thanks to product differentiation. If this pav bhaji stall were a listed public company, this stock would likely perform better than other stalls on the stock market because of the moat that it had created for itself.

Most of the times, the economic moat is a qualitative factor and is not quantifiable. For example, customer loyalty cannot be expressed in terms of numbers. Though not quantifiable, the moat is a significant variable to be considered while assessing the intrinsic value of a company. This is another example of the edge that a retail investor who is willing to do his homework well has over an institutional investor who is not interested in non-quantifiable variables.

American economist Michael Porter defines the two ways in which an organisation can achieve the competitive advantage over its rivals: cost advantage and differentiation advantage. Cost advantage is when a business provides the same products and services as its competitors but at a lesser cost. Differentiation advantage is when a business provides better products and services as its competitors. The topic of sustainable competitive advantage has generated a great deal of interest among researchers (and value investors), as some firms continue to enjoy higher profitability without any apparent differentiation from its peers. The invisible strength comes from the competitive advantage.

Michael Porter's 1985 book, *Competitive Advantage: Creating and Sustaining Superior Performance* (this book was named the ninth most influential management book of the twentieth century), lists three strategic ways in which a business can create competitive advantage for itself:

1. *Cost leadership strategy.* Cost leadership is a business's ability to produce a product or service that will be at a lower cost than other competitors. If the business is able to produce the same quality product but sell it for less, this gives them a competitive advantage over other businesses. Therefore, this provides a price value to the customers. Lower costs will result in higher profits, as businesses are still making a reasonable profit on

each good or service sold. If businesses are not making a large enough profit, Porter recommends finding a lower-cost base, such as labour, materials, and facilities. This gives businesses a lower manufacturing cost over those of other competitors. The company can add value to the customer via transfer of the cost benefit to them. The intelligent investor looks for companies that use the cost advantage to build a permanent moat by way of ensuring that the low cost of labour, material, or facilities remain available to it over a long period.

2. *Differential strategy.* A differential advantage is when a business's products or services are different to its competitors. Michael Porter recommends making those goods or services attractive to stand out from their competitors. The business will need strong research, development, and design thinking to create innovative ideas. These improvements to the goods or service can include delivering high quality to customers. If customers see a product or service as being different from other products, consumers are willing to pay more to receive these benefits. The risk that differential advantage carries is that of the competitor creating a similar product by imitation or reverse engineering. The economic moat comes by various means, such as patents and copyrights, making the manufacturing process difficult to replicate or even keeping the recipe secret. The Coca-Cola formula is the Coca-Cola Company's secret recipe for Coca-Cola syrup, which bottlers combine with carbonated water to create the company's flagship cola soft drink. The company's founder, Asa Candler, initiated the veil of secrecy that surrounds the formula in 1891 as a publicity, marketing, and intellectual property protection strategy. While several recipes, each purporting to be the authentic formula, have been published, the company maintains that the actual formula remains a secret, known only to a very few select (and anonymous) employees.

3. *Focus strategy.* Focus strategy ideally tries to get businesses to aim at a few target markets rather than try to target everyone. This strategy is often used for smaller businesses since they may

not have the appropriate resources or ability to target everyone. Businesses that use this method usually focus on the needs of the customer and how their products or services could improve their daily lives. In this method, some firms may even let consumers give their inputs for their product or service.

This strategy can also be called the segmentation strategy, which includes geographic, demographic, behavioural, and physical segmentation. By narrowing the market down to smaller segments, businesses are able to meet the needs of the consumer. Porter believes that once businesses have decided what groups they will target, it is essential to decide if they will take the cost leadership approach or differentiation approach. Small players are known to operate in niche segments, where larger companies may find it difficult to compete because of proximity of the smaller player to the customer and its greater agility.

The economic moat (created by using any of the three strategies listed above) can manifest itself in various forms. If it is expensive or inconvenient for a customer to switch from the company's products or services to that of competitors, the company has a moat. Software companies and telecom companies enjoy this advantage. Resistance to change is a closely linked factor that helps a company to retain its customers. A large entry barrier could be another competitive advantage. Companies which have built large infrastructure over time or have created a considerable brand loyalty enjoy this advantage; a new player finds it difficult to break the barrier.

The conomic moat is important because it is impossible to predict the sustainability of revenue in the future. If the moats were to be removed, the profitability would no longer remain predictable. Hence, an intelligent investor will rely on future projections only if he is sure that the economic moat will continue during the period of his investment. From this discussion emerges one important principle: if the economic moat may not continue to exist in the future, an intelligent investor will not buy that asset unless it is being sold at a significant discount to its intrinsic value.

Here are examples of economic moats in some Indian businesses.

Let us consider businesses that have a wide moat. Hindustan Unilever enjoys a wide and strong moat thanks to the trustworthy brands it has created during 80 years of its presence in India. Some of these brands are Lux, Lifebuoy, Surf Excel, Rin, Wheel, Fair & Lovely, Pond's, Vaseline, Lakmé, Dove, Clinic Plus, Sunsilk, Pepsodent, Closeup, Axe, Brooke Bond, Bru, Knorr, Kissan, Kwality Wall's, and Pureit.

Parle is the largest biscuit manufacturer in the world. It enjoys a large economy of scale, which makes its biscuits cheapest in the world and gives it cost leadership that no one else is likely to replicate in the future.

Every four out of five cigarettes sold in India are made by ITC, giving it a virtual monopoly in the cigarette business.

Nescafe, Maggi, and KitKat are great brands that provide a wide economic moat for Nestlé India. You will recall the recent incidence when Maggi was found to contain excess lead and was asked to discontinue production and the market shelves were without Maggi for six months. Other companies, like Patanjali, saw this as a great opportunity to fill the gap, and they flooded the market with similar products. However, when Maggi came back, it came back with a vengeance. Customers bought Maggi even more fervently, almost getting emotional about the product they had missed for six months; this is proof of the existence of an almost inaccessible moat.

Pidilite Industries—the company that makes Fevicol, Fevikwik, Dr. Fixit, M-Seal, Fevistik, and Fevicryl—has a virtual monopoly in almost all product categories, so much so that the customer asks not for resin but for Fevicol by brand and many don't even know that it is a brand name and not the generic name of the product.

While each investor might have his own way of finding the existence and size of an economic moat based on how deep inside his circle of competence a business is positioned, I have tried to summarise the criteria here in the form of questions that I like to ask for the purpose:

1. Can the company raise the price of its products? Does it have the pricing power? Is it the price leader, or does it have to go by the price determined by the price leader? (As an example, Tata Steel sets the price in the steel industry; others have no choice but to

follow.) Will the customers still come back to the company if it decides to raise the price? If there is an increase in input cost, can the company pass it on to the customers?

2. How big is the market size of the product? Does it have space enough for the company to grow? You might have perfected the technology to make the best mousetrap in the world, but does the world need so many mousetraps?
3. How loyal are the customers to the company? If the product is broken or damaged, will the customers return to the same company, or will they switch over to another brand?
4. Is it easy to copy the company's products? If so, is there any legal protection against copying?
5. Is it a commodity company or does it operate in a niche segment?
6. How did the company cope with the previous down cycle? Did it continue to make profits or run into losses? And what about the down cycle previous to that? (I do not like to invest in a company that does not have an uninterrupted track record of profit-making for at least 10 years; it also follows that I will not invest in a company less than 10 years old.)
7. Does the company have a management team that is focused on future growth?
8. Is there a high switching cost involved for the customers to move away from the company? Microsoft enjoys this advantage, as the cost of migration from Windows and Office are way too high.
9. Does the company enjoy the network effect? Companies like Twitter, Facebook, and Instagram have built a large network of users. The cost of building this network far exceeds the cost of infrastructure required to run a company. A new company trying to compete with Facebook must build a similar network, which seems like a Herculean task.
10. If the company has access to a unique technology which makes it a superior company in its class, does the technology have the government's protection? It must protect the intellectual property rights, else soon another company might replicate the specialised process and the technology advantage will wither away.

A qualitative factor which is too important to be ignored is the stability of the business. A business which has excellent financial statements but is losing customers is cheap for a reason. Since books of accounts only reflect the historical information and not the bad days that lie ahead for a business, the knowledge of business within your circle of competence becomes the most important determinant of the future stability of a business.

CHAPTER 10

Cryptocurrencies, Gold, Diamonds, and Other Fads

"Don't be gullible, use life before it uses you. Understand there are no free lunches, and for every action you take, there's a reaction."

Sylvester Stallone

In December 2017, Vidarbha Industries Association invited me to deliver a talk on cryptocurrencies in general and bitcoin in particular. Bitcoin was being traded at US$19,000 (₹12,35,000 at the prevailing rate of exchange). Experts were predicting a price of US$100,000.

The auditorium was packed to capacity. The audience eager to hear my analysis. I disappointed many when I said the true value of bitcoin was a big *zero*. I received a series of invitations from various organisations requesting my speech on the topic. I checked on YouTube and on the Internet. The dissenting voices were few, just two or three experts saying that cryptocurrencies was a bubble. All others agreed that bitcoin was a game-changer and predicted the price based on some matrix they used.

Bitcoin has fallen to US$4,200. It is falling like ninepins (My earlier draft of this manuscript 15 days back had the price of US$6,400 written here.) Speculative tendencies don't change. People are still speculating if this is the right price to enter since some of them missed the earlier rally.

People are again investing in bitcoin, and here are newspaper headlines:

> Bitcoin bubble or boost: $30,000. (Bitcoin price prediction 2019 from a financial analyst)
>
> It has dropped in price, this is good. Surely, bitcoin is headed up. (John McAfee, the founder of McAfee, predicts bitcoin price will be $1 million by 2020)
>
> Volatile bitcoin to touch $50,000. (Jeet Singh, cryptocurrencies portfolio manager)
>
> Bitcoin is the future; Fiat is past. (Tim Draper, venture capitalist)
>
> Bitcoin will hit $40,000. (Llew Claasen, executive director, Bitcoin Foundation)

Bitcoin will hit $320,000 someday. (Cameron Winklevoss, co-founder, Gemini)

Bitcoin will reach $1 million. (Bobby Lee, CEO, BTCC Exchange)

Since people don't understand bitcoins and blockchains and cryptocurrencies, they make great speculations about the fair market price of the currencies. As you can see from the headlines above, estimates range from $30,000 to $1 million. Read the following description to understand why they all are wrong.

The true intrinsic value of any cryptocurrency is *cipher*. Not a penny more. Cryptocurrencies in 2018 are what the Internet was in 1990 and what tulips were in 1634! Few understood the Internet in the 1990s, nor did many understand why tulips were so expensive in the seventeenth century. Few understand cryptocurrencies. People still invest. A fool and his money are soon parted. I googled to find the opinions of experts on bitcoin (as a representative cryptocurrency). Out of the top 100 results, 97 predicted the future price, differing with each other by a wide margin. Just three said that bitcoin is doomed to fail. When a bubble builds up, sane voices are seldom heard. Read this chapter if you want to be better informed than most of the experts out there.

What Are Cryptocurrencies?

A cryptocurrency is a digital asset designed to work as a medium of exchange that uses strong cryptography to secure financial transactions, control the creation of additional units, and verify the transfer of assets. Cryptocurrencies are a kind of alternative currency and digital currency (of which virtual currency is a subset). Cryptocurrencies use decentralised control as opposed to centralised digital currency and central banking systems.

The decentralised control of each cryptocurrency works through distributed ledger technology, a blockchain that serves as a public financial transaction database.

Bitcoin, first released as an open-source software in 2009, is the first decentralised cryptocurrency. Since the release of bitcoin, over 4,000 altcoins (alternative variants of bitcoin or other cryptocurrencies) have been created.

The features of a cryptocurrency are:

1. The system does not require a central authority; its state is maintained through distributed consensus.
2. The system keeps an overview of cryptocurrency units and their ownership.
3. The system defines whether new cryptocurrency units can be created. If new cryptocurrency units can be created, the system defines the circumstances of their origin and how to determine the ownership of these new units.
4. Ownership of cryptocurrency units can be proved exclusively cryptographically.
5. The system allows transactions to be performed in which ownership of the cryptographic units is changed. A transaction statement can only be issued by an entity proving the current ownership of these units.
6. If two different instructions for changing the ownership of the same cryptographic units are simultaneously entered, the system performs at the most one.
7. The validity of each cryptocurrency coin is provided by a blockchain. A blockchain is a continuously growing list of records, called blocks, which are linked and secured using cryptography. Each block contains a hash pointer as a link to a previous block, a timestamp, and transaction data.
8. By design, blockchains are resistant to the modification of the data. It is 'an open, distributed ledger that can record transactions between two parties and in a verifiable and permanent way'.

9. For use as a distributed ledger, a blockchain is managed by a peer-to-peer network collectively adhering to a protocol for validating new blocks. Once recorded, the data in any given block cannot be altered retroactively without the alteration of all subsequent blocks, which requires collusion of the network majority.
10. Blockchains are secure by design.
11. Cryptocurrencies use various timestamping schemes to 'prove' the validity of transactions added to the blockchain ledger without the need for a trusted third party.
12. In cryptocurrency networks, mining is a validation of transactions. For this effort, successful miners get new cryptocurrency as a reward. The reward decreases transaction fees by creating a complementary incentive to contribute to the processing power of the network.
13. A cryptocurrency wallet stores the public and private 'keys' or 'addresses' which can receive or spend the cryptocurrency. With the private key, it is possible to write in the public ledger spending the associated cryptocurrency. With the public key, it is possible for others to send currency to the wallet.
14. Bitcoin is pseudonymous rather than anonymous in that the cryptocurrency within a wallet is not tied to people but rather to one or more specific keys (or addresses). Bitcoin owners are not identifiable, but all transactions are publicly available in the blockchain.

To summarise, cryptocurrency is a robust medium of exchange that does not need the intervention of any centralised agency like a bank for transfer of money from one person to another. The blockchain technology it uses is a more secure method than the existing digital system of authentication of transactions.

Still that does not make a cryptocurrency a valuable asset because:

1. Cryptocurrencies have *zero* intrinsic value. They are a medium of exchange and not the currency. It is a folly to think that the medium is a currency. It is like putting a money value to a cheque

used of transferring money from one person to another—not only putting money value on it, but speculating on and trading the value of the cheque. Nothing could be more laughable.
2. If cryptocurrencies had value, they should have reduced the value of existing currencies. It does not happen. How could an alternative emerge and rise to $20,000 a coin with no effect on the value of existing currencies? The bubble is right in front of us to see.
3. Cryptocurrencies are neither gold-standard nor fiat currencies. Those advising you to buy bitcoins tell you that mining bitcoin is akin to mining gold and that the quantity mined goes down as more and more coins get mined, thus maintaining a good demand–supply ratio. Thus, they argue, bitcoin will always have value. What they don't want to understand is that while bitcoin will be mined at a reducing rate, bitcoin is not the only currency. There are 4,000 altcoins already in the market, competing with each other. Why would you prefer bitcoin over any other coin? None of them have the backing of the government, so all of them are at par. Thus, there is an unlimited supply of cryptocurrencies possible. It will fail in the demand–supply game too.
4. Cryptocurrencies are the new tulips. They are worse than the tulips. When the tulip bubble crashed, you were left holding a tulip, and you did not know what to do with that. When the cryptocurrency bubble bursts, you won't even have a tulip; it will be a string of 0s and 1s sitting on your computer which will have to be trashed.
5. It is a great technology. The blockchain will have hundreds of applications that will change the way we do things. Perhaps it will also create the government-backed fiat currency of the future. Bitcoin will be dead soon, but the blockchain will survive and will prove to be one of the best innovations of the twenty-first century. They will write praises of the blockchain over the tombstone of bitcoin.

To cut it short, this book is all about value investing, which is buying assets at a price way below its value so you have a sufficient margin of safety. In cryptocurrencies, there is none since their intrinsic value is zero. Any price you pay above zero is the excess you have paid over the value.

Gold

The intelligent investor does not buy gold; it has no intrinsic value. The love for gold is so deep-rooted in Indian minds that whatever arguments you give, people feel gold is a worthwhile investment class. Let us debunk the myth. What we talk about gold here applies to all metals and stones.

The traditional Indian view has a root in the times when the banking system was not developed and was not accessible to all and when there were not enough investment avenues. People trusted metal more than anything else. It was easy to store and carry and could be sold or pawned when you ran out of money. Women were happy to flaunt the jewellery. In the minds of most people in our country, gold has continued to be the most solid investment and that its value would never go down to zero.

The reason gold is not to be considered as an investment is that gold produces no return. It has no intrinsic value. It fetches the price based on demand and supply. If the investors were to shift to gold as their favourite investment, its price would shoot up; but if the investors found another metal, say platinum, more attractive and sold gold to buy platinum, gold's price would plummet.

Gold performs no economic function. It is static wealth. It in fact has a negative intrinsic value: the investor pays storage charges to safeguard gold. It does not contribute to the economy and to building the nation. When you buy the shares of a company, you are transferring your savings to a company which will use the money to create value. It will generate employment, pay taxes to the government, produce goods and services which will be consumed by the economy, and so on. Gold performs no such function; your wealth lies static, producing no real gain.

Warren Buffett says:

> You could take all the gold that's ever been mined, and it would fill a cube 68 feet in each direction. For what that's worth at current gold prices, you could buy all—not some—of the farmland in the US. Plus; you could buy 16 Exxon Mobils, plus have $1 trillion of walking-around money. Or you could have a big cube of metal. Which would you take? Which will produce more value?

On another occasion, he says:

> Gold gets dug out of the ground in Africa, or someplace. Then we melt it down, dig another hole, bury it again and pay people to stand around guarding it. It has no utility. Anyone watching from Mars would be scratching their head.
>
> The major asset in this category is gold, currently a huge favourite of investors who fear almost all other assets, especially paper money (of whose value, as noted, they are right to be fearful). Gold, however, has two significant shortcomings, being neither of much use nor procreative. True, gold has some industrial and decorative utility, but the demand for these purposes is both limited and incapable of soaking up new production. Meanwhile, if you own one ounce of gold for an eternity, you will still own one ounce at its end.
>
> What motivates most gold purchasers is their belief that the ranks of the fearful will grow. During the past decade that belief has proved correct. Beyond that, the rising price has on its own generated additional buying enthusiasm, attracting purchasers who see the rise as

validating an investment thesis. As 'bandwagon' investors join any party, they create their own truth—for a while.

As for those who would still like to buy gold because it appreciates, it would interest them to know that as per a study, over 35 years in India, gold grew at a pathetic rate of 2.54%, silver at even lower than that at 1.35%, while equity had a double-digit rate of growth.

If you have access to modern financial systems, never invest in gold. If you live in a village which is not yet electrified and where a mobile phone and the Internet do not exist, gold can be a great investment. Gold is a great alternate currency. Recall the demonetisation announcement on 8 November 2016, when the first thing people did was to run to the jeweller to convert unaccounted cash into unaccounted gold. But if you are a part of the formal economy and modern financial systems, gold is not for you. Gold does not generate cash; it is not a money-making machine.

The Biggest Scam of the Century: The Diamond Industry

Diamonds are no better than cryptocurrencies as an investment. The moment we speak of diamonds, 'Diamonds are forever' echoes in our minds. Engagement rings must be diamond rings. It was not so just a few years back. It all started in 1938 when De Beers ran a massive campaign in the USA, bringing diamonds into the culture. Public memory is short. Diamonds have not been forever, and they won't be forever. They have been creating a demand for diamonds the world over as the only stone that can express romance.

A diamond is a depreciating asset masquerading as an investment. Diamonds have no intrinsic value. Try selling a piece of diamond, and you will recognise how illiquid it is. You may get a fraction of what you paid for buying it. Since diamonds have no intrinsic value, the sales are backed by heavy promotions and exorbitant retailer margin. The typical markup of a retailer ranges from 100% to 200%. (You should realise this when your favourite jeweller offers you a 30% discount on diamond jewellery.) There is a series of middlemen involved between De Beers and you, each adding to his markup.

I am not getting into the unethical aspects of diamond trade here (blood diamonds, bonded labour, child labour, unhealthy working conditions in the mines, etc.), but I am considering purely the investment angle.

Diamonds are not fungible, which means they cannot be exchanged with each other. You will need to sell it at a fraction of its price if you want to buy another. So let us be clear: diamond is not an investment. Do not fall victim to the scam.

Paintings, Antiques, Watches, Horses, and Other Collectibles

A distinction must be made between assets which generate cash flows and those which do not. Paintings and other collectibles do not have any economic function to perform and do not generate any cash flows. They need to be maintained. They need to be insured and stored safely. Vintage cars cost a hell of a lot of money to maintain. Horses need a hefty daily allowance to maintain.

Like beauty that lies in the eyes of the beholder, the price of these assets also lie in the minds of the buyer. A painting with the signature of M. F. Hussain may sell for US$1 million. It has no relationship to the cost. There is no intrinsic value, except perhaps the money spent on paint and canvas.

We are not interested in anything that has no intrinsic value and which does not perform any economic function. Since these assets have no intrinsic value, there is no benchmark price. If there is no buyer or if the preference changes, they won't sell. Not within our domain. Let's stay away from the ego products.

Real Estate

Mark Twain once said, 'Buy land, they are not making it anymore.' The greed to own land has existed since time immemorial. Kings have fought wars to gain more land and to defend their territories. A distinction has always been made between people who own land and people who do not. The landlords have always been the ruling class and consider themselves superior to the tenants. This has made us greedy for land. Until recently, we carried the notion we never lose money in real estate. The greed for real estate created a big bubble which burst a few years back, and the investors are yet to recover from the shock. Thousands of flats are lying unsold. Builders have defaulted; many of them are bankrupt. The bubble has burst.

Though the market will recover, real estate is still not the best of investments. Till a few years back when financial markets were not very developed, people invested in gold and in real estate. Unaccounted money, which goes by the euphemism 'black money', is the key feature of the Indian economy. What better avenue to put your money in than gold and real estate? Till recently, it was not uncommon for the seller to use terms such as 60 : 40, which meant 60% 'white money' and 40% 'black money'. Things have changed a great deal over time, though the sector still remains a parking place for unaccounted money.

Contrary to what people believed, a long-term return on real estate has been less than the interest on fixed deposits. Excess short-term returns were possible during the periods of irrational exuberance. The collapse of the market has shattered that myth.

A key criterion to gauge the intrinsic value of real estate is the rent it derives. In India the ratio of annual rental value to property price is low. Payback period based on rent is long, which makes real estate an unviable asset class.

Gains come from capital appreciation and not from rent. Capital appreciation is random and erratic. Some properties may appreciate because of proximity to the market or for whatever reasons, while others may not appreciate as much. It is a gamble. This book moves its readers away from gamble and speculation. If it is speculative, however good it may be, we do not recommend it.

Among all asset classes, the most illiquid is the real estate. Laws in India are complicated. The government records are far from perfect. Impersonation and forged signatures were not too uncommon in the past; many properties continue to be tainted because of past bad transactions. Though there has been a marked improvement in the procedures in recent times, still the past defects continue. Sale of properties requires clearance from dozens of authorities. The typical period of the realisation of a sale proceeds is one year. Litigations and non-receipt of NOCs from authorities may extend this period indefinitely. Money from properties may not become available to you when you need it.

Real estate cause much of the family litigations that happen in India. Litigations continue for generations. I know of a property dispute that has been pending in the courts for over a hundred years. Properties carry a bundle of emotions, nostalgia, and egos with them. Most property disputes are ego driven and may defy logic.

Property maintenance cost is high. Taxes and supervision costs are high. Encroachment on vacant properties is common, and the cost of keeping a property free from encroachment and encumbrance is exorbitant, unless you are occupying the property.

Sale price is a matter of haggling; there is no quote of prevailing price, unlike shares and other securities where you can find the current market price on a day-to-day basis. Deals are done through a broker, often in secrecy. After the contract is executed, you discover that unscrupulous brokers have taken you for a ride.

Property does not come in small pieces, and you need a larger capital investment. In Mumbai, the minimum price for the smallest apartment starts at ₹1 crore. In comparison, you can buy shares at as low as ₹500.

The Bottom Line

Real estate is not a worthy investment proposition. You should consider real estate as an investment only if you can put them to actual use. If you do not own a house, buying a house is a recommended property investment for you. Buying factory land and buildings, office space, shops for your actual business requirements is recommended. Stay away from real estate for any other reason.

CHAPTER 11

Efficient Market Hypothesis

I can calculate the movement of the stars, but not the madness of men.

           Sir Isaac Newton

When we say investors like Warren Buffett have been beating the market year in and year out, we get lots of frowns from the academics who believe beating the market is a random event and that it is out of sheer luck that some investor has done so at some point in time. The market is efficient in factoring all information in the price quote, so there are no superprofits to be made. Warren Buffett is often dubbed as 'the monkey on a typewriter of the infinite monkey theorem' by academics who swear by the efficient market hypothesis (EMH).

The infinite monkey theorem states that a monkey hitting keys at random on a typewriter keyboard for an infinite amount of time will almost surely type a given text, such as the complete works of William Shakespeare. In fact, the monkey will almost surely type every possible finite text an infinite number of times. However, the probability that monkeys filling the observable universe will type a complete work such as Shakespeare's *Hamlet* is so tiny that the chance of it occurring during a period of hundreds of thousands of orders of magnitude longer than the age of the universe is low (but technically not zero). Put in other words, is Buffett a monkey who has produced *Hamlet* by sheer randomness?

Whatever the financial theories might say, the fact remains that some investors continue to outperform the market and will continue to do so, and it is they who have the last laugh to the embarrassment of some of the most respected academics.

Let us first understand what EMH is, what its implications are, and then we find out how investors can consistently beat the market.

The efficient market hypothesis (EMH) is a theory in financial economics that states that asset prices fully reflect all available information. A direct implication is that it is impossible to 'beat the market' consistently on a risk-adjusted basis since market prices should only react to new information.

EMH was developed by Professor Eugene Fama, who argued that stocks always trade at their fair value, making it impossible for investors to either purchase undervalued stocks or sell stocks for inflated prices. It should be impossible to outperform the overall market through expert stock selection or market timing, and the only way an investor might get higher returns is by chance or by purchasing riskier investments. His study revealed that abnormal returns generated by some successful investors and outperforming mutual funds is not because of any special skills and that if they did not have the special skills, they would have still succeeded. The excess return is attributable to short-term anomalies that creep in during the time new information is syncing in.

There are three variants of the hypothesis: the 'weak', the 'semi-strong', and the 'strong' forms. The weak form of the EMH claims that prices of shares already reflect all past publicly available information. The semi-strong form of the EMH claims that prices reflect all publicly available information and that prices instantly change to reflect new public information. The strong form of the EMH additionally claims that prices instantly reflect even hidden 'insider' information.

Thus, prices follow a random walk, price quotations have no memory, and the price at any point in time is the price arrived at after factoring in all information and has no relationship with the previous price quote. Professor Malkiel conducted an experiment to prove that share price trend was a pseudo trend and the price could be as random as flipping a coin.

The theory is inspired by 'the invisible hand of the competitive market' of Adam Smith. Smith talked of the unobservable market forces that act invisibly in a market because in a free market, each rational investor is guided by greed and his own good. His purchase or sale represents his best interest; thus, the price determined by the interaction of these diverse self-interests is the perfect price.

Only unforeseeable events (like mergers, a change in technology, spin-offs, an announcement about new products or services) can give an opportunity for superprofits. Since these events are random and unpredictable, price movement is also random and unpredictable, as random as the walk of a drunken man. Seeing the clear logical soundness of the EMH, Michael Jensen stated, 'There is no other proposition in economics which has a more solid empirical evidence supporting it than the efficient market hypothesis.'

If EMH were true, how do hundreds of investors continue to outperform the market year after year? Warren Buffett's market performance makes a mockery of the theory. He has been right all these years and has consistently beaten the market every year of his long-standing professional career. Investors, including the likes of Buffett, have disputed both theoretically and empirically the EMH. The prerequisite for EMH is a presumption of the perfect market and a rational man. The market is seldom perfect, and man is seldom rational. Perfection in the market is distorted by several factors, such as overconfidence, overreaction, representative bias, information bias, and various other predictable human errors in reasoning and information processing.

Buffett explains this in his inimitable style: 'I'm convinced that there is much inefficiency in the market ... When the price of a stock can be influenced by a "herd" on Wall Street with prices set at the margin by the most emotional person, or the greediest person, or the most depressed person, it is hard to argue that the market always prices rationally. In fact, market prices are frequently nonsensical.'

'By and large I don't think too much of finance professors. It is a field with witchcraft,' says Munger.

Finance professors place too much reliance on EMH. They believe superprofits are not possible come what may. They do not understand that in the life of a company, many situations of mismatch between price and economic value will arise. There will be investors trying to exploit those mispriced situations using multiple strategies. The interaction of such strategies may create further mispricing.

To explain, if a group of investors belonging to a particular investment school sell a share short because they feel it is overpriced, constant onslaught by those bears may hammer the price down to a low level, so low that value investors find it a great buy and start 'bottom fishing'. As this value buying starts pulling the share up again, the bulls notice the uptrend and decide to ride on it, and the price soars. The share thus remains mispriced for a long period. Professors do not understand this simple behavioural aspect of the market and its constituents.

Let us see why EMH fails in the real world (despite so many Nobel laureates backing the theory).

First, information that becomes available is likely to be perceived and interpreted by people in different manners. Your experience, qualification, temperament, extent of exposure to the investment, and a host of other factors will decide how you react to a particular information. The aggregate of such varied individual responses is far from rational. In simple words, the average of irrational behaviour of constituents does not make an intelligent price quote.

Second, under EMH, no investor should be able to get a larger long-term average return than the market. How would the theory explain the vast variance in the performance of various mutual funds where the return could vary from −20% to +50%?

Third, and related to the second, if no investor is able to consistently beat the market, then how have investors like Buffett done it successfully for years?

To conclude, markets are not as efficient as theorists believe them to be. They remain inefficient more often than they remain efficient. Irrational exuberance is an important feature of the market, and as long as the market is driven by a herd mentality and the countering forces of greed and fear, anomalies will keep appearing. Intelligent investors will continue to exploit those anomalies to their advantage, notwithstanding what academics believe.

Common sense continues to be the scarcest commodity. Despite the information explosion, the ability to analyse the information rationally and objectively has not developed. Manic depressive Mr Market will keep knocking at your door in a state of wild optimism or pessimism. The performance of your portfolio will depend on how you evaluate his offers and take advantage of his irrational behaviour.

The market is not a laboratory and will always be a mix of variables—some predictable, some unpredictable, some behaving rationally, some behaving totally irrationally. The total of all this makes a curious mix devoid of any logical explanation. If the market were so mathematically accurate as propounders of EMH want us to believe, it would not have attracted billions of investors. It continues to attract investors, all trying their different investment strategies; some succeed, while a lot many underperform in the market. This irrational behaviour keeps the market off balance most of the time. It remains tilted up or down. The intelligent investor is likely to find value deals in most market conditions. And if the market is overheated, the intelligent investor does what he should do: he sits quietly, refusing to play to the euphoria of Mr Market. Sooner or later, the bipolar disorder of Mr Market will throw an attractive ball at him, and it will reward him. Patience makes an investor successful.

Speculators get investment guidance from Mr Market. They substitute his judgement for theirs. He is a wise man and can't be wrong. ("Trend is the best friend.") In reality, Mr Market knows nothing. He is the average of all contradictory forces that operate in the market. The speculator reads the daily market fluctuations with the seriousness of a doctor reading an ECG report, sometimes his heartbeats mimicking the daily fluctuation graph. Price rise on any day is a positive reinforcement of his buy decision and the price fall, a negative reinforcement. He feels happy when he thinks Mr Market is endorsing his judgement. When the price falls, he doubts his own judgement instead of challenging the wisdom of Mr Market. How can Mr Market be wrong? By the time he gets over the remorse of having made the wrong decision, the market has fallen more. He often ends up selling at the lowest price.

With 8 out of 10 players relying on Mr Market's verdict, the verdict has been influenced by the speculative intent of the speculators who then rely on that verdict as the final word. This is the fallacy of *circulus in probando*, the circular logic.

Price is determined by the equilibrium between demand and supply. Demand on a particular day is determined by various factors, such as the availability of cash with an investor, his perception about the market, his expectations about the future events, his moods, his perception about a particular stock, the opinion of the TV anchor, the latest tweet by Porinju Veliyath, and the sum total of these crazy behaviours reflected in the moods of Mr Market.

Since the speculator does not have any benchmark (such as intrinsic value) to compare the market price to, he relies on the combined forces of demand and supply to be more accurate. It is the biggest folly to think it reflects the fundamentals. A distinction has to be made between the day-to-day price fluctuations and the underlying fundamentals of a business. Both are not correlated in the short run. Prices go down when the underlying fundamentals are getting stronger. Short-term fluctuations are caused by a wide variety of causes and non-causes. Mr Market knows nothing; he is as stupid as the people who believe him.

Public memory is short. What shows on TV is what people remember. Research means googling the keyword and scrolling through the first fifty results. As long as people will have short memories and no inclination towards systematic research, stock prices will keep oscillating between greed and fear. This will always create opportunities for intelligent investors.

Charlie Munger has a take on this: 'My idea of shooting a fish in a barrel is draining the barrel first.' Munger likes the barrel to be drained first before he can shoot the fish inside. Water in the barrel is the herd of investors and speculators in the market. When they flee the market, he knows it is the best time to hunt for fish.

CHAPTER 12

Some Investment Follies

Every day, self-proclaimed stock market "experts" tell us why the market just went up or down, as if they really knew. So where were they yesterday?

Author Unknown

Search for the Holy Grail of Investment

The lure of quick money leads many to a search for a formula to succeed in the market. Human beings look for simple correlations, simple formulae to complex problems. A search for investment books on Amazon shows interesting titles, such as *Street Smart Trading, Swing Trading, Hot and Run Trading, Goodman Wave Theory, How to Trade Like a King, Master Swing Trader, High Probability Trading, Ripple Trading*, and so on. The fact that such books exist, and are sold, proves that investors are always on the lookout for a magical formula, the holy grail of investment. Looking into the complexities of the investment process, it is natural for people to believe that there must be some secret recipe that makes some investors succeed.

One magic formula is to apply your recent market success in the future. If you have succeeded because of a secular uptrend in the market, using whatever formula, you are likely to apply it in the next phase of the market as well. You apply it till you rise to your level of incompetence. History only rhymes; it does not repeat itself.

Investors would be better off learning about value investing reading books such as this instead of basing their investment decisions on unsubstantiated pseudo correlations.

Super Bowl Indicator

During my childhood days, there lived a lunatic who lived in a village an hour's drive from Nagpur. People visited him with a feeling of devotion. They thought him to have divine power, and the visitors would ask him questions concerning important aspects of their life, to which he would give absurd answers. The devotion and belief were so strong they would pick up clues from his meaningless replies and would feel he had answers to their problems. The mad god-man was always right!

The stock market has many such god-men, many such theories that people rely on. Let us pick up one such absurdity to explain how funny the market participants behave: the Super Bowl Indicator. You may have heard of it. It is so well known; it has its own entry at both Wikipedia and Investopedia. Investopedia says the Super Bowl Indicator is a not-so-serious market barometer based on the theory that a Super Bowl win for a team from the National Football League's American Football Conference (AFC) foretells a decline in the stock market the coming year. A win for a team from the National Football Conference (NFC) and teams from the original National Football League (NFL) before the merger of NFL and American Football League (AFL) in 1966 means the stock market will rise in the coming year.

Wikipedia says as of January 2017, the indicator has been correct *40 out of 50 times*, as measured by the S & P 500 Index, a *success rate of 80%*. What? The indicator has been correct 40 times out of 50? It means I will be right 80% of the time if I bet on the stock market based on the win of a particular football team!

The Hemline Index

Hold your breath. There is a theory in economics which says that the hemline of women's dresses rises with the stock market prices. In good economies, we get such results as miniskirts (as seen in the 1920s and the 1960s), or in poor economic times, as shown by the 1929 Wall Street Crash, hems can drop almost overnight. Non-peer-reviewed research in 2010 supported the correlation, suggesting that 'the economic cycle leads the hemline with about three years'.

The research concluded with these words: 'Supporting the urban legend, we find that poor economic times make the hemlines to decrease, which means that women's dresses get lower, and that prosperity is correlated with a reduced hemline (more miniskirts). At the same time, and this is new to the available evidence, we find that there is a time lag of around three years. This explains why at present, in an economic downturn, the skirts are short, as this is simply due to the fact that the economy was in a boom about three years ago.'

You may laugh, and you can see through the stupidity of the conclusion. I have presented this example to explain that there are hundreds of such models in economics and finance which use technical jargon to impress users but are no different from the Hemline Index. We believe what is published as research from a leading institute to be true because we cannot understand its premises. This example should encourage you to doubt anything that is presented in a manner that you cannot understand.

Correlation Does Not Imply Causation

This is a typical example of a post hoc fallacy. Since event Y occurs after event X, event Y must have been caused by event X. If AFC has won Super Bowl, the market must decline in the coming year. When the two variables are correlated, it is tempting to assume the causal relationship between the two. This is the classic case of a spurious correlation. The stock market is full of false theories, false indicators, and false predictors. I picked an extreme example to bring home the point.

With big data and supercomputing powers at our command, the situation is likely to worsen, and we are likely to find more such random coincidences. Unless we have our basics right, we will continue to break open fortune cookies to find our luck. Many of the best analytical models that traders use are nothing but sophisticated-looking versions of the Super Bowl Indicator, neatly hidden behind complicated calculus, graphs, and charts.

Technical Analysis Is Fundamentally Flawed

Technical analysts believe past trading activity and price changes of a security can be valuable indicators of the security's future price movements. They believe there is a predictable pattern in the price movements. The past data can be plotted on a chart and can be extrapolated to draw a trend line. This way, future price can be predicted.

If you do not know what technical analysis is, congratulations. It is better you do not know it. It is a pseudoscience which wears the cloak of a high-quality scientific work with profuse use of scientific-looking terms (like 100 days moving average, Bollinger Bands, candlestick patterns, support level, double bottom, double top) thrown in to impress the user.

If you know and understand technical analysis, unlearn it. It may not be good for your long-term financial health. It is something similar to someone playing a slot machine, thinking that since the last three balls have fallen to the left side, the next must also fall on the same side. Remember all those who sell snake oil or the quacks selling crystals to cure cancer? Or aromatherapy using aromatic oil for therapeutic purpose? Or astrology trying to predict future events based on the relative positions and movements of various real and construed celestial bodies? Tune in to business channels, and you will find 'expert technicians' discussing complicated charts and patterns, suggesting you which shares to buy and sell. Let it be clear. Technical analysis works no more than astronomy does nor market timing works.

I am amused when I watch technical experts air their opinion on business channels. 'Based on 100 days moving average, the price of this share should rise from ₹643 to ₹728.' Two days later, if there is a sudden shake-up in the market and the price has gone down to, say ₹618, the same expert has now noticed a downtrend, and now you must sell with a price target of ₹593. This is nothing more than pure entertainment. It is amusing to see people follow these advice.

If you can predict the market with a scientific accuracy, you should not invest the value-investing way. Why should you invest the boring way? You should buy on margins. You should be indulging in derivatives where you can buy big on a small margin.

The problem is, most people who think they can predict the market believe themselves to be prophetic. If you come across someone who can predict, befriend him. He is soon to become the richest man in the world. Till you find one, please continue to invest the way I suggest. I have worked hard to ensure you don't lose your shirt.

Sometimes technical analysis becomes a self-fulfilling prophecy. If a well-known analyst predicts that the price of a stock will be up by 20% in a few days, that prediction will make people buy the stock, and it will go up soon. However, the moment the gas is out of the balloon, it will fall again. Rise and fall without change in fundamentals may not endure long, and it is, at the most, speculative. Ignoring all those chatter that happens on TV will be good for the investor.

Apophenia

Technical analysts make the mistake of finding correlations where there are none. There is a term for such behaviour: *apophenia*. Apophenia is the experience of seeing meaningful patterns or connections in random or meaningless data. Neurologist Klaus Conrad coined the term. He defined it as the 'unmotivated seeing of connections'.

Apophenia may take the following forms:

1. *Clustering illusion.* Clustering illusion is the cognitive bias of seeing a pattern in what is a random sequence of numbers or events. Technical analysts make the mistake of projecting future price based on the past random patterns.
2. *Confirmation bias.* Confirmation bias, also known as observational selection or the enumeration of favourable circumstances, is the tendency for people to (consciously or unconsciously) seek information that conforms to their existing viewpoints and ignore information that goes against them, both positive and negative. It is a cognitive bias and selection bias towards confirmation of the hypothesis under study. You look for evidence to support the story that is already formed in your mind, and when you find one, it reinforces your story. In the days of big data analytics and information explosion, it is easy to fall prey to this bias. If you have a symptom which looks like cancer to you, you do a google search and will find many evidence to prove that it is cancer. If you have already formed an opinion that a company is a great buy at the present price, you can gather enough evidence to convince your mind that your belief was correct.
3. *Gambler's fallacy.* The gambler's fallacy (also the Monte Carlo fallacy or the fallacy of statistics) is the logical fallacy that a

random process becomes less random and more predictable as it is repeated. This is most commonly seen in gambling, hence the name of the fallacy. For example, a person playing craps may feel that the dice are 'due' for a certain number based on their failure to win after multiple rolls.

Separating Skill from Luck

Some analysts claim to know it all. They claim they are right all the time. To prove it, they show a track record of predicting the market over a long period. Let us understand how this scam operates.

In one version of this scam, let us call it the email scam. The analyst sends out unsolicited email to 1 million people. With everything on sale in the digital age, getting 1 million email addresses is no big deal. To half of them, he gives a tip: a particular share will be up within a fortnight. To the other half, the email is worded differently; it says the same share will fall. Half of the recipients will know he's wrong, while the other half will know he's right, though many will attribute his prediction to sheer luck. He will package his product in a complicated mathematical equation, using some scientific-sounding method to make it look like an exact science.

The next fortnight, he removes half a million from the database and sends the second mail to half the people who thought he was right the first time. He plays the same trick again. To 2.5 lakhs people, he sends a prediction about the rise of a particular share and, to the other 2.5 lakhs, the fall of the same share. He is smart enough to pick a share that has a high beta value (i.e. the share has an active movement up or down). He will be right to half of the recipients. If some people had not noticed his first email, it is time they notice the second one. He again eliminates the people to whom he proved wrong.

In the next iteration, it is 1.25 lakhs people and the same method. But now he can say he has been right four times in a row. The next three iterations make him right seven fortnights in a row, and the number is now 15,625. This may look like a small number, but they are likely to treat him like a god, someone who has been damn right at every prediction, that this is the man to be trusted. And this number is not too small because this is the set of people who are already sold to the idea, so the strike rate is high. It is at this point that he offers subscription to the exclusive club. No prize for guessing: people will queue up to be in. At the next prediction, if he is again at his game, he will disappoint half of his followers.

There are variations to the scheme. An astrologer makes ten different, unrelated predictions and posts them on different social media. If one prediction turns out true, he shares it in every social media to claim he had already predicted it, while the predictions proving him wrong are deleted from social media. In the digital age, public memory is short, and you don't feel the need to remember anything. You think you can also dig into social media and Google to retrieve past events. We know this as survivorship bias and is the logical error of concentrating on the people or things that made it past some selection process and overlooking those that did not because of their lack of visibility.

The mutual fund salesman who comes to you, showing schemes that have grown at 32% per annum for past seven years is resorting to the same scheme. He has eliminated loss-making schemes from out of hundreds his company has floated and is showing the success of a handful that are still surviving. Lord Keynes knows it well when he advises, 'If you can't forecast well, forecast often.' Forecast so much that there are more instances where you have been right!

Predictions often tell more about the forecaster than they tell about the future. Buffett once said, 'My own investment philosophy has developed around the theory that prophecy reveals far more of the frailties of the prophet than it reveals of the future.'

Be a sceptic; know that none can have a clear view of the future. The more an expert claims to know, the less he knows. Understand this, and it will save you a lot of stress and money you would have spent on the advice of experts. Once you learn you cannot outsource decision-making and understand that experts know less about your investments than you do, it will be the beginning of a successful investing career.

Munger explains, 'I know one guy; he's extremely smart and a very capable investor. I asked him, "What returns do you tell your institutional clients you will earn for them?" He said, "20%." I couldn't believe it because he knows that's impossible. But he said, "Charlie, if I gave them a lower number, they wouldn't give me any money to invest!"'

Professional money managers know they know nothing. (If someone does not know he knows nothing, he is in a state of bliss; ignorance is bliss.) But they are ready to make an irresponsible promise. They know they are throwing a dart. If it hits the target they get accolades; if it doesn't, they still get their pay cheque. That's the advantage OPM (other people's money).

I am convinced that an amateur investor is better equipped to make more money than the professional manager if he learns the discipline taught in this book and learns not to make stupid mistakes. In earlier times, when information was expensive and was available to only a select few, professionals had an edge. The Internet has made the playing field level for everyone, and now you have access to the same information that a professional has. You get it as fast as he gets it, if not faster. The cost of buying and selling is a fraction of what it used to be, again because of the Internet. Every single advantage that professional money managers had over the individual investors has vanished. There never was a better time for people like you and me to succeed in the stock market.

Confusing a Great Company as a Great Stock

You may find a company to be a great company and may be tempted to invest in that. Unless you study the financials, this approach is fraught with perils. The company may be good, but the 'good' may already have been factored in the price, and however good it may be, it is no good since it is overpriced. Remember, price is what you pay; value is what you get.

Sometimes what looks like a great company may not be all too great. You visit a hotel property and conclude that the hotel company is a great investment, not realising that the property you visited might be their only money-making property. They might lose money in all other properties.

Unless the feel-good factor of the company is reflected in the financial statements, it is an unreliable variable for decision-making.

Penny Stocks

Stock market tips to suggest the next Infosys and the next Wipro keep coming to you from all and sundry. With the digital technology attached to your person 24/7, tips keep pouring in on Facebook and WhatsApp and Twitter and Instagram and SMS and every other social media. Some of these tips come from the 'insiders', people who are in the knowledge of things that few know of. They know a penny stock has a potential to rise by 1,000% in a short time, from ₹0.85 to ₹8.50. To prove their credentials, they site penny stocks that have risen 1,000% to 10,000% in just one year.

When you have no research methodology of your own, you are likely to follow the 'tips'. People fail to realise that if tips were so useful, why would they reach out to you in the first place? Most tips come to you free of cost from clandestine sources, and you believe them to be true! Instead of waiting for the magic of compounding to create unlimited wealth for you, you buy or sell on impulses guided by greed and fear. Such behaviour cannot create wealth.

Some stocks rise. They may bring you a windfall. It is an 'easy come, easy go' situation.

Penny stocks are stocks that are trading at a low price, at less than ₹10. Having understood the concept of value investing after reading this book, you may argue that if it is selling at less than the intrinsic value, is it not a value buy? We answer the question after we discuss the pitfalls of investing in penny stocks.

There are plenty of penny stocks available on the bourses.

About 25% stocks on BSE and 10% stocks on NSE trade below ₹10. Market capitalisation of a third of the companies on NSE and two-thirds of the companies on BSE is below ₹100 crores. Most of the stocks on BSE trade in the 'T2T' category. Liquidity in T2T is low. When you want to buy, there may not be enough sellers. When you want to sell, there may not be enough buyers. The spread between buy and sell is high, and if you buy and sell on the same day, you lose a great deal of money in the spread.

It is easy to manipulate the price of penny stocks. Since they are low-priced and since most of the stocks are held by the insiders, with low floating stock, small investment in such stocks is enough to pump up the price.

Penny stocks are a great vehicle for the 'pump-and-dump scheme'. In a pump-and-dump scheme, the speculator (most of the time, the promoters of the company themselves) buys shares from the market and corner a substantial portion of floating stock. They now spread good news about the company, using email, social media, and a dedicated team of sub-brokers who give 'hot tips' about the company to their clients. Obliging journalists carry favourable stories about the company.

Many a time, a cartel spread across various cities carries out concerted action. Circular trading is resorted to. Broker A sells shares through the stock exchange for ₹50, which are lapped by broker B, who is part of the cartel. The next day, he offers it for sale at ₹60, which broker C, another cartel broker, is happy to buy. All the transactions happen through the recognised stock exchanges. Money changes hands through the settlement mechanism of the exchange. While all these trading is taking place, the media management network is busy creating goodwill for the company; the latest quarterly results show impressive growth, and the press reports show a 'turnaround' in the company.

Now the real money comes in, real people place the buy orders, the price surges, and the buyer buys more the next day, happy with the uptrend. The scheme is ready for the final act. Now there are enough buyers to buy out all cornered stocks; the cartel dumps it and takes the moolah home. The story has a tragic ending, the gullible investors are left with shares that won't sell. They might sit on the shares for the rest of their life, hoping (if not the real profitability) for the cartel to push the price again. The cartel would not do that again to the same company because they know the floating stock now belongs to outsiders. They have hundreds of other companies to play with. Next time, it will be another company. And perhaps some of the same investors who feel that 'this time it's different'.

Whenever the market rises, new theories are invented to justify the rise. Since the price has run way beyond the valuations, you must find some justification in buying at the inflated price, else the flow of money will stop, leading to a crash. The new theories, the new justification are meant to convince the existing investors not to sell and the new investors to buy—to keep the show going. At the peak of the dot-com mania, newspapers and magazines were flooded with articles talking about the death of conventional accounting norms and the need to replace website views as the new determinant of success of a dot-com company.

This leads to a further rise and creates the mania. Mania is difficult to resist as you make a lot of money. Everything turns into gold. When the bubble bursts, the money vanishes. I am yet to meet any speculator who came out of a bubble burst unhurt.

The surveillance teams of SEBI and stock exchanges often suspect pump and dump and other illegal activities taking place in some penny stocks. You would wonder why they don't suspend trading in these stocks. The reason is that if the trading is suspended or the company de-listed, the genuine investors would suffer as it will close the exit route of their investment. SEBI fines the insiders, bans them, names and shames them, but the show still goes on.

Having understood the risks, let us address the questions about value investing potentials of penny stocks. No denying, many start-ups who are penny stocks today may be the Infosys of tomorrow. They are buried in the heap of stocks which are bad quality, and it will require a considerable expertise and hard work to separate wheat from the chaff, perhaps as difficult as finding a needle in a haystack. It requires a different competence that a few of us have. Unless you have that special acumen, penny stocks are not for you. Those who want to specialise in penny stocks should know the failure rate is high. They are not for average value investors.

CHAPTER 13

Irrational Exuberance and Stock Market Bubbles

"October: This is one of the peculiarly dangerous months to speculate in stocks. The others are July, January, September, April, November, May, March, June, December, August and February."

Mark Twain

Two emotions drive the stock market: fear and greed. Often the investor is caught in greed and wants to make as much wealth as possible in the shortest possible time. When greed drives the market, frenzy and irrational exuberance prevail. Logic and rational thinking take a back seat in a greed-driven market. It is surprising that, every few years, the market gets into a euphoric state, greed overtakes fear, a big bubble builds up, and people refuse to believe or understand that it is a bubble; they refuse to learn from the history. When the bubble bursts, they lose everything.

Many a time, the bubble becomes so big that when it bursts, it pulls down the whole economy with it. Greed has existed since time immemorial.

Alchemy, the 'science' of converting any metal into gold, has drawn the best of brains for generations. Some things alchemists tried to do were change lead or mercury into gold, make the philosopher's stone, and make the 'elixir of life', which they thought could cure any disease and make someone young again. Conmen had a great time during the alchemy days. They knew alchemy to be a fake science but also knew how to exploit the gullible who were ready to invest everything they had so they could double or triple their wealth.

Ben Jonson's drama *The Alchemist*, first performed in 1610, had a successful run for decades. In *The Alchemist*, Jonson unashamedly satirises the follies, vanities, and vices of mankind, most notably greed-induced credulity. People of all social classes are subject to Jonson's ruthless, satirical wit. He mocks human weakness and gullibility to advertising and to the greed of turning base metal into gold.

The history of financial bubbles is also as old as civilisation. Let us read about some bubbles which, in retrospect, will make you wonder why people who indulged in it were crazy enough to not recognise the irrationality. It is easy to look at a thing in retrospect; it is a tough task when you are a character in the play. Knowing about past bubbles will help you understand the greed and fallible human being so that the next time the market becomes irrationally exuberant, you know what to do.

Reading this book and assimilating the philosophy explained here should act as a great insurance against financial bubbles. The intelligent investor does not speculate. He buys nothing that does not have a margin of safety built into the price he pays; he is not likely to become a prey to the bubbles.

The Tulipomania

The first recorded bubble is the Dutch tulip mania (1634–37). It was an episode in which speculators propelled tulip bulb prices to incredible heights before collapsing and plunging the Dutch economy into a severe crisis that lasted for many years.

Here are the events leading to the tulip mania.

The introduction of the tulip to Europe is usually attributed to Ogier de Busbecq, the ambassador of Ferdinand I, Roman emperor to the sultan of Turkey, who sent the first tulip bulbs and seeds to Vienna in 1554 from the Ottoman Empire. Tulips became a coveted luxury item, and a profusion of varieties followed.

Tulips grow from bulbs and can be propagated through both seeds and buds. Seeds from a tulip will form a flowering bulb after 7–12 years. When a bulb grows into a flower, the original bulb will disappear, but a clone bulb forms in its place, as do several buds. Properly cultivated, these buds will become bulbs of their own. During the plant's dormant phase from June to September, bulbs can be uprooted and moved about, so actual purchases (in the spot market) occurred during these months. During the rest of the year, florists or tulip traders signed contracts before a notary to buy tulips at the end of the season. Thus, the Dutch, who developed many of the techniques of modern finance, created a market for tulip bulbs, which were durable goods.

As the flowers grew in popularity, professional growers paid higher and higher prices for bulbs, and prices rose. By 1634, in part because of demand from the French, speculators entered the market. The contract price of rare bulbs continued to rise throughout 1636, but by November, the price of common 'unbroken' bulbs also increased. So soon, any tulip bulb could fetch hundreds of guilders. That year, the Dutch created a formal futures market where contracts to buy bulbs at the end of the season were bought and sold. Traders met in 'colleges' at taverns, and buyers were required to pay a 2.5% 'wine money' fee, up to a maximum of three guilders per trade. Neither party paid an initial margin or a mark-to-market margin, and all contracts were with the individual counterparties rather than with the exchange. The Dutch described tulip contract trading as *windhandel* ('wind trade') because no bulbs were changing hands. The entire business was accomplished on the margins of Dutch economic life, not in the exchange itself.

By 1636, the tulip bulb became the fourth leading export product of the Netherlands, after gin, herring, and cheese. The price of tulips skyrocketed because of speculation in tulip futures among people who never saw the bulbs.

Tulip mania reached its peak during the winter of 1636–37 when some bulbs were changing hands ten times in a day. No deliveries were ever made to fulfil any of these contracts because, in February 1637, tulip bulb contract prices collapsed and the trade of tulips ground to a halt.

By the peak of the Tulipomania in February 1637, a single tulip bulb was worth about ten times a craftsman's annual income, and *a single Viceroy tulip bulb* could be exchanged for *all* the following goods:

- 2 lasts of wheat
- 4 lasts of rye
- 4 fat oxen
- 8 fat swine
- 12 fat sheep
- 2 hogsheads of wine
- 4 tuns of beer
- 2 tons of butter
- 1,000 lb of cheese
- 1 complete bed
- 1 suit of clothes
- 1 silver drinking cup

Astronomically high tulip bulb prices resulted in some astonishing anecdotes, such as the sailor who mistakenly ate an extremely rare *Semper augustus* tulip bulb, thinking it was an onion. This 'onion' was so valuable it could have fed his whole ship's crew for an entire year. They jailed the hapless sailor for several months for his innocent but costly mistake.

Another similar anecdote is of a travelling English botanist who, unaware of the Dutch tulip mania of the time, peeled and dissected a wealthy Dutchman's ƒ4,000 Admiral Von der Eyk tulip bulb, mistaking it for an unusual species of onion. The bewildered English traveller was quickly led through the streets, followed by a mob, and brought before a judge who sentenced him to prison until he could pay for the damage.

Like all bubbles, the Dutch tulip bulb bubble continued to inflate beyond people's wildest expectations until it 'popped' in the winter of 1636–37. A default on a tulip bulb contract by a buyer in Haarlem was the main bubble-popping catalyst and caused the tulip bulb market to implode as sellers overwhelmed the market and buyers disappeared altogether. Some traders attempted to support prices, to no avail. Within just a few days, tulip bulbs were worth only a hundredth of their former prices, resulting in a full-blown panic throughout Holland.

Dealers refused to honour contracts, further damaging confidence in the tulip bulb market. Eventually, the government attempted to stem the tulip market meltdown by offering to honour contracts at 10% of their face value, which only caused the market to plunge even further. The brutal popping of the tulip bulb bubble ended the Dutch Golden Age and hurled the country into a mild economic depression that lasted for several years.

Thanks to what they went through, the Dutch still look at all speculative schemes with suspicion. Perhaps the stinginess of the Dutch is also because of the loss of money and sanity during the tulip mania.

The South Sea Bubble

The South Sea Bubble is one of the largest asset bubbles that the world has ever seen. In fact, this bubble bankrupted the prosperous British economy during the seventeenth century. At one point in time, all the money in Britain was not enough to pay the debts that accrued because of the South Sea Bubble.

Although this bubble happened 300 years ago, generations of the British population have been paying this debt. Even today, a portion of the tax collected from the general population is used to pay off this debt.

The government of England had been at war with almost all of its neighbours during the seventeenth century. These wars had proved very expensive for the exchequer. Of these wars, Britain had amassed a massive debt of £31 million while it had a meagre £50,000 in reserves to service this obligation. The government was bankrupt, and it had no way to pay the next interest instalments that would be due on the loans.

A man named John Blunt came to the fore during this crisis. He offered the chancellor of the English treasury an option to get rid of all the debt at once and overnight! This could be done by creating a new company called the South Sea Company. This company would have monopoly rights to trade with the South Seas (i.e. Central and South America).

The money generated through such trade would have increased the value of the shares. But Central and South America were under Spanish rule, and Britain was at war with Spain. However, the British somehow convinced the Spaniards to allow them to load one ship of goods per year for every South American port and the right to trade slaves! Not mentioning this meagre trade agreement clearly, John Blunt declared that they had struck an agreement with the Spaniards, and the South Sea Company was ready for business.

In fact, he even gave the king and other honorary members of parliament shares in the business. This convinced the common man of the authenticity of the shares, and the price of shares skyrocketed.

As the value of each share rose, fewer shares had to be issued to knock off England's debt of £31 million. Thus, John Blunt had authorisation to create more shares and sell them at the market rate and pocket the profit. That is what the South Seas Company management did. By this time, John Blunt and anybody connected with him had become wealthy beyond imagination. The South Sea Company had a market capitalisation close to 25% of the British GDP and could be considered being valued at half the valuation of all companies listed on the New York Stock Exchange today! The South Sea Company did not earn a dime in operations, and yet it was the most valuable company on the planet!

Since the South Sea Company made no money through operations, there was only one way to keep the company in existence (i.e. ensuring that the share price went higher and higher). Only the sale of new stock could pay the dividends due to old stockholders and maintain the facade of a successful corporation.

John Blunt came with an interesting Ponzi scheme to keep the show going.

First, he declared that the people only needed to put 20% of the money down to take ownership of the stock and the balance could be paid two months later. This created an obscene amount of demand since people were buying five times as many shares as they earlier could, therefore raising the prices higher. The price of a share with a £100 face value went up to £500 in a matter of weeks.

To further prop up demand, John Blunt was loaning out money from the coffers of the South Sea Company to investors who wanted to buy the stock! Once again, artificial demand was created, and prices were now in the £800 range.

Last, John Blunt undertook an audacious scheme and sold shares for just 10% down with the balance to be paid out a year later. This time, the stock hit the roof, and the price was over £1,000 per share.

However, the public soon realised the illusion they had been living and sold off their holdings. As the prices collapsed, John Blunt offered investors an insane 30% dividends on their stock every year for the next ten years. This desperation by John Blunt confirmed the public fears that the South Sea Company was a gigantic bubble. A massive sale of the stocks took place, and within three weeks, the £1,000 shares were worthless.

Many people had lost their life savings in the South Sea Bubble. Bankruptcies were rampant, as many common people had extrapolated the trend of South Sea's past success and had borrowed money to invest in the company, hoping to make a windfall gain. The windfall gain did not happen. Instead the British middle class was wiped out and burdened with a debt which is still being paid out from tax revenues 300 years later.

Railway Mania

The Railway Mania was the earliest technology bubble in the UK in the 1840s and can be compared to the dot-com bubble of the 1990s. It followed a common pattern: as the price of railway shares increased, more and more money was poured in by speculators until the inevitable collapse. It reached its zenith in 1846, when 272 acts of parliament were passed, setting up new railway companies, with the proposed routes totalling 15,300 km of the new railway.

Around a third of the railways authorised were never built. The companies either collapsed due to poor financial planning, were bought out by larger competitors before they could build their line, or turned out to be fraudulent enterprises to channel investors' money into other businesses.

In 1825 the government had repealed the Bubble Act, which had been brought in after the near-disastrous South Sea Bubble of 1720. It had put close limits on the formation of new business ventures and had limited joint-stock companies to a maximum of five separate investors. With these limits removed, anyone could invest money (and hopefully earn a return) on a new company, and railways were promoted as a foolproof venture.

New media such as newspapers and the emergence of the modern stock market made it easy for companies to promote themselves and provide the means for the public to invest. Shares could be purchased for a 10% deposit, with the railway company holding the right to call in the rest at any time. The railways were so heavily promoted as a foolproof venture that thousands of investors on modest incomes bought large numbers of shares while only being able to afford the deposit. Many families invested their entire savings in prospective railway companies, and many of those lost everything when the bubble collapsed and the companies called in the rest of their due payments.

The British government promoted an almost laissez-faire system of non-regulation in the railways. Companies had to submit a bill to the parliament to gain the right to acquire land for the line, which required the route of the proposed railway to be approved, but there were no limits on the number of companies and no real checks on the financial viability of a line. Anyone could form a company, gain investment, and submit a bill to the parliament.

Since many MPs were heavy investors in such schemes, it was rare for a bill to not pass during the peak of the mania in 1846. Although the parliament rejected schemes that were misleading or impossible to construct, at the mania's peak, there were several schemes floated for 'direct' railways which ran in vast, straight lines across swathes of countryside that would have been difficult to construct and impossible for the locomotives of the day to work on.

Magnates like George Hudson developed routes in the north and in the Midlands by amalgamating small railway companies and rationalising routes. He was also an MP, but he failed owing to his fraudulent practices of, for example, paying dividends from capital.

As with other bubbles, the Railway Mania became a self-promoting cycle based on overoptimistic speculation. As the dozens of companies formed operated and the simple non-viability of many of them became clear, investors realised that railways were not as lucrative and as easy to build as they had been led to believe. Coupled with this, in late 1845, the Bank of England put up interest rates.

As banks began to reinvest in bonds, the money flowed out of railways, undercutting the boom. The share prices of railways slowed in their rise then levelled out. As they fell, investment stopped overnight, leaving numerous companies without funding and numerous investors with no prospect of any return on their investment. The larger railway companies, such as the Great Western Railway and the nascent Midland Railway, bought up strategic failed lines to expand their network. These lines could be purchased at a fraction of their real value as given a choice between a below-value offer for their shares or the total loss of their investment, shareholders naturally chose the former.

Many middle-class families on modest incomes had sunk their entire savings into new companies during the mania, and they lost everything when the speculation collapsed.

America's Stock Market Crash of 1929

On 29 October 1929, Black Tuesday hit Wall Street as investors traded some 16 million shares on the New York Stock Exchange in a single day. Investors lost billions of dollars. In the aftermath of Black Tuesday, America and the rest of the industrialised world spiralled downward into the Great Depression (1929–39), the deepest and longest-lasting economic downturn in the history of the Western industrialised world up to that time.

During the 1920s, the US stock market underwent rapid expansion, reaching its peak in August 1929 after a period of wild speculation. By then, production had already declined, and unemployment had risen, leaving stocks in great excess of their real value.

Among the other causes of the eventual market collapse were low wages, the proliferation of debt, a struggling agricultural sector, and an excess of large bank loans that could not be liquidated.

Stock prices declined in September and early October 1929, and on 18 October, the fall began. Panic set in, and on 24 October, Black Thursday, a record 12,894,650 shares were traded. Investment companies and leading bankers attempted to stabilise the market by buying up great blocks of stock, producing a moderate rally on Friday. On Monday, however, the storm broke anew, and the market went into free fall. Black Monday was followed by Black Tuesday (October 29), in which stock prices collapsed and 16,410,030 shares were traded on the New York Stock Exchange in a single day. Stock tickers ran hours behind because the machinery could not handle the tremendous volume of trading.

After 29 October 1929, stock prices had nowhere to go but up, so there was considerable recovery during succeeding weeks. Overall, however, prices continued to drop as the United States slumped into the Great Depression, and by 1932, stocks were worth only about 20% of their value in the summer of 1929. The stock market crash of 1929 was not the sole cause of the Great Depression, but it acted to speed up the global economic collapse of which it was also a symptom.

By 1933, half of America's banks had failed, and unemployment was approaching 15 million people, or 30% of the workforce.

Black Monday of 1987

Monday, 19 October 1987, is called the Black Monday. It was when stock markets around the world crashed in unison. The crash began in Hong Kong and spread west to Europe, hitting the United States after other markets had already sustained significant declines. The Dow Jones Industrial Average (DJIA) fell 23% in a single day.

On Thursday, 15 October 1987, Iran hit the American-owned supertanker *Sungari* with a Silkworm missile off Kuwait's main Mina Al Ahmadi oil port. The next morning, Iran hit another ship, the US-flagged MV *Sea Isle City*, with another Silkworm missile. On Friday, 16 October, when all the markets in London were unexpectedly closed due to the Great Storm of 1987, the DJIA fell 108.35 points and closed at 2,246.74 on record volume. The then treasury secretary James Baker stated concerns about the falling prices.

The crash began in Far Eastern markets the morning of 19 October and sped up in London time because London had closed early on 16 October due to the storm. By 9.30 a.m., the London FTSE100 had fallen over 136 points. Later that morning, two US warships shelled an Iranian oil platform in the Persian Gulf in response to Iran's Silkworm missile attack on the *Sea Isle City*.

By the end of October, stock markets had fallen in Hong Kong (45.5%), Australia (41.8%), Spain (31%), the United Kingdom (26.45%), the United States (22.68%), and Canada (22.5%). New Zealand's market was hit hard, falling about 60% from its 1987 peak and would take several years to recover.

The Black Monday decline was and remains as the largest one-day percentage decline in the DJIA.

A popular explanation for the 1987 crash was computerised selling dictated by portfolio insurance hedges, the culprit being programme trading. In programme trading, computers execute rapid stock trades based on external inputs, such as the price of related securities. Common strategies implemented by programme trading involve an attempt to engage in arbitrage and portfolio insurance strategies.

As computer technology became widespread, programme trading grew dramatically within Wall Street firms. After the crash, many blamed programme trading strategies for blindly selling stocks as markets fell, exacerbating the decline.

The Dot-Com Bubble

The dot-com bubble was a historic economic bubble and period of excessive speculation that occurred from 1995 to 2000, a period of extreme growth in the usage and adaptation of the Internet. The Nasdaq Composite stock market index, which included many Internet-based companies, peaked in value on 10 March 2000 before crashing. The dot-com crash lasted from 11 March 2000 to 9 October 2002.

When the story was building, the investors thought the Internet was the panacea to all world problems, and any company that had dot-com at the end of its name (or any Internet-related prefix or suffix) was a potential goldmine.

Venture capital was easy to raise. Investment banks, which profited from initial public offerings (IPO), fuelled speculation and encouraged investment in technology. A combination of increasing stock prices in the quaternary sector of the economy and confidence that the companies would turn future profits created an environment in which many investors were willing to overlook traditional metrics, such as the price–earnings ratio and base confidence on technological advancements, leading to a stock market bubble.

Between 1995 and 2000, the Nasdaq Composite stock market index rose 400%. It reached a *price–earnings ratio of 200*, dwarfing the peak price–earnings ratio of 80 for the Japanese Nikkei 225 during the

Japanese asset price bubble of 1991. In 1999, shares of Qualcomm rose in value by 2,619%, 12 other large-cap stocks each rose over 1,000% value, and 7 additional large-cap stocks each rose over 900% in value.

An unprecedented amount of personal investing occurred during the boom, and stories of people quitting their jobs to engage in full-time day trading were common.

The news media took advantage of the public's desire to invest in the stock market; an article in *The Wall Street Journal* suggested that investors 'rethink' the 'quaint idea' of profits, and CNBC reported on the stock market with the same level of suspense as many networks provided to the broadcasting of sports events.

At the height of the boom, it was possible for a promising dot-com company to become a public company via an IPO and raise a substantial amount of money even if it had never made a profit or, in some cases, realised any material revenue.

People who received employee stock options became instant paper millionaires when their companies executed IPOs; however, most employees were barred from selling shares immediately due to lock-up periods.

Most dot-com companies incurred net operating losses as they spent heavily on advertising and promotions to harness network effects to build market share or mind share as fast as possible, using the mottos 'Get big fast' and 'Get large or get lost'. These companies offered their services or products for free or at a discount, expecting they could build enough brand awareness to charge profitable rates for their services in the future.

The 'growth over profits' mentality and the aura of the 'new economy' invincibility led companies to engage in lavish spending on elaborate business facilities and luxury vacations for employees. Upon the launch of a new product or website, a company would organise an expensive event called a dot-com party!

On 20 March 2000, *Barron's* featured a cover article titled 'Burning Up; Warning: Internet Companies Are Running Out of Cash—Fast', which predicted the imminent bankruptcy of many Internet companies. This led many people to rethink their investments. That same day, Microstrategy announced a revenue restatement due to aggressive accounting practices. Its stock price, which had risen from $7 per share to as high as $333 per share in a year, fell $140 per share, or 62%, in a day. On Friday, 14 April 2000, the Nasdaq Composite Index fell 9%, ending a week in which it fell 25%. This forced the investors to sell stocks ahead of Tax Day, the due date to pay taxes on gains realised in the previous year. On 9 November 2000, Pets.com, a much-hyped company that had backing from Amazon.com, went out of business only nine months after completing its IPO. By that time, most Internet stocks had declined in value by 75% from their highs, wiping out $1.755 trillion in value.

Many dot-com companies ran out of capital and went through liquidation. Supporting industries, such as advertising and shipping, scaled back their operations as the demand for services fell. Several companies and their executives were accused or convicted of fraud for misusing shareholders' money, and the US Securities and Exchange Commission levied large fines against investment firms, including Citigroup and Merrill Lynch, for misleading investors.

Indian Stock Market Crashes

India experienced its first stock market crash in 1865. Although the Bombay Stock Exchange had not yet been formed, Gujarati and Parsi traders often traded shares mutually at the junction of Rampart Row and Meadows Street. In the preceding years, speculation about the results of the American Civil War had led to irrational increase of stock prices of new Indian companies. Shares of the Backbay Reclamation (face value ₹5,000) touched ₹50,000, and those of Bank of Bombay (face value ₹500) touched ₹2,850.

Money made from cotton was pumped into the stock market, driving prices of stocks higher. Banks loaned money to speculators, further fuelling the bull run, and wealthy merchants like Premchand Roychand dispensed advice that led to ordinary people placing their bets on shares.

New companies were floated with new share issues publicised in the newspapers. Forward contracts further promoted speculative purchases. However, the market crashed in May 1865 when the civil war ended, causing cotton prices to fall. Shares of the Backbay Reclamation fell by 96% to under ₹2,000, and several merchants including, Behramji Hormusji Cama, went bankrupt. The crash not only led to a dwindling of the financial fortunes of many; it also led to a decrease of the city's population by 21% due to the closing down of many enterprises. On 1 July 1865, when hundreds of 'time bargains' had matured (as the future contracts were then known), buyers and sellers alike defaulted, leading to the burst of the bubble. A share of Bank of Bombay, which had touched ₹2,850 at the peak of the market, slumped to just ₹87 in the aftermath of the bust.

After the liberalisation of India in 1991, the stock market saw several cycles of booms and busts. Some were related to scams such as those engineered by players like Harshad Mehta and Ketan Parekh. Some were due to global events. And a few were due to circular trading, rigging of prices, and the irrational exuberance of investors, leading to bubbles that burst.

Considering the world financial crisis of 2007–2008, the stock markets in India fell frequently in 2007 and 2008. In 2007 alone, there were five sharp falls in the stock markets.

On 21 January 2008, the BSE fell by 1,408 points to 17,605, leading to one of the largest erosions in investor wealth. The BSE stopped trading for a while at 2.30 p.m. due to a technical snag, although its circuit filter allows swings of up to 15% before stopping trading for an hour.

Referred to in the media as Black Monday, the fall was blamed by analysts at HSBC Mutual Fund and JP Morgan on a large variety of reasons, including a change in the global investment climate, fears of the United States' economy going into a recession, FIIs and foreign hedge funds selling to reallocate their funds from risky emerging markets to stable developed markets, a cut in US interest, huge build-ups in derivatives positions leading to margin calls, and many IPOs sucking out liquidity from the primary market into the secondary market.

CHAPTER 14
Value Investing

"The stock market is filled with individuals who know the price of everything, but the value of nothing."

Philip Fisher

Value investing refers to buying and selling shares on the basis of a perceived gap between their market price and intrinsic value. Almost all successful investors in the world practise some form of value investing. There are as many variations of value investing as there are value investors, each investor adopting the version that suits his inclinations.

It is fashionable to speak of yourself as a value investor—quite safe also. Nobody understands it anyway. The term is prone to be misused. *Value investing* is a bait mutual funds use to lure the investors; when investment analysts find that an investment is not behaving the way they expected it to behave, they take refuge in the term *value investing*. Despite its fan following, few have a clear idea of what it is.

Few mutual funds are value investors. Value investing is a subset of fundamental analysis. Fundamental analysis requires patience and long-term commitment. Mutual funds managers must prove their work every quarter and every year. Fundamental analysis is the casualty. They find support in academic models such as efficient market hypothesis, for which at least three academics have won the Nobel Prize. Value investing for most mutual funds is only a sales gimmick.

There is nothing mysterious about value investing. It is simply finding the intrinsic value of an asset and then buying it at a considerable discount to that value. It is as easy as ABC. The challenge is in having the requisite discipline to buy it at a discounted price and to sell it when the discount has vanished. The challenge is also in not giving up to short-term noises and fluctuations.

Other investors do not have a benchmark value. They risk losing their capital. The first principle of a value investor is to buy with a margin of safety so that he is able to protect his capital. The margin of safety takes care of market excesses and valuation errors.

I can categorise popular investment methods as follows:

1. value investing
2. growth investing
3. portfolio investing
4. momentum investing.

Value investing involves buying securities below intrinsic value. Value investors distinguish between value and price. They believe markets are frequently in a state of irrationality. Often there is a divergence between price and value: when the markets go euphoric, price exceeds value, and when the markets are depressed, investment is available below its price. This divergence of value from price gives rise to buying and selling opportunities.

Growth investing is a variant of value investing. Value investing looks at the present value; growth investing looks at the rate of growth, which will eventually create value. Growth investing apparently seems contradictory to value investing in that you may pay more than the value. In effect, however, a premium is paid for the growth, which will generate value in the future. Warren Buffett explains this by saying, 'Growth and value investing are joined at the hip.' Another very famous investor, Peter Lynch, pioneered a hybrid of growth and value investing with what is now referred to as a 'growth at a reasonable price (GARP)' strategy.

Momentum investors go by the trend. They are also known as technical investors or technicians or chartists. They believe that a trend, once established, will continue forever unless some force changes its course. Using the charting techniques, they try to predict the future price. Technical analysts also use market indicators of many sorts, some of which are mathematical transformations of price, often including up and down volume, advance/decline data, and other inputs. They use these indicators to help assess whether an asset is trending and, if it is, the probability of its direction and continuation. Technicians also look for relationships between price–volume indices and market indicators.

Portfolio investors determine their risk appetite and create a diversified portfolio based on their individual risk appetite. The inventor of the strategy is Burton Gordon Malkiel, an American economist and writer most famous for his classic finance book *A Random Walk Down Wall Street*. He is a leading proponent of the efficient market hypothesis, which contends that prices of publicly traded assets reflect all publicly available information. Malkeil believes that since the market is efficient, active intervention with the market does not help.

Thus, the value investors look for shares below their intrinsic value. Growth investors seek companies whose near-term growth will cause value, thus justifying current price. Portfolio investors don't bother about divergence in value and price; in fact, they believe price is the true reflection of value, so they buy a mix of stocks that will mitigate the risk. Momentum investors are unconcerned with value. They look for shares much in demand so they can sell off and book profits.

A technical investor charts the trend line, which is historical price data. Price at any point in time is determined by demand and supply. On an *X–Y* table, the technical analyst charts the price movement of the past. So far so good. But now he uses his chart as a tool for price prediction. He extrapolates the data to project the future price. He believes that the clue to the future price is already there in the present price line. He disregards the fundamentals of the company he is analysing. To him, the company is just a name with a trend line. Name is not as important to him as the trend line is.

From the point of view of value investors, technical investing is nothing more than a speculation. How can you predict price while disregarding the fundamentals? Published annual accounts received by a technical analyst find their way to the wastepaper basket at the first opportunity.

If price were so detached from fundamentals, that fundamentals were inconsequential; absurd consequences could follow. In the short run, divergence between price and value does arise. The market is far from being perfect. Small and inconsequential events get amplified, and major events sometimes remain unnoticed. Many 'non-events' also get factored in the price in the short run. However, in the long run, price line crosses the value line many a time. These irrational price movements give rise to many bargain situations for purchase and sale of shares. A value investor waits patiently to exploit such irrationality in the market.

Value investing is more about an attitude, a state of mind. If you have ever travelled by a Mumbai suburban train, you can understand the following example. (Search Google images for 'Bombay local' to know what I mean.) Since the whole of the working population travels from suburban sites to the business district every day during peak hours, passengers squeeze themselves in the coaches like a can of tuna. In the morning, everyone travels to the business district, and in the evening, everyone moves out. There is no traffic if you travel against the current: going away in the morning and towards the commercial centre in the evening.

If you want to board a train from, say, Sandhurst Road to Dadar in the evening when the whole traffic is moving in that direction, you can do either of two things.

First, and this is what people do, use all your muscle power to hold the support bar of the coach as the train stops for a couple of seconds, and be part of the crowd and push your way in the already-crowded train. In fact, much of the muscle work is done by the people behind you, who will push you in the train; it's almost like a synchronised motion since people behind them are pushing them in!

Or you can take a contrarian stand. You take the train to the opposite direction: to the Victoria Terminus (now rechristened as the Chhatrapati Shivaji Terminus, or CST). Since there is no flow of traffic towards the business district at that hour, you can find a comfortable seat. You travel to CST, which is two stations away, and when everyone gets off, you remain seated. You take the best seat option available. At CST, a crowd throngs the coach. Since you have a comfortable seat already, you smile when the crowd jostles one another!

If you have the patience of the contrarian traveller, you have all the virtues of becoming a value investor. A contrarian traveller travels against the crowd. He knows he will take more time than the crowd, but he also knows he will arrive comfortably and in better shape.

Let us use the analogy to understand the concept of value investing. In the market, there are players who enter with different purposes and use different investment strategies. Their holding period also varies. Some of them are intraday traders, who buy during a trading session and square up the deal before the close of the session, taking home the difference as profit (or incurring a loss). There are short-term players and long-term players and hedgers and arbitrageurs and so on. While many of them take recourse to technical analysis, there are some who buy after studying the fundamentals and after assuring themselves that there is enough margin of safety for them.

The technical traders, or momentum players, are akin to the passengers on Mumbai suburban routes who join the crowd. Like the crowd that pushes the passenger into the coach and out of the coach, they also ride on the crowd. They ride on the trend. Trend is a graphic representation of the demand–supply equation, thus representing the crowd. They buy a share after they are convinced that there are numerous people who have already bought it and that more people are still buying it, thus causing a rise in price. When they sell, they wait for that point in time where many people have already sold it. This gives them a clear sign that a downtrend is established and that, once established, the downtrend will continue to take the price to lower and lower level.

A value investor behaves like the passenger who boards two stations back. He will not trust a share unless it is backed by sound fundamentals. He looks for a bargain. He finds out the shares that are selling at a discount to their real value. Market movements do not bother him, nor do the popularity or otherwise of a share. More often than not, the shares he discovers after a great deal of hard work turn out to be shares that are out of favour for some reason or are being neglected or ignored or despised by the market. This makes him a contrarian investor. He keeps buying those shares with the full conviction that someday the market is likely to recognise the true worth of the shares he is buying. He buys and sits tight on his investment till the market realises its true potential. Then he sells at a handsome gain. The strategy may look unglamorous and less appealing to many people since it lacks the lustre that is so often associated with the stock market. But he does not care about the glamour. He cares about the money, and he makes more money than his neighbour, and makes it more safely.

Benjamin Graham is considered the father of value investing. His book *Intelligent Investor* has seen many editions and reprints since it was originally published in 1949, and his other book, *Security Analysis*, has remained equally popular. His most famous student, Warren Buffett, has said whenever he is in doubt about his investment decisions that he likes to go back to *Security Analysis* for a solution.

Intrinsic Value

The long-term investor looks for value. Value is created when a stock is available at a price below its intrinsic value. While in the long term, stock prices hover around the intrinsic value, in the short run, they often digress from each other. Optimism or pessimism may cause price to rise or fall way beyond the fundamentals. Warren Buffett says that, in the short run, the market is like a voting machine but, in the long run, it is like a weighing machine. In the short run, stock prices determination is akin to a popularity contest; however, in the long run, prices must settle around the fundamental value. The earnings, cash flow, and assets quality matter in the long run.

Things that matter on a day-to-day basis are too fickle and change frequently. Add to this the role that noise has to play—noise created by news, gossips, rumours, speculation about the company, the industry, the economy, the country, and the world. Voters are fickle and change their mind at every news, good or bad, related or unrelated. When the market is bullish, good news is amplified beyond its fundamental impact, and bad news gets played down upon; however, when the sentiments are down, bad news cause more havoc than can be justified, and they seldom notice the good news. The moody Mr Market continues to show his mood swings. In the long run, however, the weighing machine measures the fundamentals more accurately.

There are two approaches to calculating intrinsic value. First, the discounted cash flow model uses future free cash flow projections and discounts them, using a required annual rate, to arrive at present value estimates. While the calculations involved are complex, the purpose of the DCF analysis is to estimate the money an investor would receive from an investment, adjusted for the time value of money.

The father of value investing, Benjamin Graham, devised the second approach: the *original Benjamin Graham formula*.

The original formula from *Security Analysis* is:

$$V = EPS \times (8.5 + 2g)$$

V is the intrinsic value, EPS is the trailing 12-month EPS, 8.5 is the P–E ratio of a stock with 0% growth, and g is the growth rate for the next 7–10 years.

However, this formula was later revised as Graham included a required rate of return.

$$V = \frac{EPS \times (8.5 + 2g) \times 4.4}{Y}$$

The formula is the same, except the number 4.4 is what Graham determined to be his minimum required rate of return. At the time of around 1962, when Graham was publicising his works, the risk-free interest rate was 4.4%, but to adjust to the present, we divide this number by today's AAA corporate bond rate, represented by Y in the formula above.

All this may look too complicated to a beginner, but as we dwell more into it, you realise that these are simple methods of finding the fundamental valuation without resorting to complex mathematical exercise. Anyway, this is of not much practical relevance in present times. The world has moved ahead, making Graham's method redundant. But the credit to instil the value investing discipline goes to Graham. The investors would remain indebted to him forever for separating scientific investing from a game of chance. Investors following his concepts continue to make unlimited wealth and will continue to do so.

Times and circumstances might have changed quite a lot since Graham wrote his book, but his key principles have stood the test of time. The core principle, 'margin of safety', continues to be the soul of value investing: paying a price far below the value to avoid erosion of capital in case of market fall. Graham was a pure balance sheet analyst. He never wished to go beyond published accounts. He invented the net–net method of finding the intrinsic value. The net–net investing method focuses on current assets, taking cash and cash equivalents at full value, reducing accounts receivable for doubtful accounts, and reducing inventories to liquidation values. Total liabilities are then deducted from the adjusted current assets to get the company's net–net value.

Primum Non Nocere

Graham was a defensive investor. His primary focus was to protect his capital. He looked for companies that were already quoting so low that they would not get battered down in a market crash. Like the medical maxim of primum non nocere, which means non-malfeasance or 'cause no harm' or 'cause no harm to the capital', was his first principle. A margin of safety ensured safety of capital.

Philip Fisher refined the value investing theory. Net–net investments were not easily available as market improved, and there arose a need to put a value to quality of management, brand recognition, and business franchise. Fisher considered these aspects while looking at value. Thus, while Graham's value was based on post-mortem analysis of annual accounts, Fisher was looking for good-quality management that follow what they now call good corporate management and has a successful business model with a strong franchise and customer loyalty.

Warren Buffett combined the two variants. He often remarks he is 85% Graham and 15% Fisher. He has practised value investing all his life. He is so obsessed with value investing that he considers the adjective *value* a redundant qualifier. To him, *investing* means 'value investing'. Everything else is speculation.

Value investing is difficult. It requires a great deal of hard work, including subjective and abstract terms as inputs for finding value is very difficult. You don't have to be a genius to handle value investing. It does not require an extraordinary IQ. However, it requires a great deal of common sense and good judgement. You need to train your mind to exercise that judgement. You also need to train your mind not to succumb to emotional breakdowns and to remain unruffled in the face of market idiosyncrasies.

The tools of value investing are easy. This book covers them all. With some practice, you will apply them. Patience and a sense of judgement need to be inculcated. It requires the relevant frame of mind, which needs to be cultivated. It comes with practice. Read books on Buffett, Graham, Fisher, and others. Read the communications Buffett addressed to the shareholders of Berkshire Hathaway. They have been archived on the website of the company. Learn their principles, copy them, and put them in practice. There is no other investment style that comes close to value investing.

Value investing is applied common sense. As Charlie Munger says, 'People are trying to be smart—all I am trying to do is not to be idiotic, but it's harder than most people think.' Have the mindset and discipline of a prudent investor. Learn how not to make stupid mistakes, and you are already on the road to success.

The key to value investing is the fact that the market behaves irrationally. Instead of reason and rationality guiding the market, bouts of greed and fear causing excesses run the market.

Value investors do not predict market price. They are unconcerned with the direction of the market. Technical indicators like 'head and shoulder' (to them, it is just a shampoo brand) and 'dear cat bounce' are just funny terms for them. They are not amused by support and resistance. To them, candlesticks are no more useful than wax candles.

They look for only one parameter: the divergence between the price and value of the scrip they are concerned with, irrespective of the market movement, notwithstanding the war in the Gulf and the petroleum crisis.

The value investor remains unperturbed because he has strong research to back him. He has done a thorough homework, and his purchase and sale decisions are supported by the fundamental knowledge of the company. A value investor takes a bottom-up approach. He examines the company he wants to invest in first and as the most important part of his analysis. The analysis of the industry the company is operating in and analysis of the economy come later. The latter analysis may not be necessary in most of the cases and is done with the sole aim of confirming the results.

Fundamental analysis means knowledge of finance and accounting, a knowledge which is a prerequisite to value investing. Anyone with an inclination can master the knowledge required to master the accounting concepts. This book will equip you with sufficient basic knowledge, and you can keep adding to your knowledge base as you make further progress.

As a chartered accountant whose foundation of knowledge is the concepts of accountancy, I have guided thousands of people to master bookkeeping and accounting during my long career, and I find people of all backgrounds can learn it in a few days. There are dozens of books on finance for non-finance people; there are great courses on edX, Coursera, Udacity, and iTunes University. Knowledge is within easy reach of someone who has the yearning.

A value investor does not invest in a company which does not fall within his circle of confidence. He knows what he knows and also knows what he does not know. If he comes across an attractive investment idea but one which falls outside the domain of his own circle of competence, he will stay away, however attractive that idea may be.

One of the keys to Warren Buffett's financial success is his belief in the circle of competence. The circle of competence is the theory that an investor should choose one particular area in which to focus his efforts. This should be an area in which his skills and experience are above that of the average investor. According to Warren Buffett, a successful investor need not have a large circle of competence; he needs to know when he is acting in stupidity (i.e. outside of his area of competence).

'I don't understand what car companies are going to do 10 years from now, or what software or chemical companies are going to win/do ten years from now but I do understand that Snickers bars will be the number one candy company in the US—like it's been for 40 years. So, I look for durable competitive advantage and that is hard to find. I look for an honest and able management and I look for the price I'm going to pay,' says Warren Buffett.

The circle of competence develops over time as you learn more of the economy and the industries. You need to identify your circle of competence before you embark upon an investment plan. Every investor can identify his circle of competence. If you cannot define your circle of competence, you should not be investing.

Developing a strong circle of competence, however, does not mean you need to have a degree in business or economics. To find your circle of competence, think about your education, personal interests, and past work experience. If you have a degree in computer science, you're qualified to understand how a software company makes its money. If you've spent ten years working as the manager of a large clothing store, you have an edge in understanding investments in the retail area. If you're an avid hiker, you are more apt than most to determine which companies have items that will appeal to hiking and camping enthusiasts. Even paying attention to which products your family uses regularly can give you valuable insight into what stocks you may wish to purchase.

'You don't have to be an expert on every company or even many,' says Buffett. 'You only have to be able to evaluate companies within your circle of competence. The size of that circle is not very important; knowing its boundaries, however, is vital.'

Buffet's own circle of competence is large but not all-encompassing. For example, he avoids technology stocks, saying, 'If there's a lot of technology, we won't understand it.' He did not invest in any technology stock till late in his career. He had no exposure to the technology during the dot-com boom and bust. Much later, he invested in Apple, and this investment added billions to the wealth of his company Berkshire Hathaway. Perhaps by that time, Buffett had gained sufficient insight into the technology or the specific aspect of technology that Apple uses and Apple was within his circle of competence. You can teach an old dog a new trick if he has a strong desire to learn.

Warren Buffett has over a period donated US$24.5 billion to the Gates Foundation, run by his old friend Bill Gates. For those who are inquisitive, this means ₹17,50,89,25,00,000. You will find it equally interesting that he has not invested a penny into Bill Gates's company Microsoft.

At Berkshire Hathaway's annual shareholder meeting, Warren Buffett called his decision to pass on Amazon and Google a mistake. A shareholder then rose from the audience to ask: if Buffett regrets turning down those companies, does he feel the same way about not investing in Microsoft? It was an embarrassing question since Bill Gates was seated in the front seat. Buffett gave a candid reply that it took a lot of time for him to understand that Apple was a consumer company and not a tech company. He missed investing in Microsoft for the same reason in the initial days, which was a hint that it is a great company but no longer available at the price at which he would like to buy it. So much to learn about controlling your emotions and about detachment from the Oracle of Omaha!

Business cycle upheavals and market gyrations may cause many industries and businesses to perform poorly. In identifying the companies to invest in, a value investor always looks for the companies insulated from the vagaries of economic downtrends. He eliminates companies where recession, cut-throat competition, and technology changes may cause uncertain results. Value investors look for businesses which are protected from such uncertainties by an economic moat. The moat stops enemies from attacking the castle; the economic moat stops competitors from taking away customers. The economic moat could take many forms, such as a strong entry barrier, trademark, patent or copyright protection, market strength, captive source of raw material, etc. Usually, the economic moat is reflected by a stable and consistent high return on capital.

Value investors distinguish between a commodity company and a non-commodity company. A commodity company has no control over the price, which is determined by other players in the market. It can earn superprofits only by internal efficiencies of which there is a limited scope. Non-commodity companies have a say in the price determination and are thus able to enjoy higher profitability.

A good example of a continuing competitive advantage is Coca-Cola. The customer asks for a Coke by name; they do not buy a 'cola'. Coca-Cola is a long-time investment of Berkshire Hathaway and one that Warren Buffett has constantly said is never for sale.

Gillette sells shaving blades, which is not a specialised product. The marketing and constant R & D makes it a unique company, giving it a competitive advantage.

In 1993, Warren Buffett had this to say about companies with a continuing competitive advantage: 'Is it really so difficult to conclude that Coca Cola and Gillette possess far less business risk over the long term than, say, any computer company or retailer? Worldwide, Coke sells about 44% of all soft drinks, and Gillette has more than a 60% share (in value) of the blade market. Leaving aside chewing gum, in which Wrigley is dominant, I know of no other significant businesses in which the leading company has long enjoyed such global power.'

The value investor looks for a margin of safety in the investment he buys. He will never compromise on this tenet. He may sometimes forgo one or more of the other tenets, but the margin of safety is the soul of value investing. A value investor will invest in a share only if he is getting it at a considerable discount to the intrinsic value. This gives him a cushion against his error of judgement and of a sudden change in circumstances. A higher margin of safety also means the possibility of reaping higher profits.

A value investor does not treat shares as a commodity for making profits. When he buys the shares of a company, he imagines himself to be a fractional owner of the business, however small that fraction may be. He applies the same criteria that an owner of a business will apply while buying a business. This gives him many advantages. Since he is now the owner of the business, he will hold on to his investment the way an owner does: for a long time. He is not concerned with day-to-day price movement as long as he knows he has made a wise investment. He is concerned about the quality of management and other fundamentals of the company.

The Benjamin Graham Approach to Stock Market Investing

While a majority of individual investors in India have no clear road map and they speculate, as distinguished from investment, there are a few focused investors who would take one of the roads to success. The most usable investment style comes from the investor Benjamin Graham, who has been followed by the most successful investors in the world, including the legendary Warren Buffett, who learnt the basics of investing under Graham's tutelage. Graham's greatest contribution to the investing community was a common-sense yet powerful tool called margin of safety.

Graham knew a stock selling at $1 today might sell at either $1.5 or at $0.50 cents tomorrow. He also understood that the current valuation could also be flawed; the $1 price could be off the mark. He distinguished between the intrinsic value and the market price and was looking for a divergence between the two. If the market price was below the intrinsic value, it created a margin of safety. This is likely to limit the losses to a great extent. While buying at a discounted price does not guarantee profits, a margin of safety curtails the losses to the minimum.

To give an example, if the prevailing price of a stock is ₹120 and it has an intrinsic value of ₹150, buying that stock at ₹120 would give a margin of safety of 20%. If the price rises above ₹150, the investor would not consider buying it. However, if the price again falls below ₹150, he may consider buying again unless the fall has been for a change in fundamentals of the company.

One has to create an attractive risk–reward situation so that downside is limited by creating a sufficient margin of safety. The upside is vague and uncertain and is likely to take care of itself. The basic philosophy is simple: don't lose money. If you don't lose money, the probability of you making a gain is higher. It's a simple theory but is one of the most important constituents of stock market success.

Graham explained that intrinsic value and price do occasionally coincide, but most of the time, because of the exuberance prevailing in the market, the price is likely to hover up and down the value curve. An investor who can understand this divergence may find a buying opportunity with a margin of safety. Graham introduced the concept of a hypothetical being called Mr Market in his book *Intelligent Investor* to explain this point.

Mr Market suffers from bipolar disorder. At any given time, he is driven by panic, euphoria, and apathy, depending upon his mood. He approaches the investor as a reaction to his mood, which has nothing to do with the fundamentals of the stock. He may offer absurd buy and sell quotes. One day he may quote stocks at a discount. The next day he quotes the same stock at a higher price. Mr Market is manic depressive, randomly swinging from bouts of optimism to moods of pessimism.

The good thing about Mr Market is that he is a gentleman. He makes an offer, it is for the investor to accept the offer or reject it. Mr Market is indifferent to your reaction and does not pester you, unlike Mephistopheles of Dr Faustus, to buy or sell. He makes an offer and leaves you at that. It is for you to evaluate his offer as good. Someday you might find Mr Market making an attractive offer. It's time for you to grab the stocks.

Greed and fear are the two important hallmarks of any capitalistic system. Mr Market is a personification of those phenomena. Warren Buffett says an investor ought to be fearful when others are greedy and greedy when others are fearful.

Investors following Benjamin Graham's approach to investing continue to be the most successful investors.

Warren Buffett Changes Graham's Theory to Meet the New Situation

Graham was not interested in the quality of management of a company or in the nature of its business. He was interested in statistical-based screening. He looked for the stocks whose current market price was way below the book value.

Things were different during Buffett's time. Graham's screen would now return few stocks, and those stocks had poor quality management and other issues which would keep the prices depressed. He found that if he could find a company that meant good business rather than rely on pure statistical screening, the reward was likely to be higher. This small tweak in approach made Buffett the most successful investor in the world.

Buffett invests in businesses he can understand. He looks for companies that have a competitive advantage over other companies through a strong franchise, niche product, brand name, or any other factor that makes an economic moat for the company. Buffett's approach has an added superiority over Graham's. While Buffett looked for the present value, he also considered quality of management, sustainability of business, and competitiveness of the company, which provides for an added margin as these factors are likely to contribute to an increased profitability and margin of safety in the future. Graham stocks had to be sold off when the price rose and the margin of safety vanished. Buffett could hold his shares for a lifetime. The better revenue-earning capacity of his stocks would ensure a continued margin of safety. Buffett has often said that his best investment period is 'forever'.

Statistician George Box hits the nail on the head when he says, 'All models are wrong but some are useful.' The use of a mathematical model for valuation may mislead. Most mathematical models use a large number of variables and an equal number of assumptions. The equations are valid only if the conditions prevail. They seldom do. The result looking like an exact result derived to six decimal points is as faulty as it can be. Behind the facade of exactitude lies the most untrusted truth.

Aiming for a precise valuation will be an exercise in futility. It may serve no purpose. Just tweak one assumption, and the whole model fails. For example, the recent weakening of the Indian rupee has affected the valuation equation to an extent not expected by many. The best solution is to find a range instead of a value, and if you have a margin of safety at the higher end of the valuation scale, you can be comfortable investing in that security since the actual valuation lies somewhere between the higher and the lower end.

Check the analysts' estimates of equity valuations. No two analysts would agree, and the valuation would differ by as much as 50%. If the top B-school graduates, armed with the best analytical tools, can err so much in calculating the value, precise valuation becomes a mirage. Your own valuation range regarding companies falling within your circle of competence is likely to be more logical than the experts' valuation.

Warren Buffett defines intrinsic value as 'the discounted value of the cash that can be taken out of a business during its remaining life'. This is the textbook definition using the discounted cash flow model. However, Buffett is talking about the philosophy rather than the mathematics here. He is thinking like the owner of a business or like the buyer who wants to buy the whole business and would like to be sure he can get his money back from future earnings. Theoretically, if the valuation is quantifiable, market uncertainty will still cause the future price to also deviate from the value, again proving the futility of exact measurement.

It is expected that in time the price may equal intrinsic value or may even exceed that, as more and more investors discover the gap, and that would be the moment of truth for the long-term investor. Many times the divergence may continue for long. However, there is a pattern in that divergence. The percentage change in book value in any year is likely to be reasonably close to that year's change in intrinsic value.

Growth is one more variable to be factored into the equation. However, this is rarely considered because it is difficult to project or the tools of analysis may not be intricate enough to incorporate this. This comes as a bonus to the investor. Good companies often grow at a fast and speeding-up rate of growth. If you have bought an investment with a good margin of safety to the intrinsic value, the future growth will make your investment deliver better returns than calculated.

Whether measurable or not, growth is a key component to be considered by the investor. If you buy a company with a good margin of safety to the intrinsic value and the company does not grow at a good rate of growth, sooner or later the price might rise to intrinsic value; at that point, you might have to exit that investment and look for another one which has a margin of safety.

Your present investment does not have the margin of safety based on the current market price. However, if the company keeps growing, the growth will keep creating a margin of safety every year, and you can hold on to the investment forever. No investment is better than growth at a reasonable price. If the future growth is negative, it may destroy value.

The Peter Lynch Approach: Stocks You Understand

No other modern-day investor is respected as much as Peter Lynch. Peter Lynch advocates that an individual investor investing for himself has a distinct advantage over institutional investors. An individual investor is closer to the market to understand the companies he is investing in and is more flexible in his approach, unbridled by approvals and bureaucratic hurdles. They don't have the pressure to show an impressive quarterly performance, nor do they have to publish the details of the assets they are buying. Countless empirical evidence suggest that an individual investor, if methodical in his approach, can beat the institutional investor hands down.

Peter Lynch's approach, like Buffett's, is the bottom-up approach.

No wonder, Fidelity Magellan Fund remained the highest-ranking fund during the entire duration the fund was under Lynch's stewardship, clocking an impressive growth of 29% per annum. He is known for his saying that you should never invest in an idea you cannot explain with a crayon, meaning you should not own a business that is not simple enough to be described in a few sentences. Coca-Cola makes its profit by selling sugar syrup; it is an example of the simplest business model. High-quality businesses can be explained in easy terms.

A class of seventh graders at an American primary school did a social studies project on stocks. The kids had to do their own research and dig up stocks for a paper portfolio. They sent their picks to Peter Lynch, who later invited them to a pizza dinner at the Fidelity executive dining room, illustrating their portfolio with little drawings representing each stock. Lynch just loved this because it illustrates the principle that you should only invest in what you understand. The kids' portfolio comprised toy manufacturers, makers of baseball swap cards, clothing manufacturers and outlets, Playboy Enterprises (Boys are boys!), Coke, and other stocks of that ilk. With a portfolio lacking in glamorous technology ventures and entrepreneurial risk-taking (they went for solid stocks with excellent profits), their portfolio returned 69.6% against a background of a 26.08% gain in the S & P 500 in 1990/91. A bunch of schoolkids could beat the market by following the common-sense approach of understanding the companies they were buying. I am sure if we pitted them against professional money managers armed with Excel sheets, calculus, candlestick charts, indicators, and oscillators, the former would have done better.

Peter Lynch sums up his ideas in his book *Beating the Street* with humorous quotes which are worth pondering over. We would like to call them the Peter (Lynch) Principles:

1. When the operas outnumber the football games three to zero, you know there is something wrong with your life.
2. Gentlemen who prefer bonds don't know what they are missing.
3. Never invest in any idea you can't illustrate with a crayon.
4. You can't see the future through a rear-view mirror.
5. There's no point paying Yo-Yo Ma to play a radio.
6. As long as you're picking a fund, you might as well pick a good one.
7. The extravagance of any corporate office is directly proportional to the management's reluctance to reward the shareholders.
8. When yields on long-term government bonds exceed the dividend yield of the S & P 500 by 6% or more, sell your stocks and buy bonds.
9. Not all common stocks are equally common.
10. Never look back when you're driving on the autobahn.
11. Never bet on a comeback while they're playing 'Taps'.
12. The best stock to buy may be the one you already own.
13. A sure cure for taking a stock for granted is a big drop in the price.
14. If you like the store, chances are you'll love the stock.
15. When insiders are buying, it's a good sign—unless they happen to be New England bankers.
16. In business, competition is never as healthy as total domination.
17. All else being equal, invest in the company with the fewest colour photographs in the annual report.
18. When even the analysts are bored, it's time to start buying.
19. Unless you're a short seller or a poet looking for a wealthy spouse, it never pays to be pessimistic.
20. Corporations, like people, change their names for one of two reasons: either they've gotten married or they've been involved in some fiasco that they hope the public will forget.

21. Whatever the queen is selling, buy it. (When a company is privatised, it is worth buying.)

More than eighty years have passed since Benjamin Graham proposed value investing as a safe alternative to speculative trading. Economists thought it was a short-term window of opportunity, which would go away as soon as more players appeared on the scene and bridged the value gap. They have been proven wrong. The mispricing continues in the market, and with the advent of computer-based trading, the mispricing has increased instead of reduced. The perfect market is a far cry. Value investors in the foreseeable future will continue to earn higher returns than investors following any other approach.

It does not matter what approach to value investing you take. Each may have a different payoff, but one thing is sure, value investing wins hands down over any other approach to investing. As Seth Klarman puts it, 'While it might seem that anyone can be a value investor, the essential characteristics of this type of investor—patience, discipline, and risk aversion—may well be genetically determined.' I might add here that you should identify your dominant traits and select the version of value investing which go well with your personality type.

CHAPTER 15
The Margin of Safety

The function of margin of safety is, in essence, that of rendering unnecessary and accurate estimate of the future.

Benjamin Graham

A value investor has no interest in buying stocks at a fair market price; he looks for a bargain. He would buy something worth ₹100 for ₹50. He is least interested in buying at a fair price. If something worth ₹100 is being sold at ₹100, he is not interested. The greater the discount, the more confident he is in buying it. Warren Buffett says, 'When you build a bridge, you insist it can carry 30,000 pounds, but you only drive 10,000-pound trucks across it. And that same principle works in investing.'

A value investor stands alone, especially during the prolonged period when the market remains overpriced. Many with a shaky foundation give in when everyone else is making higher profits. In the long run, however, it works with so much success; those who understand it never abandon it.

The principle of margin of safety presumes there are two different numbers for each security: intrinsic value and price. Price is what you pay for; value is what you get. If the price you pay for is less than the intrinsic value of the security, your purchase gives you a significant margin of safety. Margin of safety is the protection against downside risk. The higher the margin of safety, the lower the downward risk. Graham wrote in his celebrated work, *The Intelligent Investor*: 'Confronted with a challenge to distil the secret of sound investment into three words, we venture the motto, MARGIN OF SAFETY.'

Graham's concept of margin of safety is based on simple truths. He knew a share priced at ₹100 today might get priced at ₹50 or ₹150 tomorrow. It is impossible to predict the price at any point in time, especially in the short term. 'If I buy this stock at ₹50, I will reduce the probability of a substantial fall, though price may fall to any level. If I have done my homework well and if the price falls further, unless the fall is because of changed fundamentals of the company, I will buy more instead of the usual reaction of a panic sale.'

'Buy low, sell high' seldom works unless you understand your company well and understand the concept of intrinsic value.

Graham knew well the behavioural aspects of investors much before the discipline of behavioural economics developed in its present form. He knew the market was irrational more times than it was rational, that price determination was a complex process and not the simple equilibrium that economists were so fond to defend, and that the best way to guard against the 'unknown unknowns' was to buy with the highest possible margin of safety.

Speaking in the context of bonds, Graham observed (the concept applies as much to equity): 'The function of the margin of safety is, in essence, that of rendering unnecessary an accurate estimate of the future. If the margin is a large one, then it is enough to assume that future earnings will not fall far below those of the past in order for an investor to feel sufficiently protected against the vicissitudes of time.'

Efficient market theorists are sceptical of the existence of a margin of safety and believe that any divergence between value and price is just a momentary phenomenon and that the gap gets is filled in in no time. Empirical evidence proves otherwise. The market may remain irrational at more periods than it is rational, and while price line may cross the value line in the long term, in the short run, it may hover around the value line. Sometimes the price goes way above the value; at other times, the price goes below the value. Remember Mr Market and his mood swings.

The intelligent investor constantly evaluates all securities within his circle of competence that are constantly available at a discount to their fair market value. In an overpriced market, he waits patiently for the right ball to fall on the sweet spot of the bat. If it does not, he remains inactive. Self-discipline in the face of temptation is the most important trait that makes you a successful investor.

He swings his bat when he has to. There is no 'clean bowled' in investing. But when the market is panicky, it may throw open dozens of opportunities to the investor. He now swings at many balls, sometimes at every ball (within his circle of competence, keeping his diversification policy in mind).

This may sound easy in theory; however, finding the intrinsic value is perhaps the most difficult part in fundamental analysis and requires a careful consideration of various factors, both quantitative and qualitative. Quantifying the qualitative factors is perhaps the most intricate part of the process. It does not require mathematics, but it requires an ability to weigh—if not quantify—each qualitative variable and factor it into the valuation. This ability to identify and include such factors makes successful investors successful.

Know that when I say 'quantifying the qualitative factors', I do not mean arriving at a precise figure. It means forming the mental picture of divergence between the *price*, which is a precise mathematical term, and *value*, which is vague and any attempt to make it precise will only make it unreliable. The moment you insert too much mathematics into things which do not need mathematics, you mess up things, a common mistake that the modern breed of laptop-carrying number crunchers are likely to make.

Thus, a margin of safety is no guarantee that the price will rise in the future to fill the gap. There are various reasons for the same. First, the market is likely to be irrational for a longer time. Second, even when the market is rationally priced, the particular scrip you have purchased may continue to languish below its value for a considerable period (if you are unlucky, during the entire period of your holding). Third, finding value is subjective because of qualitative variables involved, and value arrived at by different investors is likely to be different. This brings out the importance of the circle of competence. It is futile to find the intrinsic value of something outside of your circle of competence. Stick to your circle of competence, where you know what you are doing.

A margin of safety is no guarantee, yet it is a powerful tool. It provides a solid defence against downside risk, and it increases your probability of gain. On the day the market recognises that a stock is trading below its realistic price (i.e. its intrinsic value), the price is likely to catch up with the value. This may not happen overnight and may test the patience of the investor. That is the reason most value investors are 'buy and hold' investors; they buy a good share at a price below its value and sit over it for a long time. Warren Buffett has been known to apply as much as a 50% discount to the intrinsic value as his price target.

Different investors use variants of this philosophy that match their investment style. Benjamin Graham used to run a mechanical screener of finding the net-net stocks. The net-net investing method focuses on current assets, taking cash and cash equivalents at full value, then reducing accounts receivable for doubtful accounts, and reducing inventories to liquidation values. Total liabilities are deducted from the adjusted current assets to get the company's 'net-net' value. Dividing this by the number of shares gives you net-net per share. If a stock is trading at a price less than its net-net value, there is value to be had to the extent of the difference.

Since Graham started his career when the US economy had just faced the severest recession ever and was emerging out of it and was rebuilding itself, the mechanical screener was enough to identify undervalued scrips. There were many undervalued companies, and the screener helped Graham identify the ones that had the highest margin of safety.

Philip Fisher adopted a different approach. He was not content with the mechanical filter that Graham used and first looked for companies that had quality management, a high growth potential, and a robust business model. In his outstanding book *Common Stocks and Uncommon Profits*, he created a 15-point criteria to identify great companies and great managements. Fisher recommended targeting businesses for investment that had growth orientation, high profit margins, high return on capital, a commitment to research and development, superior sales organisation, a leading industry position, and proprietary products or services.

Fisher relied on scuttlebutt to test the quality of management and the business model of the company. Scuttlebutt (meaning 'gossip' or 'rumour') is a method that Fisher used for gathering information about the company. He travelled beyond the published accounts of the company and talked to the people who could give insights about the company that were not sometimes reflected in the published reports. He thus talked to the management, customers, vendors, employees, ex-employees— everybody who could give inputs about the company. Once he identified a great company, he rarely sold his shares and stayed invested for life. He would say, 'If the job has been correctly done when a common stock is purchased, the time to sell it is—almost never.'

Warren Buffett realised that while Graham's mechanical scanner worked fine for Graham, it might not act as the right filter in changing times, and a mix of Graham and Fisher worked for him. The chief difference between Graham and Fisher was that Graham bought undervalued shares based on the balance sheets of the companies and sold them when the price reached the intrinsic value; Fisher went beyond the balance sheet and discovered companies which continued to grow, and thus he created a margin of safety even when the earlier price target was reached.

'It's waiting that helps you as an investor, and a lot of people just can't stand to wait,' says Charlie Munger. It is the wait that makes this investment style boring and unglamorous for most investors. People love activities. They like action. They like to buy and sell every day. In the investing suggested here, you will buy not more than a handful of scrip in your lifetime. You will keep adding more and more quantity of the same stocks to your portfolio. You will study the balance sheets of those few companies with more attention than the company management. It is about knowing more and more about less and less. You will wait for an opportunity to buy, and you will wait for an opportunity to sell, even if that wait is forever.

The mathematician Pascal said, 'All of humanity's problems stem from man's inability to sit quietly in a room alone.' Few people have the patience to do so in the world of investment. If you develop that ability, you will make more money than many others, and there won't be many copying your style because few have the required patience, though I hope many readers of my book will develop that mindset.

Buffett looked for businesses whose intrinsic value would increase. To him, those shares were like bonds: risk-free. For example, when he bought Coca-Cola stock, the company had earnings of $0.18 a share and was growing its per share earnings at a rate of 16% a year. They paid $3.24 a share, which equates to a P/E ratio of 18. This P/E ratio looks expensive with little margin of safety. But he knew something which Graham would not have considered in his calculations of margin of safety. He could see that the company was growing at 16% per annum, which would lift the rate of growth from the present 5.55% ($0.18 / $3.24) to an increasing rate. This will have a positive impact on the intrinsic value and on the future price. Coca-Cola proved to be a multi-bagger for Berkshire Hathaway, and it continues to grow. These stocks have a name now: growth stocks. Growth stocks may be considered value stocks with the rate of growth factored in.

Buffett, in his inimitable style, explains the concept of margin of safety using the analogy of a bridge: 'You have to have the knowledge to enable you to make a very general estimate about the value of the underlying business. But you do not cut it close. That is what Ben Graham meant by having a margin of safety. You don't try to buy businesses worth $83 million for $80 million. You leave yourself an enormous margin. When you build a bridge, you insist it can carry 30,000 pounds, but you only drive 10,000 pound trucks across it. And that same principle works in investing.'

In another occasion, Buffett uses the same analogy of the bridge but with a more interesting explanation: 'If you understood a business perfectly and the future of the business, you would need very little in the way of a margin of safety. So, the more vulnerable the business is, assuming you still want to invest in it, the larger margin of safety you'd need. If you're driving a truck across a bridge that says it holds 10,000 pounds and you've got a 9,800 pound vehicle, if the bridge is 6 inches above the crevice it covers, you may feel okay; but if it's over the Grand Canyon, you may feel you want a little larger margin of safety.'

Speculators and day traders who remain fully invested all the time are without any margin of safety. Buyers of synthetic derivative products usually carry no margin of safety. Investors who do not do their homework before buying a stock may not be left with a margin of safety because even if there is safety in their investment, during the next market fall, they are likely to panic and sell it.

Buffett includes intangibles like intellectual properties, goodwill, and such factors while calculating the margin of safety. Another legendary value investor, Seth Klarman, prefers to be more conservative. In his book *Margin of Safety* (now out of print; it used copy selling at US$14,950 at Amazon when I last checked it), he explains it thus:

> The problem with intangible assets, I believe, is that they hold little or no margin of safety. The most valuable assets of Dr Pepper/Seven-Up, Inc., by way of example, are the formulas that give those soft drinks their distinctive flavours. It is these intangible assets that

cause Dr Pepper/Seven-Up, Inc., to be valued at a high multiple of the tangible book value. If something goes wrong—tastes change, or a competitor makes inroads—the margin of safety is quite low.

Tangible assets, by contrast, are more precisely valued and therefore provide investors with greater protection from loss. Tangible assets usually have value in alternate uses, thereby providing a margin of safety. If a chain of retail stores becomes unprofitable, for example, the inventories can be liquidated, receivables collected, leases transferred, and real estate sold. If consumers lose their taste for Dr Pepper, by contrast, tangible assets will not meaningfully cushion investors' losses.

In short, there are as many ways of calculating margin of safety as there are investors. You can take the most conservative approach of Graham as one end of the spectrum to Buffett's approach as the other end. It does not mean Buffett's margin of safety has more margin of error than Graham's. It only means Buffett's area of competence is different and that operating within his area of competence makes Buffett's calculations equally—or perhaps more—dependable.

The true test of a margin of safety comes in a market crash. In a bull phase, everything rises. The rising tide lifts all ships. Mistakes get ignored, and however foolish you may be in your investment choice, you still make money. Every boom produces a new set of 'experts' who believe they have the Midas touch. High risks pay off; penny stocks rise faster than good stocks. But when the market falls, everything falls like a house of cards. It is only when the tide goes off that you discover who has been swimming naked.

In a falling market, the stocks that were running way beyond their intrinsic value are the ones that fall the most. They have been rising up incessantly, the bubble gaining more gas as it moves up. When the crash occurs, they are the first ones to be ditched by the speculators, and they are the ones that have the free fall. The impact of the fall is likely to be the lowest in the stocks that carry a margin of safety.

The recent fall in the Indian markets will explain this point. The run-up of indices saw even insignificant mid-caps and small-caps spiral up. When the market fell, the fall in the shares with dubious fundamentals and uncertain intrinsic value was as high as 70%. Almost entire portfolios of investors like Porinju Veliyath, who's been dubbed as the small-cap king (the news of Veliyath buying a share would shoot the price through the roof) plummeted. The 10–15% fall in the market caused a 70% fall in the price of scrips that had run ahead of their valuations, but fall in strong shares is correlated to the fall in the market. Most of them held the fort; some of them rose when the market was falling.

Buying shares with a clear margin of safety but without due diligence and research can be dangerous. More often than not, the margin of safety is illusionary, and the share may be fairly priced.

The Risk

The first thing an intelligent investor should focus on is not the expected value of future profits but the risk. By keeping the risk low, you can protect yourself from potential downside. The positive outcome is bound to follow soon. In the short run, the price may go down, but you have protected yourself from the long-term risk by buying shares at a discount to their value. What an average investor thinks of risk is not the risk; it is volatility. Volatility is a feature of the stock market and not a defect, and it is the intelligent investor's great friend.

From this understanding of risk, the conventional wisdom that 'the higher the risk, the higher the reward' is flawed. It may be true in casinos or in Russian roulette, and it is true in day trading and speculation. However, as you increase the time frame for which you stay invested, with every year added, you lower the risk, so much so that for a long term, the risk approaches near zero.

Let me redefine risk for you in a much better way. Risk is not about volatility; it is about price. It is about what you pay and what you get.

The higher the margin of safety, the lower the risk. Most speculators don't want to understand this definition and are focused on the short term. The boring task of understanding risk for the long term is left to the value investors. It is not without reasons that wealth is created by long-term investors.

This approach requires a paradigm shift on what you think about risk and reward. Sensex has fallen from 38,896 on 28 August 2018 to 33,690 on 25 October 2018. Search for investment advice by analysts by scrolling back to the *Economic Times* and *Moneycontrol.com*—the analysts who were recommending a strong buy on certain shares and now recommending a strong sell on the same shares. Should you be buying or selling at ₹70 what was being recommended as a buy at ₹100? This sums up the irrationality and fallibility of human beings.

The academics define *risk* differently, and the concept is so deep-rooted in the academic and practical world that low-risk long-term value investing is understood by few. If you are a value investor, you will continue to be in a minority till more people read this book and change their mindset and understanding about risk. You will continue to beat them all in investment return till they do that.

Declining prices are a boon to a value investor. It helps you lower your average cost of acquisition. If the price of a share were to remain constant or keep on rising, your average cost of acquisition will be higher, thus lowering your returns. If the market behaved irrationally and the price of the scrip you want to buy is volatile, you may use volatility to lower your average cost of acquisition, thus increasing your long-term returns.

There are two ways you, as a value investor, can mitigate risk: first, by buying at a price which creates a high margin of safety and, second, by properly diversifying your portfolio.

The Black Swan Risk

We also need to discuss another form of risk, the risk of rare and unpredictable outcome, which the well-known thinker Nassim Nicholas

Taleb called the black swan event in his bestseller book *The Black Swan: The Impact of the Highly Improbable*.

The term *black swan* is a Latin expression. Its oldest reference is in the poet Juvenal's expression that 'a good person is as rare as a black swan'. It was a common expression in sixteenth-century London, a statement that described impossibility, derived from the Old World presumption that all swans must be white because all historical records of swans reported that they had white feathers. Thus, the black swan is an oft-cited reference in philosophical discussions of the improbable.

In simple terms, it means that black swan events occur and that when they occur, most people are caught napping. It is something they have never imagined will happen. In the stock market, black swan events cause much havoc. Investors thought tech stocks would keep rising forever until the dot-com bubble burst. The sub-prime crisis was next in line, and the recent banking and NBFC crisis in India is another black swan event. The technical analysts can make impressive price charts based on price momentum to predict where the market will be next week, but the intervening black swan event can disrupt the whole equation.

Black swans arrive unexpectedly; disruptions occur without warning. In retrospect, black swan events are easy to interpret. You may find causal relationships that lead to the event, but when the event occurs, it causes massive destruction. Since a black swan event is unpredictable, there is no way you can be prepared for it. The only way to handle a black swan event is to buy quality stocks at a margin of safety and to stay invested, unruffled by the intervening event. Value investors lose the least if the market falls because of a built-in margin of safety.

Be prepared for the market to fall 10%, 20%, 30%, or even 40% in some years. Some years may be so bad that speculators and traders may close shop. The long-term investor remains unruffled. The fall in his stocks is likely to be lower than the market fall because of the margin of safety. And he looks at this temporary period of fall as an opportunity to find stocks at a bargain price. I have always used the market crash as an opportunity to up my holding and have always been rewarded. The markets always recover.

Warren Buffett explained his investment philosophy in his letter to the shareholders way back in 1962: 'Specifically, if the market should be down 35% or 40% in a year (and I feel this has a high probability of occurring one year in the next ten—no one knows which one), we should be down only 15% or 20%. If it is more or less unchanged during the year, we would hope to be up about ten percentage points. If it is up 20% or more, we would struggle to be up as much. The consequence of performance such as this over a period of years would mean that if the Dow produces a 5% to 7% per year overall gain compounded, I would hope our results might be 15% to 17% per year.'

Munger puts it even more bluntly: 'If you're not willing to react with equanimity to a market price decline of 50% two or three times a century you're not fit to be a common shareholder and you deserve the mediocre result you're going to get compared to the people who do have the temperament, who can be more philosophical about these market fluctuations.'

If you do not have this mindset, you may panic at the fall and may end up selling low. Researches prove that more money is made by investors who buy and hold and learn to insulate their investments from market sentiments. Benjamin Graham puts this aptly in these words: 'The investor who permits himself to be stampeded or unduly worried by unjustified market declines in his holdings is perversely transforming his basic advantage into a basic disadvantage. That man would be better off if his stocks had no market quotation at all; for he would then be spared the mental anguish caused him by other persons' mistakes of judgment.'

It Is the Price You Pay That Matters

It is the price you pay that determines the margin of safety. If you pay a higher price, the margin will be lower or may be lost. If you can find a quality stock at a reasonable price, you have mitigated the downside risk; the price may go up subsequently. It is impossible to determine the exact value of any investment in a dynamic world; a higher margin of safety also provides a cushion against human judgement errors.

What if a good-quality stock that falls within your circle of competence is not selling at the price at which you would like to buy it? It is possible to buy that stock if you have the patience to wait. Volatility is an investor's best friend. The price soars, and the price falls. If you are tracking a few good-quality stocks, you are likely to find an investment window sooner or later.

One more myth needs to be cleared here. Being overvalued or undervalued has nothing to do with the historic high or historic low price of a stock. A stock may trade at its historic high but may still be undervalued.

'You're looking for a mispriced gamble. That's what investing is. And you have to know enough to know whether the gamble is mispriced. That's value investing,' explains Charlie Munger. A stock is a mispriced gamble when its price diverges from its long-term valuations. Mispricing may be positive or negative from the point of view of an investor. If it is positive, it means the pricing is creating a margin of safety. Any fall from that price further will increase the margin of safety even more, and any move upwards will reduce the safety margin. The negative mispricing, which means price moving ahead of the valuations, does not interest a value investor. He may not be interested in that stock, however good that may be fundamentally, unless the price goes down, creating a margin of safety.

If you can understand the business of the company and can assert with confidence that the gamble is mispriced in your favour, you have discovered a value buy.

A great business at a fair price is superior to a fair business at a great price.

Let us take an example to understand this important concept. The EPS of a company is ₹5 a share, and the company is growing at 20% per annum. The price-to-earnings ratio of the company is 15 (i.e. it is selling at 15 times its earnings of ₹5 a share, or ₹75). Now there is another company which also earns ₹5 per share but is growing at 10% per annum. This company is selling at 10 times its earnings—that is, at ₹50. Based on these parameters, many are likely to conclude that the second is a better buy since it is cheaper. However, since the rate of growth of the first company is double that of the second company, in 10 years, the earnings of the first company will grow to ₹30 per year, while the earnings of the second company will only be ₹13. If we presume the same multiplier to earnings, the price of the first company will be ₹450, while that of the second company will be ₹130. That is the difference growth can make on your investments.

CHAPTER 16

Don't Trust Your Broker for Investment Advice

"Stop listening to professionals! Twenty years in this business convinces me that any normal person using the customary three percent of the brain can pick stocks just as well, if not better, than the average Wall Street expert.

Peter Lynch

The worst investment advice you can get is from your investment broker. Your broker is likely to call you with investment advice every other day. Just decline. In the first place, Indian firms are not known to do good research. The record of some firms who do research is not impressive at all. Even advice from international firms is bad.

When someone armed with a top B-school degree generates voluminous data on his laptop, giving an aura of mysticism to the whole process, it scares the amateur investor. You need to understand that in the stock market, smart money is not as smart as it looks, nor is dumb money as dumb as the amateur thinks it is. You need to break the shell and know you will soon beat the smart money in the game.

There are fundamental flaws in this recommendation business. The analysts bring out research reports at the behest of brokerage firms, which are perennially interested in new buy recommendations. You are likely to find more buy recommendations than sell and hold recommendations. The brokerages make no money in your decision to hold on to your investment. You have in your basket only a limited number of stocks to sell unless you are a short-seller. The domain of 'buy' is as large as the total number of scrips listed and trading. Obviously, more commission is made from a buy recommendation.

The analyst has a target to churn out a given number of recommendations every month. Imagine the number of recommendation a single analyst will produce during his professional career. This will be many times the number of scrips you are likely to buy during your entire life. If stock market experts were so expert, they would be buying stock, not selling advice.

Because of the compulsion to create a research report periodically, the researcher is racing against time. He does not have access to the real people and is more likely to talk to the investors' relations and public relations officers, whose job is to showcase the best their company can give. This produces an optimistic bias.

If the general analyst community gives a buy recommendation to a scrip, it requires a considerable amount of research by an analyst who wants to disagree—and not merely the backing of research, it requires considerable courage for a lone researcher to disagree with the research reports of prominent researchers. The safe course for him is to fall in line.

It does not pay for a brokerage firm to initiate research in a company unless that company has numerous floating stocks to justify the potential commission to be earned. Smaller companies or companies with less liquidity are likely to be skipped. Also likely to be skipped are the companies which are undergoing a major transformation at the moment because the safe researcher prefers stability rather than uncertainty. These are the areas where the pot of gold lies. Multi-baggers are likely to be sitting among these ignored and neglected stocks.

Don't get me wrong. Brokers are not bad people. I have broker friends who are great human beings. The problem is that they are not investment advisers. They are not researchers. They are salesmen. They make money not by advising you but by selling shares to you and by buying shares from you.

A 'cardiologist' used to visit Nagpur to give free consultation to heart patients. This was when few hospitals in Nagpur were doing cardiac surgeries. This doctor represented a leading heart hospital in Hyderabad. If you sought her advice on undergoing cardiac procedures, she invariably recommended the bypass surgery. She was a salesperson wearing the garb of a doctor. An LIC agent acting as life insurance adviser does the same. The broker is no different. His cash register clicks when you buy or sell.

You may trust your broker with your money. He may be a good man, but don't trust him with your investment recommendations. His recommendations are not to be taken seriously. They won't work. They may work sometimes, but throwing up a die to get recommendations will work as well.

There are reasons you should do your own research.

You alone will be responsible for your investment decisions. If you follow the advice everyone follows on the stock market, you do not differ from an average player in the market whose reward will be nothing more than average. If there is a consensus in the market that a stock, let's assume ACC, will rise, that consensus itself will cause the stock price to rise in the short run, ignoring the fundamentals. While it may be party time for all participants who join the bandwagon, there are no superprofits to be made. Real return accrues for the player who has his fundamentals right and has been sitting on the stock before the bandwagon drove it to greater heights.

The 'momentum players' lose money as often as they make it. They trade on momentum, the upward or downward movement in the market. They do not bother about fundamentals, and their investment decisions are guided by the trend. We often hear on the street 'Trend is a trader's best friend' and 'Keep it simple. Trade with the trend'. The problem with this approach is that you do not know if the stock you bought deserves the price you paid for it or the price you sell it at. While you may be lucky to make money on the trend, your gains may reverse on a sudden trend reversal, which happens more often than not. One quick shake-up in the market, and all your gains vanish. But if you know your fundamentals and know the reasons you are buying a particular asset for, short-term market hiccups won't bother you. You will remain invested as long as the fundamentals are intact. Any change in the fundamental parameters of your stock should prompt you to revisit the reasons for the investment decision.

CHAPTER 17

Why Dividends Matter

The only thing that gives me pleasure is to see my dividend coming in.

John D. Rockefeller

One of the best ways a company can update its shareholders of its progress is to inform a shareholder that they are pleased to credit dividends in his bank account. However small the amount may be, it is bound to give a smile on the face of a shareholder.

A dividend is a share in the profit of a company distributed to the shareholders. Not all profits earned by a company are distributed as dividends. The decision to declare a dividend is a policy matter, and the board of directors of the company are the ones to make that decision. The decision has a crucial impact on the future of a company. The company may keep the amount not distributed as dividends for its capital requirements as money belonging to the shareholders, thus adding to the value of shares owned by them. It is not unusual for good companies to declare over one dividend in a year (interim dividends and final dividends). A company's track record of consistent dividends over the years is one of the greatest indicators of strength of a company.

Dividends matter to the shareholders for the several reasons.

1. Dividends Reflect Fundamentals

While there may not be much of a direct relationship between the fundamentals of a company and the dividend payout, it still matters. Sometimes a profit-making company may decide not to pay dividends; this could be for a host of reasons, like it has growth opportunities ahead where the money can be utilised, creating further wealth for the shareholders.

There are companies which will, in the absence of profits, dig into past reserves to pay dividends. They often do this to show to the shareholders that all is well with the company.

Dividends distribution has a great impact on the psyche of the shareholders. Some of whom do their fundamental analysis based on only one parameter: how much is credited into his bank account through dividends.

For an investor, dividend is the only real thing; everything else is delayed gratification. A company which earns ₹10 a share on a ₹10 share and distributes ₹2 as the dividend has utilised the remaining ₹8 for future growth; it will fructify later. The future is uncertain, and the future earnings will depend upon a host of internal and external factors. The ₹8 is not what matters for most shareholders, but the ₹2, which is real money.

2. Dividend Yield

Many investors watch the dividend yield as an indicator. Dividend yield is arrived at by dividing the dividend amount per share by the current market price.

$$\text{dividend yield} = \frac{\text{annual dividends per share}}{\text{price per share}}$$

Let us dwell a little into this topic. I have listed companies with the highest dividend yield in India, based on the current market price (as of 22 October 2018).

Company	Price	% Div.	Div. Yield
Gitanjali Gems	1.55	8	51.61
Ingersoll Rand	520.9	2,080	39.93
IOC	131.25	210	16
Pincon Spirit	5.2	7.5	14.42
Vedanta	215.15	2,120	9.85
Power Finance	81.55	78	9.56
21st Cen Mgt	26.3	25	9.51
REC	104.6	91.5	8.75
ILandFS	6.9	30	8.7
NALCO	67.8	114	8.41
SJVN	25.45	21	8.25
HPCL	212.55	170	8
Polyplex Corp	502	400	7.97

BPCL	273.5	210	7.68
Manaksia	39.3	150	7.63
Oil India	201	150	7.46
Chennai Petro	261.9	185	7.06

Some conclusions are obvious from the above statistics:

a. Some of the companies with the highest dividend yields are not the best of the companies. Gitanjali Gems, a company owned by fugitive Mehul Choksi, shows a dividend yield of 51%. This looks too good to be true because it is. This company is under the scanner of enforcing agencies for loan default and financial frauds. Presumably, the dividend was declared before the scam broke, and pitted against the current price, which has fallen from ₹104 to the present ₹1.55, it shows absurd results.

b. IL&FS is another company which went through troubled times, and the dividend yield looks higher for the same reason.

c. Ingersoll Rand has declared a whopping dividend of 2,020% or ₹202 per share. This is a one-off event since in the past, the company has declared 30% dividend consistently. This results in a higher yield compared to the market price. Further investigation might lead you to an attractive investment opportunity. Every ratio is a lead to something good, which needs further study.

d. The list includes some good companies. A high dividend yield coming out of some of these companies is a lead to market mispricing. Mr Market might be pricing them lower, and it may be a great investment opportunity.

e. Some companies are 'dividend stocks'. Every year they continue to give high dividend yields. After a due study of the fundamentals, they may be considered for investment.

f. Some stocks in the list are public sector undertakings (PSUs). They often have a high dividend yield because the market does not pay much pricing premium on them. They also fall in the category of 'dividend stocks'.

3. Dividend Stickiness and Dividend Coverage Ratio

As discussed earlier, managements would often keep paying out the same or increasing dividends just to show to the shareholders that their company is growing. Even in the situation of lowering profitability, the dividend is likely to stick. We call this as stickiness of the dividend. For a majority of the shareholders, the financial statements have no relevance and are to be consigned to the trash can (computer trash can in the electronic era) in the first possible opportunity but not before turning to the page which says, 'The board of directors are pleased to declare a dividend of ₹XX per share.'

Since most companies (except companies involved in large projects and exploration, where revenue is erratic) stick to a stable dividend policy, a cut in the dividend often causes panic in the market. It has sometimes to do with psychology than economics. While an increasing dividend is a reassurance, a constant dividend is also not looked down upon. But if a company which has been declaring a constant dividend, irrespective of the percentage of dividend per share, declares a lower dividend for the year, this is bound to set off the panic button. It is not unusual for managements of struggling companies to borrow and pay dividends. (Legally, dividends can be paid only out of current and past accumulated profits.)

A tool that the intelligent investor must use to find out what percent of the profits is being distributed as dividends and whether the profits will suffice to cover the dividend is the dividend coverage ratio, also known as the dividend cover. This simple tool can help a shareholder understand the robustness of a company in terms of its capacity to service the shareholders' equity.

$$\text{dividend cover} = \frac{\text{earnings per share}}{\text{dividend Per Share}}$$

Let us pick up a real-life example.

The EPS of ACC for the year 2018 is ₹49, and the company declared a dividend of ₹26 per share.

$$\text{dividend cover} = 49 / 26 = 1.88$$

It means that for every ₹1 of dividend paid, the company has ₹1.88 available out of the current year's profits. After paying the dividend, the remaining amount will be kept by the company as the shareholders' funds. The higher the cover, the more confidence it should give to the shareholders.

4. **Dividends Bring Discipline**

History shows that the more the cash a company keeps, the more it is likely to use it for executive compensation and mindless diversification. In India, where a majority of the businesses are headed not by a professional manager but by the promoter himself, the temptation to compensate himself to the detriment of other shareholders is not uncommon. Dividends act as a balance.

Manipulation of the books and resorting to creative accounting to show a picture better than reality is again not uncommon. But a dividend is actual money that has to be paid and is not a book entry that's prone to manipulations. The dividend is a reality; manipulation becomes more challenging when the company has to meet the obligation of paying dividends.

Dividends are an implied public promise by the management. Reduce dividends, and investors feel cheated, almost like a breach of promise. It is only the dividend that a shareholder can get from the company in terms of cash inflow; the capital appreciation comes from the market when he sells off the share and is only notional till shares are sold. Dividends carry a great deal of emotional value for shareholders.

There is only one worthy exception: Warren Buffett's company, Berkshire Hathaway, which pays no dividends.

Why Berkshire Hathaway Pays No Dividends

Berkshire Hathaway does not pay dividends because its chairman, Warren Buffett, believes it is more beneficial to allocate the company's earnings in other ways. In particular, Buffett prefers to reinvest profits in things that allow his company to improve its efficiency, expand its reach, create new products and services and improve existing ones, and further separate itself from competitors. Buffett feels that investing back into his business provides more long-term value to shareholders than paying them, because the company's financial success rewards shareholders with higher stock values. While the company does not pay a dividend, it does, however, have a prudent stock buy-back policy that works to put cash into shareholders' pockets.

The company has paid only one dividend during his reign, in 1967, and Buffett later joked he must have been in the bathroom when the decision was made. Statistics give credence to Buffett's stance that using profits to buttress the company's financial position results in greater wealth for shareholders than paying dividends. Berkshire Hathaway's profits increased by almost 700,000% between 1964 and 2014.

But that's the stuff legends are made of. Few investors trust other managements like they trust Buffett.

CHAPTER 18

Stock Splits, Bonus Shares, and Buy-backs

"When I was young, I thought that money was the most important thing in life; now that I am old I know that it is."

Oscar Wilde

Does the Stock Split Enhance Value?

A stock split is a decision made by the company management to split the shares into multiple shares. A company may split its ₹10 share to two shares of ₹5 each. Companies resort to a split when the price per share has gone beyond the range deemed appropriate by investors. It is a pure psychological game. An investor is likely to feel a share trading at ₹2,000 (face value ₹100) more expensive than a share trading at ₹150 (face value ₹5). He does not understand that a share with a face value of ₹5 is trading at 30 times the face value, while the other one is trading at 20 times. We often end up comparing apples to oranges.

Investors often greet the stock split decision with extreme joy, and the price rises after the split. The reasons are more in human psychology than in economics. Speaking logically, a split should not add any value. When a company which has 1 crore shares of ₹10 each splits its shares into ₹5, it would now have 2 crore shares of ₹5 each. The pizza remains the same. Instead of splitting it into 4 slices, you split it into 8 slices. Now there are more slices; perhaps more people can share it. It's the same with the stock split. Earlier, I held 500 shares; now I have 1,000 shares. I am likely to be tempted to sell the 'additional' 500 that I received because of the split (even though it is nothing more than splitting the pizza slice). This generates more floating stock in the market at an affordable price. More floating stock and lower price—the market is likely to receive it favourably.

When a split happens, the trading price of the share is adjusted in the markets. Thus, a share trading at ₹100, when split in two, should trade at ₹50. However, as showed above, the cognitive factors often drive the price higher.

Some people like to buy the shares on split announcement and sell them after the split. There is no real unlocking of value in the split, so it is a non-event as far as a value investor is concerned. Split changes none of the economics of the share; it remains the same share, just cut into a lower denomination. Knowing a split is often welcome by investors, unscrupulous managements often resort to stock splits at the peak of the boom so that the psychology keeps driving their stock prices higher, though prudent managements would also resort to the stock split to keep the price in the range. Some of these companies have split so many times that the face value is now ₹1. A split less than ₹1 is not permissible.

There are notable companies which understand that split creates no real value. In the present market scenarios, institutional investors dominate the market. A split is inconsequential to them. A split is of no consequence to retail investors too since there is no marketable lot in digital environment and you are free to buy just one share. Unless the price of one share itself is beyond your reach, Berkshire Hathaway has never split its shares, and the price is beyond the reach of many. On the date of writing this, I checked up Berkshire's price, and it was trading at $15,525 (₹3,23,935). In 1996, with Berkshire Hathaway selling for $33,000 a share, outsiders planned to buy Berkshire shares and resell them to investors in $1,000 pieces through unit investment trusts. Not wanting small investors to pay sales charges and other administrative expenses that such trusts would entail, Berkshire Hathaway issued class B shares (dubbed Baby Berkshires) each without voting rights and worth 1/30 of the regular class A shares. In January 2010, they split class B shares 50 to 1, making each worth 1/1,500 the value of class A shares. The latest trading price of Berkshire B is $9.67.

In the Indian markets, the current trading price of MRF is ₹65,129 (face value ₹10), Page Industries ₹29,650 (FV ₹10), 3M India ₹19,440 (FV ₹10), Eicher Motors ₹22,500 (FV ₹10).

Bonus Shares

The news of the issuance of bonus shares brings cheer to the investors. Companies like to reward the shareholders without affecting the cash flows. Investors like to invest in companies that give bonus shares. They consider bonus shares a sign of good health of the company.

Let us understand how bonus shares work. Bonus shares are issued out of accumulated profits of the company. The accumulated profits belong to the shareholders, and when not issued as bonus shares, they are still a part of the book value of the shares.

An example will help us understand. A company has issued 10,000 equity shares of ₹10 each. Thus, the total paid up capital is ₹1,00,000. The company has accumulated profits (also known as reserves and surplus) of ₹5,00,000. Thus, the total monies belonging to shareholders is ₹6,00,000, or ₹60 per share. The company utilises ₹1,00,000 out of the accumulated profits to issue bonus shares at the ratio of one share against one share held (1 : 1) The total capital is now ₹2,00,000, and the accumulated profits is ₹4,00,000. You now have two shares instead of one you owned before. The book value of each share is ₹30 per share, and since you own two shares against each held before, the total book value of the original share plus bonus share put together is ₹60. As you can see, it created no real wealth. The claim of one share was ₹60; now you own two shares. The claim of two shares put together is ₹60. The proportionate right of a shareholder has not changed.

The issue of bonus shares does not impact the profitability of the company in that bonus shares are akin to a stock split; the only difference is that the split changes the face value. Instead of one share of ₹10, now you have two shares of ₹5. The bonus creates additional shares. Instead of one share of ₹10, you now have two shares of ₹10 each. There is no difference in the bundle of rights and obligations.

There is another difference important for an investor to recognise. A company can split shares any time; it need not be backed by any reserves. It is akin to changing a ₹10 note for two ₹5 notes. Bonus shares can be issued out of accumulated profits alone, which means the company needs to have sufficient reserves before it capitalises them as bonus shares.

On the issue of bonus shares, as the shares become ex-bonus, the market price adjusts to the new price. For instance, a company trading at ₹100 issues a 2 : 3 bonus. (This means two new shares against three held by a shareholder.) For ₹300, a shareholder that had three shares earlier now owns five shares. Thus, the stock should now trade at ₹60 per share.

Does the price rise after the bonus announcement? It does. The reasons are not psychological as with a split. Let us explore the reasons.

1. The rise in liquidity brings more floating stock. Some people feel they have 'free' shares now. It is positive for the investors. Higher floating stock is often correlated with price.
2. Bonus shares are issued out of reserves; it is a celebration of the success of the company. It is a confirmation to the investors that the company is successful.
3. A very important reason that a bonus is important from the point of long-term investors has to do with future payouts. A stable or increasing rate of dividends is what most investors look for in companies as a measure of stability and growth. There is a certain amount of 'stickiness' in the dividend that companies pay out. A constant rate of dividends assures the shareholders that all is well with the company. If a company reduces dividends, it sends bad signals to the investors. A company which pays out an increasing rate of dividends must continue to do so. If it does not increase the payout in a particular year, the market becomes alarmed. Company managements are particular not to cause any scepticism by changing the dividends policy.

When a company issues bonus shares, the total share capital is increased to that extent. Keeping the same rate of dividends means paying out more. Dividends being sticky is, in most cases, a corporate policy; a bonus implies higher amount of dividends in the future.

This is one factor which makes the bonus superior to splits from the point of view of shareholders. A split is often a gimmick to boost the share prices in the short run; bonus shares are long-term commitments.

Buy-Back of Shares

Companies often resort to buy-back of shares to reward the shareholders by utilising its surplus cash. There are two ways in which a company can return the cash to shareholders: first is dividends, where cash gets distributed proportionately to all shareholders. The second is buy-back. Let us understand the differences between the two.

As explained earlier, there is a certain degree of stickiness in dividends. Once a company distributes dividends at a specific rate, that rate becomes the benchmark for the future dividend rates. Buy-backs do not come with any such conditions attached. The company does not have to repeat it the next year.

Buy-back benefits the company and the shareholders. On distribution of dividends, the company is required to pay a dividend distribution tax of around 17.5%. This is besides the normal corporate tax the company has already paid on the amount that is to be distributed. Buy-backs do not attract tax liabilities.

A prudent company would like to buy back its own shares when it knows the market is pricing the shares below its value. Who else can be the judge of true value than the management of the same company? If its share is undervalued, the company may resort to buy-back, which serves two purposes. First, the excess cash lying in the company gets utilised in buying a good underpriced investment: its own stocks. Second, the act of buy-back often boosts up the market price of its shares, as it reduces the floating stock in the market, and it sends positive signals to the market. If a company is buying its own shares, it has to be good. Why would they buy otherwise? Buy-back can also be used as a means to fortify the company against a potential hostile takeover.

The management must weigh various factors before deciding to buy the shares. Since buy-back will entail returning cash to the shareholders, how much cash can it spare, keeping its current and future requirements in mind? If the company has growth opportunities where money can grow at a rate higher than the present rate of growth, returning the money would not be good for the shareholders in the long run, and the company should keep the money. This money can grow faster in its own hand rather than in the hands of shareholders. This would cause higher future profitability. However, if the company has no expansion plan or does not need any further capital expenditure or working capital requirements, it will do well to return it to shareholders. The money can thus grow better in the hands of the shareholders.

When a company offers to buy back your shares, should you offer or decline? It all depends upon the price at which the company is buying compared to the prevailing market price. It is also a price-versus-value consideration. As a rule of thumb, it is more beneficial not to accept the buy-back offer if you are a long-term investor. Buy-back results in reducing the number of issued shares in the market. This increases the future EPS since there are fewer shares among which to distribute the profits. Buy-back is also known as float shrink since it reduces the float in the market.

Take for example a company which earned profits of ₹5 crores last year. If it has 50 lakhs shares outstanding, the EPS is ₹10 per share. The company decides to buy back 20% of its shares. After the buy-back, the outstanding shares are 40 lakhs. Assuming that this year the profits remain same, the EPS will be ₹12.50. This is a simplified version of the process. A company which buys back its shares has a growing cash balance because of its increasing profitability. A company which keeps buying shares from the market regularly continues to grow stronger.

In India, There are two ways in which a company can buy back its shares:

1. *Open market purchase.* If a company opts to buy shares from the open market, it makes an offer to shareholders, showing the maximum price and the number of shares it wishes to purchase. However, the company is at liberty to pay less than the offered price and is not obligated to purchase the entire quantity as announced in the repurchase plan. Only public shareholders may take part in the open market buy-back. A word of caution: it is not uncommon for managements to announce a buy-back to support the share price, to which news the market often reacts positively, and later not to buy anything or buy just a fraction of the total quantity for which it has received approval.
2. *Tender route.* Here the company directly purchases shares from the shareholders proportionately. The biggest plus is, the company fixes the price at which it intends to buy the shares, which is higher than the market price, thereby benefiting shareholders. Both promoters and public shareholders take part in the process.

Buy-backs may cause value destruction when the company buys shares at a price higher than the value. In that way, the buy-back does not differ from the investment decision that any investor must make. Buy low is the criterion. If the management buys out shares at a price higher than the value, it throws good money after the bad, and it may hurt its future profitability.

CHAPTER 19

What to Look for in Companies You Buy

"If we become increasingly humble about how little we know, we may be more eager to search."

Sir John Templeton

An investment is a long-term decision. Unlike a speculator, who buys to make a quick buck by throwing a dart in the dark and hoping that it lands at the right spot, an investor buys a share as if he is buying a piece of ownership and will wait with patience for the company to grow so that the shareholders are rewarded. The decision to buy a stock being a long-term decision, coupled with the fact that you will buy just a handful of companies during your entire investing life, it is important that you pay careful attention to various factors that go in making your investment a long-term success.

This information is not available in the quarterly accounts or annual accounts of the company. Studying these factors will make you more informed about the company than most investors, including institutional investors and large fund managers, who seldom go beyond the published information and conference calls.

Here is what you should look for in the company you invest in.

How the Company Treats Its Stakeholders

How the company treats its employees, customers, vendors, lenders, and shareholders is an important factor for determining the long-term health of the company. A company which does not treat its employees well is also not likely to treat its shareholders well. Most companies are focused on treating their customers well since customers bring in money, and often the employees are ignored. A happy employee is the key to productivity and efficiency in an organisation, employees with low morale will pull the organisation down. Employees are the most important resource of the organisation. Philip Fisher would use the scuttlebutt method to find out what was going on inside the company. You don't have to go to the cafe (or a *chai tapri* in an Indian scenario) near the factory premises to check the grapevine. Keep an eye on online resources (websites like Glassdoor.com and LinkedIn) to read reviews about the company given by the employees, the ex-employees, and the disgruntled employees. Publications like *Business Today* and *Business*

India carry out a survey to come up with a list of the best companies to work for.

When a company faces rough weather, employees are more likely to stay with the business which has been good to them in good times. A business which builds the loyalty of employees finds it easier to steer itself clear of bad situations. A business which treats its employees as its first customers builds a great deal of internal strength.

How a company treats its employees is an important window to know the culture of the company. Company culture is the personality of the company; it comprises a wide variety of elements, including work environment, company mission, values, ethics, and company vision.

An important test of the culture of a company is employee turnover: how long the employees stay in the company. In this era of hire and fire, where employees resign just for a change or are fired just because they could not meet the March target of 10% quarterly growth, the company which values its employee and the employees which value the company together make the long-term winning team. The data is difficult to find, but if you can find this out, it is a valuable tool for assessing the future of the company. The annual accounts of the company may throw light on the number of employees leaving during the year; some companies address the shareholders about attrition rate through the chairman's communication. For companies that do not, you will need to keep your ears and eyes open to look for clues.

Equally important is how the company treats its vendors and customers. While this information is difficult for an individual investor to find out, the company website and other online resources might give clues. Creditors' turnover ratio and figures pertaining to amount outstanding to creditors might throw light on this aspect. Debtors' turnover ratio, a classification of debts into those outstanding for a period of over six months and less than six months, may help you draw a conclusion about the satisfaction level of customers. Social media is a great place to find customer satisfaction level. How fast a company responds to a customer query and how it deals with customer grievances can be easily traced on social media.

Corporate culture refers to the beliefs and behaviours that determine how a company's employees and management interact and handle outside business transactions. Often, corporate culture is implied, not defined, and develops organically over time from the cumulative traits of the people the company hires. A company's culture will be reflected in its dress code, business hours, office setup, employee benefits, turnover, hiring decisions, treatment of clients, client satisfaction, and every other aspect of operations.

A company builds its culture over a lifetime. It does not happen overnight. The business ethos of the founders set the cultural foundation of the organisation; it takes conscious efforts by subsequent managements to enhance the organisational culture. Research has proved that there is a direct correlation between the cultural values of a company and its stock performance. To take an example, in India, Tata Group companies enjoy the trust of investors because of the presence of a positive corporate culture. Tata Group has built its culture over generations and is one of the inherent invisible strengths of the group.

As explained earlier, analysing corporate culture is something that few analysts are interested in. Analysts look for quantifiable parameters; culture is not prone to quantification and mathematical expressions. It cannot be expressed as a number on the spreadsheet, making it irrelevant for investment decision-making, which is based on complicated mathematical equations these days, making it look like rocket science. In a quest for exactitude, they lose the bigger picture, and the analysts end up paying too much importance to quantifiable variables, ignoring the non-quantifiable ones. Analysing corporate culture is one such key factor, which is too important to be ignored, sometimes perhaps more important than financial statements.

'In the corporate world, if you have analysts, due diligence, and no horse sense, you've just described hell,' says Charlie Munger. Investment is all about common sense. It is easy to understand. People armed with impressive degrees from top B-schools make it complicated because that is how they earn their bread. Mathematical models launch the rockets; they do not win on the stock market.

Remember Union Carbide, the company which in 1982 was responsible for the biggest industrial disaster in the history, killing 3,787 people, permanently incapacitating 40,000 people, and exposing over 500,000 people to deadly gases? The government of India sued Union Carbide and agreed to an out-of-court settlement of US$470 million in 1989. The plant site has not yet been cleaned up. Warren Anderson, CEO at the time of the disaster, and Union Carbide refused to answer to homicide charges and remained fugitives from India's courts. The US denied several extradition requests. Anderson died on 29 September 2014 in Florida. Seven Indian employees of Union Carbide were convicted of criminal negligence in 2010 and fined $2,000 each.

The financial statements of the company were great, and the company continued to make great profits for its investors. (It was owned 51% by Union Carbide, USA, and 49% by Indian investors). There were red flags by auditors and whistle-blowers about the workers' safety and the risk of exposure to lethal gases; the company paid no heed to it.

A gas leak had not occurred in the Bhopal plant of Union Carbide, but it had a history of disaster. In 1976, two trade unions complained of pollution within the plant. In 1981, a worker was accidentally splashed with phosgene as he was carrying out a maintenance job of the plant's pipes. In panic, he removed his gas mask and inhaled a large amount of toxic phosgene gas, leading to his death just 72 hours later. Following these events, the journalist Rajkumar Keswani investigated and published his findings in Bhopal's local paper *Rapat*, in which he urged, 'Wake up, people of Bhopal. You are on the edge of a volcano.'

In January 1982, a phosgene leak exposed 24 workers, all of whom were admitted to a hospital. None of the workers had been ordered to wear protective masks. One month later, in February 1982, an MIC leak affected 18 workers. In August 1982, a chemical engineer came into contact with liquid MIC, resulting in burns in over 30 percent of his body. Later that same year, in October 1982, there was another MIC leak. In attempting to stop the leak, the MIC supervisor suffered severe chemical burns, and two other workers were severely exposed to the gases. During 1983 and 1984, there were leaks of MIC, chlorine, monomethylamine, phosgene, and carbon tetrachloride, sometimes in combination. In 1982, Carbide's auditors warned of a possible 'runaway reaction'. Carbide didn't supply an antidote, maintaining that MIC was 'nothing more than a potent tear gas'. This case highlights the importance of analysing corporate culture.

Can an investor afford to stay indifferent? The obvious argument is that it is up to the company management to make policies and implement them; as long as the shareholder gets a handsome return on his investment, he should remain unconcerned. This tragedy made the investors realise that corporate culture is a key ingredient in corporate success. You cannot cut corners on that. This may bring you short-term money, but the long-term survival, growth, and success of a company depends upon how it treats its various stakeholders. Union Carbide was a bankrupt company after the Bhopal gas tragedy and was taken over by Dow Chemicals.

This example should bring home the point that corporate culture is easy to know if you wish to do so, though it is vague and has to be felt rather than quantified. You might grade it, but you have no set formula for factoring it into the value calculations. Given a choice between two companies with an equal margin of safety, you should opt for the one which has a more sustainable culture. It is the difficulty to quantify that gives you an edge over institutions and funds, for they will buy nothing based on something that cannot be converted in money terms.

Based on the above discussion, let us define the factors we should look at to identify a *great corporate culture*.

First, the attitude of the founders and the present management of the company plays a key role in determining the culture that the top management likes to percolate down from the top. What is the composition of the board of directors of the company? Does it look balanced and diversified in terms of people having diverse expertise, or is it a bunch of people handpicked by the founder to act as figureheads? How independent are independent directors? They choose more often than not the independent directors—not on account of their technical expertise, but as a means of statutory compliance. Looking at the profile of independent directors may give you clues if they are independent or are there just to collect their sitting fees.

Second, the vision document and the mission statement of the company may help you identify the long-term vision and growth prospects of the company.

Third, look for the policy of the company vis-à-vis employees' motivation, how the company handles employees' grievances, how it incentivises them, and the growth opportunities the company offers to its employees. Do the employees love the company? Would the employees recommend their friends to join the company?

Fourth, look for factors to find out the company's attitude towards its relationship with vendors and customers. Are the vendors likely to stick with the company in bad times? Is the company loyal to the customers and vice versa? Do the customers love the products of the company?

Last, find clues about the employee retention policy and attrition rate. How long are employees likely to stick with the company?

It is easier to find the management's attitude in a company, which is still headed by the founder of the company. Know the founder, and you will know the culture of the company. If the top management no longer includes the founder, an important determinant of the management's attitude is the involvement of executives who hold meaningful stakes in the company. Despite the separation of ownership and management in the modern corporate world, some old-fashioned things still work. Top management without a stake in ownership is likely to be reckless and speculative in their behaviour.

CHAPTER 20

Buying a Share Is Like Buying a Business

"Details create the big picture."

Sanford I. Weill

The biggest mistake of investors is to think of a share as an instrument independent of and unrelated to the business it represents. The first thing to realise is that the stock derives its value from the underlying business and that what you are buying when you buy a share of a billion-rupee company is one part of the ownership of the company.

You become an owner of the company to the extent of the money you invested in the company. This is not an academic conclusion but something that has a great impact on your investment decision.

To understand the valuation process and the concept of ownership, you will apply the same criteria as you would when buying a small business across the lane. Let us say there is a small ready-made-clothes store in your neighbourhood up for sale. (We will use this example to understand the concept and apply the principles learnt to buying a share in a large listed company.)

The owner approaches you with an offer to sell it to you for ₹50 lakhs. There are two different ways you can value this business. First, you can sum up the market value of all its assets and reduce the liabilities from it. Let us say the value of the shop is ₹20 lakhs, the business has a stock of goods worth ₹30 lakhs, and has cash and cash equivalents of ₹10 lakhs. This totals up to ₹60 lakhs. Against this, there is a bank loan of ₹20 lakhs. Thus, the net sum of all assets is ₹40 lakhs. Why would you pay ₹50 lakhs for something worth only ₹40 lakhs? There is an invisible factor not reflected in the financial books, which is the key determinant here, the goodwill of business. This is the best shop in the locality, and the owner is known to be an honest and a sincere businessman who sells quality stuff. The owner knows every customer personally. Shopping here is a pleasant experience, and customers love to come back to this shop. Since our tool is inadequate to give the right valuation to this business, let us try an alternate way.

You may ask this question: 'How much will I earn every year if I invest ₹50 lakhs in this business, or in short, what is my return on investment (ROI)?' From the books of accounts, you find that last year the owner earned a post-tax income of ₹5 lakhs. Thus, your ROI is 10%, which looks like a fair amount. You find that the net income has been flourishing and during past three years, it has grown from ₹4 lakhs to ₹4.50 lakhs then to ₹5 lakhs. (I am keeping it simple to explain the point.) Presuming that the income for the next year will be the same as the current year (a conservative estimate since there may be disruptions because of the change of ownership), by paying ₹50 lakhs, you are paying ten times the earnings. Your price-to-earnings ratio, known as P/E ratio, is 50 : 5 or 10 : 1 or simply 10 (also called P/E multiple when expressed as a single number instead of a ratio). This, in simple terms, means that, other things being equal (they won't be—they should improve), your payback period is 10 years. Or to put it in other words, you will recover your investment in 10 years out of the income that you accrue every year.

This concept of P/E is crucial to your understanding of investment valuation. The higher the P/E ratio, the more time it will take for you to recover your investment. Some stocks are fancily priced; it is not unusual to find a P/E multiple of 100 sometimes. In simple terms, you will take 100 years to get your money back. (It is not as simple as that. There are more variables, like increase in future earnings, that need to be factored in, yet this gives you a fair idea of the utility of P/E as an important determinant of your investment decision.)

By now you know a big business does not differ from a small one regarding valuation method as long as you apply the ownership test (i.e. you treat yourself as the owner of the business even when you are buying just one share out of 10 million floating in the market).

Let us take the same example a step further to explain more concepts. You find this an attractive deal but don't have money to pay to the owner. You circulate the idea of investment among your friends, and 9 of your friends will come forward and be your partners in this business, each contributing 1/10 of the required capital (i.e. ₹5 lakhs). Now there are 10 shareholders with an investment of ₹500,000 each. However, some of your investor friends would like to further divide their ownership into even lower units so they can invite some of their family members to invest. Since it may become too complex because of so many divisions, you all agree to split the required capital into 50,000 shares of ₹100 each (thus totalling to ₹50 lakhs). Now things are easy. Someone who wants to invest only ₹2,00,000 will be allotted 2,000 shares, one who wants to invest ₹1,00,000 will be allotted 100 shares, and so on. This is how share capital is split in a joint-stock company. (Now you know why it is called a joint-stock company.)

Having divided the capital into shares, now we can do all our analysis based on one share. The current year's earning of ₹5,00,000 translates into earning per share of ₹10 since there are 50,000 shares. This is known as EPS in stock market language. Bingo! Things are so easy. They looked so confusing before. EPS is ₹10, and the market price of this share is ₹100. The P/E ratio is thus 10 : 1 (We also calculated the same ratio by using global figures.)

EPS and P/E ratio are the two factors you will keep a watch on. This is a simple but very effective tool. It helps you compare the earnings (and P/E multiple) of the company with its peers or with the industry average. The P/E ratio is portable and can be taken out of the industry your company operates in and be compared with the ratio of another company in an entirely different business group. You may also use P/E for comparing the performance of the same company over a different period. A higher P/E ratio means that investors wish to pay a higher price for the same amount of earning. It may also mean that the stock has become expensive. A low P/E may mean that investors are estimating future earnings to be lower, and so the resultant multiple is lower. It may also mean that the security is undervalued and there is a potential for that stock to rise and reach its realistic P/E ratio. Thus, P/E, when coupled with other tools, can be an important factor for an investor to know.

A more detailed discussion on P/E ratio follows in chapter 22.

CHAPTER 21

Understanding Financial Statements

"You have to understand accounting and you have to understand the nuances of accounting. It's the language of business and it's an imperfect language, but unless you are willing to put in the effort to learn accounting—how to read and interpret financial statements—you really shouldn't select stocks yourself."

Warren Buffett

As a chartered accountant with a PhD in commerce, I find this to be the most difficult chapter to write. There is always the fear of overdoing. In the business world, if there is anything that scares people the most, it is financial data and accounts. We professionals have a tendency to make it look more boring than it is because it gives us an air of having technical knowledge that only a select few can understand.

Financial Statements are easy to understand. It has a language of its own, which can be mastered if you are willing to understand it. Once you understand that language, you can talk to the balance sheet and profit-and-loss accounts. Understanding financial data is an important part of the investing process, you cannot calculate intrinsic value unless you reach out for the financial data of the company. Warren Buffett is known to spend hours reading corporate balance sheets and related data. His wife once said, 'All Warren needs is a book and a 60-watt bulb.' Buffett spends 80% of his time reading. What may look like the most boring parts of financial statements contain the most important bits of information, and Buffett reads every figure of the stocks he is invested in or is likely to invest in. He, at age 87, understands more about the stocks that interest him than most people do because of his passion for understanding numbers.

Reading a balance sheet can be fun for those who develop the right skills. Contrary to what you may believe, the skills can be gained by anyone with no previous exposure, whatever your educational background. Develop love for numbers; it is one skill that will give you a definite edge over a majority of investors, who think of the balance sheet to be just a mandatory mail that you must receive from the company every year. It is seldom opened.

Balance Sheet

First, let us understand what a balance sheet is. A balance sheet is a statement drawn from the books of accounts of a company which shows the assets, liabilities, and the shareholders' equity at a specific point in time. The published accounts in India carry the balance sheet as of 31 March each year since the financial year in India for statutory compliance begins on 1 April and ends on 31 March. A balance sheet is a snapshot of what the business owns, what it owes, and the amount invested by shareholders in the business.

In a balance sheet, the assets are written on one side, the liabilities on the other. Assets are what the business owns. Fixed assets include land and building, plant and machinery, vehicles, warehouses. Current assets include stock of raw material, work in progress, finished goods, debtors, cash balance, bank balance. Investments include stocks, term deposits. In short, all the properties and chattels and receivables are reflected on the assets side of the balance sheet. The liabilities side reflects the amount the business owes to outsiders and includes long-term and short-term loans, debentures outstanding, borrowings of all kind, expenses outstanding, and amounts due to vendors and suppliers.

Assets are what the business owns; liabilities are what the business owes. The difference between the two is obviously all the money that belongs to the owners of the business; it is represented by share capital and shareholders' reserve. The balance sheet will always balance, which means everything that the business will get by selling off all its assets and paying off all its liabilities will belong to the shareholders.

Hence, the equation:

assets = liabilities + shareholder's capital

Now things are obvious. To finance the purchase of assets, you either take a loan from outsiders or ask your shareholders to contribute. If you understand this basic equation, the concept of a balance sheet is clear to you, and this is all you have to know to understand a balance sheet. Suppose you borrow ₹10 lakhs from a bank and use that money to buy stock. Your liabilities to the bank will increase by ₹10 lakhs. This amount will 'balance' on the asset side and will be reflected in the form of increase in stock. If the company wants to purchase a new machine and takes ₹25 lakhs from the shareholders, the asset side will increase by ₹25 lakhs with an increase in fixed assets (machinery). The balance will be maintained. Now this becomes fun once you know every transaction will impact these three components in such a way that they will remain in a state of balance at any point in time, and the balance sheet you extract any day of the year will always balance.

We have talked about some components of assets and liabilities above. Assets and liabilities comprise many smaller components, which when aggregated become total assets and total liabilities. Let us have a finer understanding of what those components are.

Assets. In India it is customary to write assets in the order of liquidity. The assets which are most illiquid (land, building) are placed at the top, and the assets which are highly liquid (cash, bank balance) are placed at the bottom. The assets are classified as follows:

Non-current assets
    Property, plant, and equipment
    Capital work in progress
    Goodwill
    Other intangible assets
    Financial assets
        Investments
        Loans
        Other financial assets
    Non-current tax assets
    Deferred tax assets
    Other non-current assets

Current assets
    Inventories
    Financial assets
        Investments
        Loans
        Trade receivables
        Cash and cash equivalents

Bank balances other than cash and cash equivalents mentioned above
Other financial assets
Other current assets
Total assets

Liabilities. Liabilities are the money that the company owes to outsiders. Like assets, liabilities are also arranged in the order of liquidity. Longest-term liabilities appear at the top, and the immediate liabilities appear at the bottom.

Non-current liabilities
Financial liabilities
Provisions
Non-current tax liabilities (net)
Other non-current liabilities
Current liabilities
Financial liabilities
Borrowings
Trade payables
Dues to micro and small enterprises
Dues to others
Other financial liabilities
Other current liabilities
Provisions
Total liabilities

Equity. As explained earlier, the difference between assets and liabilities is the capital of the owners of the business. It is shown in the balance sheet as follows:

Equity
Equity share capital
Reserves and surplus
Capital reserve

Capital redemption reserve
Securities premium reserve
General reserve
Retained earnings
Other reserves
Export profit reserves
Total attributable to owners of the company

Equity and reserves are the amount that belongs to the owners of the business. If you own one share in this company, you own a small fraction of equity share capital and the sum represented as reserves and surplus. Categorisation of reserves and surplus under various heads is done to define the purpose for which the shareholders' money has been allocated.

If you have come this far, you would have realised that it was fear of the unknown. Accounting statements are drawn in a logical form meant to be read and understood by the common investor.

It's time to peep into the real world. Let us consider the balance sheet of Hindustan Unilever Limited. Below are the balance sheets for five years.

Table 1. Balance Sheet (in Crore Rupees)

	March 2018	March 2017	March 2016	March 2015	March 2014
	12 months	12 months	12 months	12 months	12 months
EQUITIES AND LIABILITIES					
SHAREHOLDER'S FUNDS					
Equity share capital	216	216	216	216.35	216.27
Total share capital	216	216	216	216.35	216.27
Revaluation reserves	0	0	0	0.67	0.67
Reserves and surplus	6,859.00	6,274.00	6,063.00	3,507.76	3,060.11

Total reserves and surplus	6,859.00	6,274.00	6,063.00	3,508.43	3,060.78
Total shareholder's funds	7,075.00	6,490.00	6,279.00	3,724.78	3,277.05
NON-CURRENT LIABILITIES					
Other long-term liabilities	666	574	395	170.11	278.82
Long-term provisions	772	485	594	956.35	838.69
Total non-current liabilities	1,438.00	1,059.00	989	1,126.46	1,117.51
CURRENT LIABILITIES					
Trade payables	7,013.00	6,006.00	5,498.00	5,288.90	5,793.89
Other current liabilities	972.00	809.00	864.00	908.05	852.94
Short-term provisions	651	387	290	2,585.87	1,957.01
Total current liabilities	8,636.00	7,202.00	6,652.00	8,782.82	8,603.84
Total capital and liabilities	17,149.00	14,751.00	13,920.00	13,634.06	12,998.40
ASSETS					
NON-CURRENT ASSETS					
Tangible assets	3,776.00	3,654.00	2,902.00	2,435.50	2,397.94
Intangible assets	366.00	370.00	12.00	22.03	24.12
Capital work in progress	430	203	386	479.01	312.08
Intangible assets under development	0	0	0	0	7.7
Fixed assets	4,572.00	4,227.00	3,300.00	2,936.54	2,741.84
Non-current investments	256.00	260.00	319.00	654.11	636.17
Deferred tax assets (net)	255	160	168	195.96	161.73
Long-term loans and advances	404	352	162	583.46	605.51
Other non-current assets	523	387	419	0.44	0.68

Total non-current assets	6,010.00	5,386.00	4,368.00	4,370.51	4,145.93
CURRENT ASSETS					
Current investments	2,855.00	3,519.00	2,461.00	2,623.82	2,457.95
Inventories	2,359.00	2,362.00	2,528.00	2,602.68	2,747.53
Trade receivables	1,147.00	928.00	1,064.00	782.94	816.43
Cash and cash equivalents	3,373.00	1,671.00	2,759.00	2,537.56	2,220.97
Short-term loans and advances	0.00	0.00	0.00	657.27	537.68
Other current assets	1,405.00	885	740	59.28	71.91
Total current assets	11,139.00	9,365.00	9,530.00	9,263.55	8,852.47
Total assets	17,149.00	14,751.00	13,920.00	13,634.06	12,998.40

Voila! The document makes sense. In fact, if you study corporate balance sheets, you will soon find it developing into a hobby, perhaps a fruitful hobby. Numbers give you a great advantage over others. If your investment decision is based on a study of financial statements, you will no longer be throwing darts in the dark.

How to interpret a balance sheet? There are various ways to do it. I will recommend common-sense tools that are not only easy to understand but are more effective as well.

As explained earlier, a balance sheet is a snapshot at a particular point in time; it is not a continuing process but is a standstill view (of a dynamic) business.

The best tool to make a balance sheet meaningful is to compare a balance sheet with previous years' figures. Here, we can see that the fixed assets of HUL have been rising from ₹2,741 crores in March 2014 to ₹4,572 in the year 2018. You don't need a complicated mathematical equation (or stratospheric IQ) to know the company is investing heavily in fixed assets. Fixed assets contribute to capacity expansion and provide enduring long-term benefits. Likewise you can draw conclusions about other items appearing in the balance sheet.

The second easy-to-use tool is ratio analysis. We can derive key ratios from the figures appearing in the balance sheet, and the figures can be used for comparing with previous periods, with peers, with average industry ratios, and so on. Using ratios, it is possible to link a balance sheet with its related profit-and-loss account.

Profit-and-Loss Account

The profit-and-loss account is a statement that shows the financial performance of a company over an accounting period. The profit-and-loss account is also known as the statement of revenue and expenditure or the revenue statement or the income statement. It shows how the business derives its income, what expenses it incurs, and various activities it goes through to make the profit for the year. A profit-and-loss account is drawn for a period; the annual profit-and-loss account in India is for the period starting on 1 April and ending on 31 March. You recall that the balance sheet is drawn on a date and is about a point in time.

The profit-and-loss account is the bridge that connects two balance sheets. The profit-and-loss account for the year ended on 31 March 2018 (which means the period starting on 1 April 2017 and ending on 31 March 2018). Connect the two balance sheets—i.e. the balance sheet for 31 March 2017 and 31 March 2018. Things are so easy now. The balance sheet is a snapshot, a point in time, a pillar at the start of the bridge. Profit and loss are the bridge that leads you to the other end, where you meet another pillar, another snapshot, the next year's balance sheet. The two statements put together make the complete story.

The profit-and-loss account shows gross revenue or gross income from operations (that means the sales) and shows various expenses incurred by the business to earn the revenue. The income may also include income that comes from non-operative sources. The expenses can also be categorised as expenses pertaining to business operations and non-operative expenses. The expenses are bifurcated into various heads, which makes it suitable for us to subject them to various analyses.

Let us take a real example to understand the profit-and-loss account. Following is the profit-and-loss account of HUL for five years (31 March 2014 to 2018):

Table 2. Profit-and-Loss Account of HUL (in Crores Rupees)

Year Ending	March 2018	March 2017	March 2016	March 2015	March 2014
	12 months	12 months	12 months	12 months	12 months
INCOME					
Revenue from operations (gross)	34,619.00	33,895.00	32,929.00	32,086.32	28,947.06
Less excise/service tax/other levies	693	2,597.00	2,430.00	1,915.82	1,538.77
Revenue from operations (net)	33,926.00	31,298.00	30,499.00	30,170.50	27,408.29
Other operating revenues	599	592	562	635.12	610.84
Total operating revenues	34,525.00	31,890.00	31,061.00	30,805.62	28,019.13
Other income	569	526	564	618.39	621.03
Total revenue	35,094.00	32,416.00	31,625.00	31,424.01	28,640.16
EXPENSES					
Cost of materials consumed	12,491.00	11,363.00	11,267.00	11,867.31	11,159.81
Purchase of stock-in-trade	3,812.00	4,166.00	3,951.00	3,697.96	3,350.19
Changes in inventories of FG, WIP, and stock-in-trade	−71	156	87	58.28	−166.38
Employee benefit expenses	1,745.00	1,620.00	1,573.00	1,578.89	1,435.95
Finance costs	20	22	15	16.82	36.03
Depreciation and amortisation expenses	478	396	321	286.69	260.55
Other expenses	9,272.00	8,538.00	8,434.00	8,394.94	7,764.30

Total expenses	27,747.00	26,261.00	25,648.00	25,900.89	23,840.45
	March 2018	March 2017	March 2016	March 2015	March 2014
	12 months	12 months	12 months	12 months	12 months
Profit/loss before exceptional, extraordinary items and tax	7,347.00	6,155.00	5,977.00	5,523.12	4,799.71
Exceptional items	−62	241	−31	664.3	228.68
Profit/loss before tax	7,285.00	6,396.00	5,946.00	6,187.42	5,028.39
Tax expenses (continued operations)					
Current tax	2,148.00	1,865.00	1,816.00	1,871.17	1,293.15
Deferred tax	−100	41	−7	−33.82	24.83
Tax for earlier years	0	0	0	34.81	−157.08
Total tax expenses	2,048.00	1,906.00	1,809.00	1,872.16	1,160.90
Profit/loss after tax and before extraordinary items	5,237.00	4,490.00	4,137.00	4,315.26	3,867.49
Profit/loss from continuing operations	5,237.00	4,490.00	4,137.00	4,315.26	3,867.49
Profit/loss for the period	5,237.00	4,490.00	4,137.00	4,315.26	3,867.49

Let us use this statement to understand the concept of profit-and-loss account.

The profit-and-loss account is divided into two 'sides', the income side and the expenditure side. In the above statement, income has been recorded at the top and the expenses below that. Let us first consider the income side.

Income

The first item is gross revenue from operations. This is the sales the company has done during the year. Thus, gross sales for the year 2017/18 were ₹34,619 crores. You can see the trend line of sales by comparing this figure with the figures of earlier years. It is easier to see that the sales have been rising from ₹28,947 crores in 2013/14 to ₹34,619 crores in 2017/18. You need not resort to any calculations to notice this trend (beyond a passion for numbers). Reduce excise duty (now GST), and you get net sales revenue. You notice that the company makes more than ₹500 crores every year from 'other income'. If you are curious to know the source of this income and whether it is likely to continue or grow in the future, you may go to the annexure attached to the profit-and-loss account, where the company gives the details. (Annexures are a means to keep secondary information out of the main sheet so that there is less clutter, and the statement remains user-friendly.)

Expenditure

From the sales, you must reduce expenses to arrive at the profit during the year. On the expenditure side, the first item is the amount spent on buying material and processing it into finished products if you are a manufacturing company or buying goods for sale if you are trading in goods. As explained above, the annexures will provide ample details about this. Expenses may be bifurcated into those directly related to the production of goods and services and those that are not directly related but must be incurred for the running of business.

This classification is important because expenses directly related to the production (raw material, power, wages, etc.) are variable. They are directly linked to the units produced. The higher the production, the higher the consumption of these variable inputs. Those not directly linked to the production, though important, are often 'overheads'. Overheads do not vary directly with the production, and they remain constant up to a certain scale. They scale up in steps rather than variably. Examples are salaries of office and managerial staff, office electricity, office expenses, which need to be incurred production or no production. The analysis helps us do a stress test on the company. We can find out at what capacity the company breaks even—that is, comes to a point of no profit, no loss. This helps us judge if the company has the means to survive the recessionary part of the trade cycle.

Deducting all expenses, you arrive at the net profit before taxes (known as EBT, or earning before tax). From the EBT, you reduce taxes, and you arrive at the net profit, also known as PAT (profit after tax). This is the net profit arrived at after paying off all expenses pertaining to third parties, including interest on loan. Depreciation on fixed assets has also been considered before arriving at this figure. The claim of the government has also been paid off (taxes).

This figure thus belongs to the owners of the business, the shareholders of the company. Everything won't be paid off to them; the company may decide on distributing a part of this as dividends to the shareholders and ploughing back the remaining amount in the business so it continues to grow in the company, bringing in higher revenue in the future. This is a fantastic source of capital for many companies and is referred to as internal accruals. You can see how much of such money the company has accumulated out of its earnings over the years by referring to the 'reserves and surplus' part in the balance sheet we discussed earlier.

Cash Flow Statement

The profit-and-loss account and balance sheet should together complete the picture for an average investor, but if you are an intelligent investor, you'll soon discover that the balance sheet and the profit-and-loss account have their limitations. To make the analysis meaningful and in-depth, the third document you must analyse is the cash flow statement. The cash flow statement is a financial statement that shows how changes in the balance sheet and the profit-and-loss account affect cash and cash equivalents and break the analysis down to operating, investing, and financing activities. It tells you how much cash flowed in and out of the company during the year. You might wonder why we need such a statement, which looks similar to a profit-and-loss account and shows how much income was received during the year and how many expenses were incurred during the year.

We sometimes come across companies which go bust though the balance sheet looks attractive. It is not unusual for a company's management to window-dress the accounts and show a better picture of the company. Many a time, when the company is in red, the management will resort to creative accounting or financial jugglery to show continued growth of the company. Income from operations may be negative, but the company may be selling the 'family silver' to stay afloat. The average investor is happy as long as he finds the black bottom line and the company continues to declare dividends. Then one day, the company goes belly up! Not all was well with the company; however, the traditional statements did not detect the abnormalities. The choice weapon in such situations is the cash flow statement. A real, meaningful analysis of a company's financial position cannot be done without a study of the cash flow statement.

Let me try to answer those of you who think the profit-and-loss account and cash flow statement look similar. They are similar in many respects. Yet they are different. The difference emerges because of a fundamental concept of modern accounting called the accrual system. The accrual concept means that expenses and revenues are recorded in the period they belong to and not in the period they are paid off or received.

The benefit of the accrual approach is that financial statements reflect all the expenses associated with the reported revenues for an accounting period. Once a business receives or makes cash payments, it reverses the accrual accounting entries and records the cash transactions. Thus, sales will be recorded in the year sales invoices are generated and not in the year in which payment is received. Salaries are accounted for in the period to which they pertain and not in the period they are paid (salary of March paid in April are recorded in March, only the cash outflow is recorded in April). The principle of accrual makes the accounting method uniform across companies and periods and makes comparison meaningful because all income and expenses pertaining to a period are clubbed together in that period, even if paid in advance or in arrears.

But this can cause serious mismatch between income earned and income received. Let us consider the case of a company which, last year, had made a sale of ₹50 crores. This year, the sale was only ₹25 crores, and the management pushed hard and made a credit sale of ₹30 crores at the end of the year. The profit-and-loss account shows the gross revenue at ₹55 crores, a 10% increase over the previous period. But where is the money, honey?

The transaction has been accounted for, but the money has not yet come in the bank. Because it has not received the money, the company either did not pay its bills or paid it out of past bank balance or took a loan to pay the expenses or sold assets. The profit-and-loss account will still look normal, because the purpose of the profit-and-loss account is to calculate profit for the year, following the accrual concept. But the investor who goes the extra mile and reads the cash flow statement will discover serious issues with the company. He will know there is a distortion of a fundamental business principle: income from operations is not enough to absorb expenses of operations.

This raises a red flag in his mind, which is to be investigated. Now he can explore further to answer various questions. Is it the usual practice in the company's business? (For construction companies and project companies, this is the usual pattern.) Does the company do this every year? Is the debt realised in the subsequent year, or is part of it written off? (There is the possibility of a dummy sales transaction.)

By now you understand the importance of cash flow analysis, and an intelligent investor will ignore the cash flow only to his peril. The cash flow statement is important because it excludes all non-cash items of income and expenditure. (Depreciation, for example, is an expenditure from the perspective of an accountant, but since it does not involve an outflow of cash, it is excluded from the cash flow statement.) As an investor, you will look at the ability of a company to generate cash. Many companies show good profitability but do not show matching cash flows, and you know in advance that the company may default sooner or later.

To see how a cash flow looks like, let us again go back to HUL and look at its cash flow statement.

Table 3. Cash Flow Statement (in Crores Rupees)

	March 2018	March 2017	March 2016	March 2015	March 2014
	12 months	12 months	12 months	12 months	12 months
Net profit/ loss before extraordinary items and tax	7,347.00	6,155.00	5,977.00	5,523.12	4,799.71
Net cash flow from operating activities	5,916.00	4,953.00	3,974.00	3,103.76	3,724.15
Net cash used in investing activities	−1,264.00	−752	−51	448.04	−513.16
Net. cash used from financing activities	−4,651.00	−4,264.00	−4,008.00	−3,450.44	−2,916.79
Net inc./dec. in cash and cash equivalents	1	−63	−85	101.36	294.2
Cash and cash equivalents at beginning of year	572	635	720	620.61	326.41
Cash and cash equivalents at end of year	573	572	635	721.97	620.61

Let us understand the terms used here. The cash flow statement is partitioned into three segments:

1. cash flow resulting from operating activities
2. cash flow resulting from investing activities
3. cash flow resulting from financing activities.

The money coming into the business is called cash inflow, and the money going out from the business is called cash outflow.

Operating Activities

Operating activities include the production, sales, and delivery of the company's product and collecting payment from its customers. This includes purchasing raw materials, building inventory, advertising, and shipping the product.

It includes:

- receipts for the sale of loans, debt or equity instruments in a trading portfolio
- interest received on loans
- payments to suppliers for goods and services
- payments to employees or on behalf of employees
- interest payments
- buying merchandise.

Items which are added back to (or subtracted from, as appropriate) the net income figure (which is found on the income statement) to arrive at cash flows from operations include:

- depreciation (loss of the tangible asset value over time)
- deferred tax
- amortisation (loss of the intangible asset value over time)

- any gains or losses associated with the sale of a non-current asset because associated cash flows do not belong in the operating section
- dividends received (because dividends are not a part of operations of the company).

Investing Activities

Examples of investing activities are:

- purchase or sale of an asset (assets can be land, building, equipment, marketable securities, etc.)
- loans made to suppliers or received from customers
- payments related to mergers and acquisition.

Financing Activities

Financing activities include the inflow of cash from investors such as banks and shareholders and the outflow of cash to shareholders as dividends as the company generates income. Other activities which impact the long-term liabilities and equity of the company are also listed in the financing activities section of the cash flow statement.

It includes:

- payments of dividends
- payments for repurchase of company shares.

Let us look at the HUL cash flow. Net flow from operating activity was ₹5,916 crores. Since this is a positive figure, it means the operating activities of the company; to reiterate, operating activities include the production, sales, and delivery of the company's product and collecting payment from its customers. This includes purchasing raw materials, building inventory, advertising, and shipping the product. These created a positive cash flow of ₹5,916 crores. If this were a negative figure (you come across negative figures in many companies), it would have rung the alarm bell for you. HUL is one of the best companies in India with strong financials.

The company was sitting on a cash balance of ₹572 crores at the beginning of the year; it received a flow of ₹5,916 crores from operations during the year, making it a total amount of ₹6,488 at its disposal. Out of this, the company spent ₹1,264 crores on investing activities (to refresh your memory, this refers to sale and purchase of land, building, plant and machinery, loans, etc.), and the company spent ₹4,651 crores in financing activities (payment of dividends, repurchase of shares etc.). At the end of the year, it is left with a balance of ₹573 crores. You might have already inferred that this company has a liberal dividend policy. It has distributed almost three-quarters of what it has received from operations. (Reason: strong consumer brand, no debts, not much amount needed for growth, wide and strong economic moat.)

I know this journey was easier than you thought. Accounting concepts can be easily mastered by anyone taking an interest in learning them. Numbers make sense when you befriend them, tame them. The ability to understand numbers is a great strength that puts you in a different category: that of intelligent investors, who understand what they are doing.

CHAPTER 22

The Financial Ratios

Financial ratios should not intimidate you. You don't need a degree in finance to understand ratios.

The intelligent investor tries a combination of measures to find the intrinsic value of securities. However, there is no such thing as absolute intrinsic value. If things were so easy to calculate, the discipline of value investing would have ceased to exist. It is easy to understand the concept of value (though few try to understand that), yet it is difficult to calculate the value. A lot of factors will go into calculating value, and every investor will have his own unique figure.

Some investors don't calculate the value; they are satisfied with the mental calculation, which tells them that there is an enough margin of safety. Some who are mathematically oriented try to work a precise number, using various formulae. Whatever method one adopts, one thing is sure: if you have understood the concept of intrinsic value and you equate the value against the price, whether in terms of actual numbers or through a mental calculation, the probability of you losing the money is reduced to a great extent.

Fundamental analysis is the discipline of analysing the fundamentals of a company. It is the basic tool an investor uses to analyse a company. The tools of fundamental analysis are easy for an average investor to learn and can be mastered with some efforts. This chapter discusses some more important tools. These tools should suffice most of your practical requirements, and you need not go beyond them. We are against using intricate mathematics for stock market analysis. Some tools loaded with intricate mathematics are so heavy they lose their practical relevance.

Anything that uses advanced mathematical formulae with complex equations requiring a scientific calculator or a computer programme to compute is to be looked upon with suspicion. As we discussed in the chapter of financial statements, accounting is common-sense reduction of business transactions into figures meant to be understood by the actual users of those figures. If you have understood the basic financial statements and how to read them, analysing them is just one more step forward. The primary tool for such an analysis is ratio analysis. Spend time understanding key accounting ratios, and you will thank me for the rest of your life for giving you one of the most important tools of stock analysis.

We must begin the discussion on accounting ratios with a word of caution. No single ratio can give the complete picture; the study of a combination of ratios will always make the analysis meaningful. Never get excited if you find a stock undervalued based on just one ratio; that should be the starting point of your investigation, not the conclusion. Handle ratios with care. Business is not precise mathematics, and so business analysis is also not amenable to an exact mathematical model. Any attempt to treat it so is hazardous. Many a time, you need to travel beyond mathematics and accounting to corroborate your findings.

The P/E Ratio

The starting point of any meaningful analysis of the fundamentals of a company is the P/E ratio. The P/E ratio is a quick test to find out if a stock is overvalued or undervalued compared to its earnings. Let us understand the concept.

The P/E ratio is the ratio between the market price of a share and its earnings. Before we understand the equation, let us calculate earnings per share (EPS). We saw earlier that the profit-and-loss account is a statement that shows you how much profit the company has earned. The net profit of the company, after providing for all expenses and taxes, is the amount that belongs to the shareholders of the company. Part of the amount may be distributed as dividends and the remaining may be ploughed back in business by the company. The amount of profit, before distribution of dividends, is the earning we are concerned about as shareholders of the company.

For the sake of example, let us take that company A earned ₹1 crore after taxes. Another company—let us call it company B—has earned ₹5 crores during the same period. Can you conclude that Company B is better than Company A? No, because you don't know the size of the companies. Company A might have made the profits of ₹1 crore on a capital investment of ₹5 crores, whereas the company B might have made the profits of ₹5 crores on a capital investment of ₹50 crores. Comparing the profits of these two companies is like comparing apples to oranges.

In order for that comparison to be meaningful, you can calculate for the earning per share. To keep the example simple, let us say that both companies have their capital divided into shares of ₹100 each. Company A has issued 10,00,000 shares of ₹100 each, totalling to ₹1 crores, while company B has issued 50 lakhs shares of ₹100 each, totalling to ₹50 crores. Now we use this information to find the earning per share. The earning per share is the total earning divided by the number of shares.

The EPS of company A is ₹1 crore divided by 10 lakhs shares.

₹100,00,000 / 10,00,000 shares = ₹10 per share

The earnings per share of company A is ₹10, or the company earns ₹10 on each share it has issued.

Now let us calculate the EPS of company B. That's ₹5 crores divided by 50 lakhs.

₹5,00,00,000 / 50,00,000 shares = ₹10 per share

The EPS of both companies is the same at ₹10 per share. The figures make sense. They are no longer a comparison between apples and oranges. They are comparable. What looked like different earning figures turned out to be the same figures per share.

Thus, EPS is useful for comparing earnings across companies or periods. Note that the issue price of a share may be different for different companies. In India you may find shares issued for ₹100, ₹10, or sometimes ₹1 (occurring because of stock splits). In order for the EPS to be meaningful, you should also know the par value of shares.

Now we take this analysis to the next level and link it with the market price of the share. We presume company A is selling at ₹250 per share. The price-to-earnings ratio will be:

current price / EPS
₹250 / ₹10 = 25

Assume that company B's latest price quote is ₹400. The P/E ratio of company B will be:

₹400 / ₹10 = 40

This ratio is almost a magical number for investors. You can also understand the ratio as a number or a multiple: price is 25 times the earnings.

What does it mean? In the simplest terms (though life does not exist in this simple form), it means that if an investor were to buy one share of company A at the present market price of ₹250, at the P/E multiple of 25, it will take him 25 years to get his money back. This is a simplistic criterion; receiving ₹10 every year for 25 years will make it ₹250. It is presuming linearity of earnings, that earnings will not grow in the future. It is also ignoring the time value of money; 25 years from now, ₹10 would be worth much less. Still it acts as a great rule of thumb, not as an absolute measure, but perhaps as a means of inter-firm comparison or comparison with industry data or even comparison arose industries. The P/E multiple makes the statistics of price and earnings portable and logical.

Conclusions are easy to draw now. Other things being equal, will you be investing in company A or company B? While A will give your money back in 25 years, B will give it back in 40 years. Compared to B, A is undervalued, or to put it in other words, compared to A, B is overvalued.

However, there is more to P/E than meets the eyes. What if company B is growing at a rate faster than the rate of growth of A? The future earnings of B will soon be higher than that of A. Does that not justify a higher P/E multiple?

Based on this discussion, we can draw two important principles:

1. Stocks with a lower P/E multiple are undervalued compared to stocks with a higher P/E.
2. The market assigns a higher P/E multiple to future growth. A company growing at a higher rate will trade at a higher P/E

multiple. It is not unusual to estimate future earnings for the next 2–3 years and calculate the future P/E multiple.

Don't these two like opposite conclusions from the same ratio? They do and they are. That is the reason I cautioned you in the beginning that drawing conclusions from one ratio in isolation can be dangerous. You may end up buying a stock with a low P/E because it is in a failing business and its future earnings will be low.

The PE is not without its drawbacks, and it is very important that you *know the limitations* of the tool you are using.

In isolation, the P/E ratio has no meaning. A P/E ratio of 12 says nothing about the valuation of a company unless you compare it to peers or the industry average. The biggest defect in the whole schema is that the benchmark itself shifts when the market becomes overheated. Keep in mind that if a stock has a lower a P/E ratio than the industry, that fact alone does not make it cheaper. The industry P/E may itself have become expensive, so at the most, one might say the stock is cheaper than the industry but may still be expensive per se.

Recollect the dot-com mania, where the industry P/E was as high as 200! A stock with a P/E multiple of 80 would have looked cheaper in comparison, and people made the mistake of buying those shares. With many companies, the denominator E was a negative, the company was in red, yet there was more demand than supply. When there is frenzy in the market, logic is the first casualty. Some people even argued that the conventional accounting ratios are dead in the dot-com era; 'eyeballs' and 'hits' on websites was all that mattered. Until the bubble bursts.

While P/E is a great, quick indicator, don't trust it fully until you are confident that E is clean. Sometimes the figure of earning may mislead. Consider a particular year when the company has sold off a part of the business; the capital gains will also reflect in the EPS, making it look better than what it is. Since we are using P/E to find out long-term growth prospects of a company, such one-off transactions might distort the results. Unscrupulous managements often resort to extraordinary items to boost up the EPS. You need to filter off unusual items to get the EPS that comes from the usual business operations of the company.

The best way to detect unusual items distorting the EPS is to look into the cash flow statements to know the sources where the cash came from. The EPS may be depressed because of an extraordinary loss booked by the company during that year. The company might have commissioned a massive plant, which though operational has contributed little to the revenue in the first year, but it has charged the expenses and depreciation to the account, leading to a lower than usual EPS for the year. This can be a great investment opportunity since those who consider P/E ratio to be sacrosanct might not probe deeper to find out the distortion. The key, again, is to look into the cash flow statement.

Certain businesses are cyclical, and the EPS would depend upon what part of the cycle it is operating in. Thus, a steel company, when it is at the top of trade cycle, will have earnings that are higher than that at the lower part. If you make a long-term decision based on one year's performance, it may give unpredictable results. A better course will be to take an average of the EPS of one full cycle and to use that to judge. But a cycle may last eight years, so the parameter will remain only for a long-term investor.

As the P/E ratio became the most popular indicator, analysts experimented with refinements. It is not unusual to equate current price against a previous period's earning and also to equate the current price with a future period's earning estimate. When the stocks become expensive, analysts try to justify it by replacing the E with a notional E, the estimated future earnings. This is entering the danger zone, and one needs to tread with caution. It is because the future is uncertain that we are using indicators like P/E to find a relative margin of safety. Quantifying the future in exact mathematical terms when one factor (the denominator) is an estimate is fraught with danger.

High inflation is another factor that may distort the efficacy of the P/E ratio as a consistent tool. When the inflation is high, the replacement cost of equipment and inventory is higher. When a machine purchased for ₹10 lakhs wears out, the replacement machinery may come at a much higher price, but the depreciation charged in accounts is based on the historical cost of machinery. The value of money in one year is not comparable to that in another year, making comparison inaccurate.

To sum up:

1. You arrive at the P/E ratio by dividing the current market price by the earnings per share.
2. Variations exist in terms of the trailing P/E, the current P/E, and the forward P/E.
3. Historically, the average P/E ratio of the market has been around 15–20.
4. Theoretically, the P/E shows how much an investor is willing to pay per rupee of earning.
5. Another interpretation of a P/E ratio could be a reflection of the market expectations about a company's prospects.
6. P/E in isolation is meaningless; use it with other ratios for the analysis to be meaningful.
7. P/E in isolation is meaningless; it is useful in comparison with industry P/E or peers' P/E.
8. Industry P/E is an unreliable benchmark, a stock with a lower PE than industry average may be cheaper but not cheap.
9. P/E ratios are lower during periods of higher inflation.

PEG Ratio

As discussed above, estimated figures are to be used with caution because they are, well, estimates. One ratio that uses estimated growth relatively rationally and can sometimes be considered an improvement over the P/E ratio is the PEG ratio. The basic component of the PEG ratio is the P/E ratio. It tries to refine the calculations further by factoring in the growth rate.

PEG is calculated by dividing the P/E multiple by the growth rate. Thus:

PEG ratio = P/E ratio / earnings growth rate

PEG takes the P/E ratio as the numerator and divides it by the annual growth rate per share. Let us consider an example.

A company has ₹200 as its market price and an EPS of ₹10. Thus, the P/E ratio is 20. For the last three years, it has grown at an average annual growth rate of 15%, and it is believed the same rate of growth is likely to continue.

PEG = 20 / 15 = 1.33

A PEG of less than 1 is considered a good value. Based on this, the stock looks overvalued. If the company were to grow at 30% instead of 15%, the PEG will be:

PEG = 20 / 30 = 0.67

This makes it undervalued and thus a value buy.

Let me reiterate that growth number is an estimate and is a subjective figure. A lot depends upon macro factors beyond the control of the company. In a growth stock, taking the last three years' average is a conservative method that can be used. Analysts' estimation often go off the mark. Since it is an estimate being fed into a mathematical equation, you should be careful not to consider the result to be the ultimate truth. Growth can be calculated by extrapolating past data or by using some method of future projection. A lot depends upon the accuracy of the estimation; it is easier to arrive at a reliable estimation if the company being studied is in your circle of competence.

Whatever method you apply for calculating growth, it is important that you apply the same method for all the companies you are studying to make the comparison meaningful. PEG is a great tool if you understand its limitations.

PEG works best when used with the P/E ratio. A stock with a high P/E may be considered as overpriced, yet when PEG is calculated, it may be found that while in absolute terms, the stock looks overpriced, when future growth is factored in, it may be underpriced. A stock with a low P/E may look like a value buy until you calculate PEG and find that the PEG is a high number, meaning that low future growth makes the investment unjustified.

To conclude, a PEG of less than 1 means the stock is underpriced, over 1 means it is overpriced, and equal to 1 means it is fairly priced. However, a lot depends upon the quality of data. Bad input will produce bad output. ('Garbage in, garbage out.')

Price-to-Free-Cash-Flow Ratio (P/FCF Ratio)

Some investors prefer to use the P/FCF ratio instead of or besides the P/E ratio, as it gives greater insight into the company. The beauty of the P/E ratio is its simplicity and ease of computing; P/FCF requires one to look for additional information found in the inside pages of the annual report.

As has been explained in the topic devoted to the cash flow statement, the profit-and-loss account is not the same thing as the cash flow statement. A company may make handsome profits but may still face the liquidity crunch, which may affect its performance. The numerator P in this equation is same as in P/E ratio. It is the current market price per share. The denominator is obtained by taking the figure for the net operating cash flow of the company (see cash flow statement) and reducing from it the cash used to fund the capital investment, thus getting the free cash available for the business operations of the company. Since this represents the free cash for the entire company, dividing it by the number of shares will give us free cash flow per share. This is analogous to EPS discussed above, with the difference that this is free cash flow per share instead of earnings per share.

Let us consider an example. Let us say the price of one share of a company is ₹200. The company has 3 crores shares outstanding. The company has free cash flow of ₹15 crores.

$$\text{FCF per share} = ₹15 \text{ crores} / 3 \text{ crores shares}$$
$$= ₹5 \text{ per share}$$

P/FCF = ₹200 / ₹5
= 40

All the discussion pertaining to the P/E ratio applies to the P/FCF and is not being repeated here. Just remember that in isolation, the ratio has no relevance and has to be read compared to the peers or industry.

Intelligent investors look for companies which have high or improving FCF but low share price and thus a low P/FCF ratio. A low P/FCF means an undervalued share (with the same caution that applies to the P/E ratio). As a general rule, a P/FCF under 5 (or price is less than 5 times free cash flow per share) is considered undervalued, which means the stock may trade at too low of a price and may rise to reflect the free cash flow generated by the firm.

Investors should know, as with the P/E ratio, that the management may resort to some means to show a better FCF too. Thus, the company may defer payments to vendors at the end of the year, may shorten the cycle of receipts from customers, and may keep the capital expansion plan in abeyance to show a healthy free cash flow.

FCF varies from industry to industry. An industry that requires constant investment in plants and equipment (like automobile or aviation) is likely to have less free reserve per share, whereas a company operating in the FMCG space or software development may not need much in terms of capital expenditure after the completion of a capex cycle and is thus likely to have a higher free cash flow.

Accounting standards cause distortions in the reported earnings of certain industries. A pharmaceutical manufacturer will write off the R & D expenditure over the useful life of a particular medicine though the expenditure is incurred in the initial years. The books may thus show higher profits, but the cash hole does not show in the profit-and-loss account. Depreciation and amortisation of expenses create similar anomalies. The intelligent investor needs to know this.

Price-to-Book-Value Ratio (P/BV Ratio)

Price-to-book-value ratio compares the market price of a stock with its book value. It is an excellent tool for value investors because it tells us how much we are paying for every rupee of book value of the company. It enables a comparison between the price at which the assets were acquired by the company and the price it is trading at. Use this ratio to compare different firms based on the premium one is paying over the purchase price (or the discount one is getting).

You can easily locate 'book value' in the 'shareholder's equity' column of the balance sheet. It represents the money that belongs to the shareholders and includes share capital and all reserves and surpluses that belong to the shareholders. The BV may be alternatively calculated by adding all assets and reducing all liabilities from there; however, you have direct access to that figure in the share capital column, so you don't have to go the roundabout way.

Let us consider an example. The share price of a company is ₹500. The BV or the shareholder's equity is ₹700 crores. The outstanding shares of the company are 1 crore. Thus, the BV per share is:

BV = ₹700 crores / 1 crore shares
= ₹700 per share

P/BV = ₹500 / ₹700
= 0.71

What does it mean? It means for every ₹1 of acquisition cost the company has incurred, the market is willing to pay only ₹0.71. This looks like a bargain. However, as stated before, relying on one ratio can lead to erroneous conclusions; you should only consider ratio as a lead to something which may or may not turn out to be true. Possibly, this is a bargain; the irrationality prevailing in the market might have brought the price down to a low level, making it a Benjamin Graham kind of stock. It is also possible that the company may be a sinking ship. For example, the technology has made it possible for a new company to produce goods cheaper, and it is left with the burden of higher capital cost and obsolete technology, so the market is discounting it below its book value.

As with all other ratios, this differs from industry to industry. Thus, an infrastructure company which needs to sink in substantial money in plant and machinery and other facilities will usually trade at a lower P/BV ratio than a software company. You can also interpret it that in the case of a software company, the market expects the company to create more value with each rupee invested and will pay more premium.

Like all accounting ratios, it is important that you understand the limitations of the P/BV as well. We need to first understand the concept of book value from the accountant's perspective. Transactions are recorded in the books of accounts based on historical pricing. A piece of land purchased in 1892 by Britannia in Mumbai, when land could be bought by acres in the villages around Mumbai (which are its suburbs now), for ₹500 might be worth ₹500 crores now. But under normal circumstances, the land will be reflected in the books as ₹500 alone. The profit will come when it is sold and might disrupt the whole balance sheet. However, till it is sold, it might look like an insignificant figure in the balance sheet. A company which has recently bought land 1/10 in size of this land at ₹50 crores, will have a higher book value.

Take a converse case. A company which had invested ₹100 crores in a machine to manufacture a CD-replicating machine (example, Moser Baer, which was heading towards liquidation when this was written) finds that the technology has changed and that there aren't enough people buying CDs now. If the company modernises and sells the equipment, the old machine (though in perfect working condition and in operation) may have to be sold to the junk dealer by kilos. Land appreciates in value; depreciable machinery, factory building, and furniture lose their value. In most cases, the appreciation and depreciation even out. However, one must still be cautious when comparing a 100-year-old company with a new business.

Accounting principles do not recognise the value of brand value, goodwill, and other intellectual properties, which are self-generated. A company which has been in business for 50 years will command considerable goodwill compared to a new business. This goodwill, generated over a long period, has no significance to an accountant and will not get recorded in the books of accounts. However, when a company pays actual cash or any other consideration to acquire a brand (for example, Coca-Cola acquiring Thumbs Up), the amount paid will be added to the asset base of the company. Thus, companies that enjoy an economic moat have a great deal of hidden reserves not visible in the balance sheet. Since they are not reflected in the BV, it gives an edge to a knowledgeable investor, the man who has the stock within his circle of competence.

The rationale in using the P/BV ratio is to find out how much is left if the company went bankrupt and everything needed to be sold off. Benjamin Graham's net-net is also inspired by the same philosophy, though it uses a different formula.

Limitations

Except for a few companies like banks and financial companies, book value has no relevance to the market value of a company. The items appearing in the balance sheet result from double-entry bookkeeping and go to the balance sheet because they did not go into the profit-and-loss account in that relevant year and are thus accumulated over different periods of time, making it a pot-pourri of varied transactions.

The P/BV does not consider the leverage. If a company is carrying a heavy debt in its balance sheet, it's not reflected in the ratio. Thus, the company may look robust based on the book value but may be on the verge of collapse because of debt burden.

As discussed above, for companies like Apple, Coca-Cola, and Monsanto, the book value has no relevance. The assets falling out of their balance sheet far exceed in value than those recorded in the balance sheet. In Benjamin Graham's days, when intellectual properties had not much value, book value could have correlated well with the market price of a company, but as the companies matured, the book value seems to have lost its relevance, except in specific industries. That is why Warren

Buffett said, 'In all cases, what is clear is that book value is meaningless as an indicator of value.'

Despite the limitations, the P/BV continues to be an important indicator, because it is easy to compute. The book value remains stable, so it makes the comparison of the same stock over different periods meaningful, and it may be useful in situations where the BV is positive but the EPS is negative, because the P/E ratio becomes irrelevant in such situations.

In simplicity and ease of use, this tool wins hands down. It will thus continue to be used by investors as a tool for analysing companies.

Debt-to-Equity Ratio (D/E Ratio)

Debt-to-equity ratio, or debt–equity ratio, is used to identify leveraged companies. Companies with high debts carry a greater risk of bankruptcy, and the D/E ratio is an important place to start the investigation. The D/E shows what portion of a company's business is financed by shareholders' money and what portion is financed by money from lenders. It is important to know the obligation shareholders of the company may have to bear in the event the business is not able to repay the debt. This becomes important in the event of economic downtrend when the company may not meet its financial obligations because of low profitability. Higher debt may create a liquidity crunch when the repayment falls due. It may also be a drain on the company's income since interest needs to be serviced timely. A sustained period of low income or losses may lead a leveraged company to bankruptcy.

A low D/E ratio denotes that a higher portion of the company's business is financed by the shareholders' money, whereas a high D/E ratio means that a higher portion of funding comes from debts.

$$\text{debt-to-equity ratio} = \text{total liabilities} / \text{shareholders' equity}$$

This ratio is easy to compute from the balance sheet of a company. Let us take an example.

Here is the liabilities side of the balance sheet of Sun Pharmaceuticals Limited for the year ended on 31 March 2018.

Equities and Liabilities	(Crores Rupees)
Shareholder's Funds	
Equity share capital	239.93
Total share capital	239.93
Reserves and surplus	19,530.17
Total reserves and surplus	19,530.17
Total shareholder's funds	19,770.10
Equity share application money	0
Share capital suspense	0
Non-current liabilities	
Long-term borrowings	1,564.69
Deferred tax liabilities (net)	0
Other long-term liabilities	0.91
Long-term provisions	345.18
Total non-current liabilities	1,910.78
Current liabilities	
Short-term borrowings	5,213.81
Trade payables	2,489.94
Other current liabilities	2,114.25
Short-term provisions	2,425.49
Total current liabilities	12,243.49
Total capital and liabilities	33,924.37

Total shareholders' funds are ₹19,770 crores. Total liabilities are ₹14,153 crores (sum of non-current and current liabilities).

D/E ratio = ₹14,153 crores / ₹19,770 crores = 0.72

And you thought accounting ratios were difficult to compute!

This means Sun Pharmaceuticals has a debt of ₹0.72 against ₹1 of equity. In the worst-case scenario, theoretically, if debt is required to be paid out of shareholders' money, the company has money to pay it, and the company will be left with ₹0.28 to the rupee, or 28% of shareholders' equity after meeting the liabilities of the outsiders.

Is Debt Bad for a Company?

A company may finance its operations out of debts or equity. The choice is a strategic management decision and impacts the profitability of the business. Debt per se may not be bad as we explain here.

1. Sometimes equity is not the best option. The company may sometimes need funds for a short term; equity is a long-term commitment. If a project has a short payback period, it makes sense to fund it by debt and repay the debt out of the profitability than increase the equity, which remains with the company forever and needs to be serviced.
2. Equity is expensive. A shareholder takes a higher risk when he invests in a business, so his expectation of return is also higher. Debt is cheaper.
3. Debt lets a company expand a business without diluting the owners' stake. Return to shareholders is likely to be higher in case of profit-making companies which uses debts to finance. For example, a company has a 20% return on investments. If it borrows at 9% per annum, the return to the shareholders will increase because the cost of additional capital is lower than the rate of return on investments.
4. Taxation is one of the most important but often ignored factors in calculating cost of funding. If the cost of servicing a debt and equity is same, it still makes debt cheaper, thanks to the impact of taxation.

Let us explain.

Let us presume the cost of borrowing and equity funding is the same. On a fund of ₹10 crores, the company pays ₹1 crore per annum.

In case of debts, the amount of interest paid is tax-deductible. The present rate of taxation in India is around 30%. On an interest payout of ₹1 crore, the company saves ₹30 lakhs on taxes. In the case of shares, there is a tax to be paid by the company (from its own funds) before it pays out dividends, known interestingly as DDT (dividend distribution tax). The present rate of DDT is around 17.5%. This works out to a tax rate of 21%. To pay ₹100, you need ₹121. Pay 17.5% of that (₹21) to get ₹100. Thus, the cost of capital in the two cases will be as follows:

	Debt	Equity
Interest/dividends	₹1 crore	₹1 crore
Tax saved	−0.3 crore	0
DDT paid	0	+0.21 crore
Total cost	0.7 crore	1.21 crore

You can now see what difference the share of the hidden partner (the government of India) can make to the cost of capital.

Having convinced you that debt is good, let me tell you that debt is not all that good. It comes with its share of hazards. Let me list out arguments to support this:

1. The cost of servicing a debt is a fixed charge. It has to be paid, come what may. Profit or no profit, debt must be serviced. The shareholder is a risk-taker; he knows that if the company does not make money, he gets no return.
2. The advantage of leverage works backwards when the business goes down. When profitability is low or there is a loss, interest becomes another burden to handle. The tax benefit explained above ceases to be an advantage since there is no tax being paid by a loss-making company.
3. Lenders are fair-weather friends. They would lend to you when the going is good. If it turns bad, they withdraw the money in the first opportunity, making the sinking ship sink faster.

The Verdict

The debt–equity mix is a matter of choice for the company management. The macro environment also plays a role. Some industries, like infrastructure, might need larger debts when handling high-value projects. Companies in the FMCG space has a linear business pattern and may not need much debt. For some companies, debt–equity is not a choice; they tap either of the two available to them.

From the investors' perspective, a high debt is to be avoided. Some investors consider a debt–equity ratio of 1.5 : 1 to be the maximum limit. That is a debt of ₹1.5 for every rupee of their own funds; others consider anything beyond 1 : 1 to be risky. Some cautious investors look for a much lower number. Investors like Warren Buffett look for companies that have near-zero interest burden. While there are advantages in having debts, as explained above, I also subscribe to Buffett-like caution. I filter out leveraged companies from my list, however attractive they may look otherwise.

Current Ratio

While the debt–equity ratio is focused on the overall leverage of the company, the current ratio (and its cousin quick ratio) focuses on short-term liquidity. It is a solvency ratio in the sense that it tries to find out if the company has enough liquidity to meet its current liabilities. It tells us if the company will remain solvent or may face the liquidity crisis.

The current ratio is easy to compute and understand. It is obtained by taking the figures of the current assets and the current liabilities from the balance sheet. In simple terms, if the current assets are more than the current liabilities, the company has enough short-term resources to pay off the immediate obligations. A ratio of less than one (i.e. current assets being less than current liabilities) is a definite cause of concern, and the company must find sources of finance to meet its liabilities.

Let us define here the components that make the current ratio.

1. Current assets. Current assets are in the balance sheet and comprise:

i. cash and cash equivalents
ii. marketable securities
iii. debtors
iv. prepaid expenses
v. inventory.

As you can see, these are the assets which will get converted into cash in a few days or months, hence the name current. These assets have an interesting characteristic. They circulate. When inventory is sold out, you realise either cash or create a right to receive money the debtors. When cash is realised from the debtors, it gets converted into cash or cash equivalents and is ready for another cycle.

inventory => debtors => cash

2. Current liabilities. Current liabilities and short-term liabilities and obligations payable by the company within one year. You can easily locate this under the head, 'Current liabilities and provisions' in the balance sheet. It comprises:

i. short-term debt
ii. accounts payables
iii. accrued liabilities and other debts.

We have defined the components. Let us define the ratio:

current ratio = current assets / current liabilities

Let us take one example. The following are the current assets of Pidilite Industries as of 31 March 2018.

Current Assets (Crores Rupees)

Current investments	1,072.01
Inventories	630.94
Trade receivables	689.59
Cash and cash equivalents	77.76
Short-term loans and advances	13.22
Other current assets	180.02
Total current assets	2,663.54

The following are the current liabilities of the company as of 31 March 2018.

Current Liabilities (Crore Rupees)

Short-term borrowings	0
Trade payables	428.16
Other current liabilities	450.6
Short-term provisions	9.78
Total current liabilities	888.54

Both charts are a part of the balance sheet of the company, and I have not taken any special effort to cull them. Contrary to what people think, most of the information are available. You need to be willing to use them.

current ratio = 2,663 / 888 = 3

(Fractions have been ignored or rounded off for the sake of simplicity.)

What does the ratio mean? It tells us that for every one rupee of short-term liability of the company, the company has resources worth ₹3. If all the money's worth ₹888 crores became due tomorrow, the company can sell off a portion of the current assets worth ₹2,663 crore and meet the obligation.

A few words of caution: as discussed for other ratios, the current ratio might be different for different industries and works better as a tool of comparison with peers or with the industry average. Comparing two companies belonging to different sectors may not be meaningful.

With the advent of just-in-time management techniques, modern manufacturing companies have reduced the size of buffer inventory, leading to a significant reduction in working capital investment and hence lower current ratios.

In some industries, the current ratio of lower than 1 might also be considered acceptable. This is true of the retail sector and companies like Big Bazaar and D-Mart. This stems from the fact that such retailers can negotiate long credit periods with suppliers while offering little credit to customers, leading to higher trade payables as compared with trade receivables. Such retailers can also keep their own inventory volumes to a minimum through efficient supply chain management.

While a high current ratio may be good from the point of meeting the obligations, it would be wrong to presume the higher the better. Too high a ratio may mean inefficient utilisation of resources, which may be fine from the liquidity perspective but may pull the profits down.

Sometimes the ratio may mislead and give a false sense of confidence. Consider the case of Pidilite Industries. As you can see, some current assets are more current than the others. Cash is the most liquid of all; current investments are a short-term application of cash and can be converted into cash in a day. Stock has a long cycle of conversion. Some stock may realise nothing ('dead stock'), some debtors may be sticky, and some bad; when you try to realise them, you may face the hurdle. Here, the quickly realisable current assets (cash and current investments) suffice to meet the liabilities. In some companies, while it may look like a healthy ratio, the company may still struggle to meet day-to-day obligations.

This leads us to a further refinement of ratio, the Quick Ratio.

Quick Ratio

Quick ratio is more conservative than current ratio and gives a better view of the short-term solvency of the company. Not all current assets are realisable quickly. Converting inventory into cash is a long process, and this ratio ignores the less liquid of the current assets and considers only fast-converting assets. Because this ratio is more accurate and conservative, it is also known as the acid-test ratio.

The formula is:

quick ratio = quick assets / current liabilities

The denominator, current liabilities, remains the same as in the equation of current ratio, only the numerator changes to a lower figure. Quick assets (also known as liquid assets) are:

i. cash and equivalents
ii. marketable securities
iii. accounts receivable.

Using the data for Pidilite Industries, let us calculate the quick ratio (fractions ignored):

quick assets (crores) = ₹1,072 + ₹689 + ₹77 = ₹1,838

The current liabilities are ₹888 crores. Thus:

quick ratio = ₹1,838 / ₹888 = 2

A quick ratio of 2 may be considered good in terms of solvency of the company.

CHAPTER 23

Know Your Taxes

"The avoidance of taxes is the only intellectual pursuit that still carries any reward."

John Maynard Keynes

It is important for you to know the correct tax implications of various transactions pertaining to stock market investment. Some people presume there are no taxes on stock market transactions. Some like to leave the complexities of taxation to the chartered accountant. Some just like to close their eyes to it ('Not my cup of tea'). No doubt taxation in India is complex, yet taxation of securities is not complex, and the provisions are unambiguous. Since tax is a cost to be factored in while calculating return on investments, it is important that you understand your taxes well. The government loves to present tax in a language incomprehensible to most of its subjects except a small tribe of tax experts. Let me hack it for you and present it in plain English.

The Income Tax Act likes to distinguish between an investor, a speculator, and a trader for tax treatment. If you are buying and selling shares intraday (i.e. you square off your transactions without taking delivery), you are considered a speculator. If you buy and sell frequently, with each stock coming in and going out of your demat account, you may consider yourself a trader.

If you are an investor, income arising from the sale of your shares is considered as capital gains. Income from trading is considered business income. We will discuss the two categories and their subcategories.

First, the investment income. Since you are reading this book, I presume, you are a long-term investor and are more interested in this section. Let us understand the taxability applicable to you as an investor. Tax depends upon the holding period (i.e. for how long you have held the share before selling it off). The government encourages long-term investment; you pay less tax when you hold a share for a long term. The law divides income from capital gains into (a) short-term capital gains and (b) long-term capital gains. Let us understand the two concepts.

The law has a simple definition of *short term*. An investment held for less than one year is considered a short-term investment, and an investment held for more than a year is considered a long-term investment. This is fantastic from the point of view of investors. Since most of you will hold many of your investments way beyond one year, so your investments will fall in the category of long-term investment, qualifying for a soft tax treatment.

Short-Term Capital Gains (STCG)

When the shares are sold within 12 months of their purchase, the profit on sale of such shares is called the short-term capital gains and is taxed at a flat rate of 15%.

Here's an example. I buy 100 shares of Maruti Suzuki on June 2018 for ₹6,000 a share and sell them off in November 2018 for ₹6,800. The short-term capital gains will be:

Sale price	₹6,80,000
Purchase price	₹6,00,000
Short-term capital gains	₹80,000
Tax at 15%	₹12,000

Please keep a couple of things in mind:

1. Short-term capital gains are taxed at a flat rate of 15%. This is likely to be lower than the rate at which your other income is taxable. Of course, this is higher than the tax on long-term capital gains. Still, tax at 15% may be considered quite a low rate of taxes. My wish is that the readers of this book change their investment strategy and stay invested for a long term so they pay even fewer taxes than this.
2. This concession on short-term capital gains is available only to a special class of assets, which includes equity shares. The concession is not available regarding other class of assets (for example, land and machines) where tax treatment is different.
3. The law requires that this concessional treatment is available only if the securities transactions tax (STT) has been paid on the sale of such shares. STT is the tax that your broker collects from you when you sell your shares through him. It implies that your shares are being sold through a stock exchange in India (your contract note from the broker will show details of STT paid) and are not off-market transactions or sale against buy-back offer

by the company, in which cases this concessional treatment will not be available to you.

Let us now consider the long-term capital gains.

Long-Term Capital Gains (LTCG)

Long-term capital gains arise when you hold your investments for over one year. The rate of tax on capital gains is 10%, but the effective tax rate is likely to be much lower, for the reasons explained below.

- If the capital gains during the year is less than ₹1,00,000, there will be no tax. LTCG up to ₹1,00,000 is exempt from tax.
- If your LTCG is ₹1,50,000, tax will be payable on ₹50,000 alone after deducting the exemption of ₹1,00,000.
- On capital gains beyond ₹1,00,000, the law allows you concessions to reduce your liability further. Suppose you had bought 100 shares of Azko Nobel in 2015 for ₹1,000 a share and you sell them on November 2018 at ₹1,500 per share, the tax treatment will be as follows;

   purchase price   ₹1,00,000
   sale price   ₹1,50,000

There is a capital gain of ₹50,000 in the transaction, but as said before, let us explore the additional concessions available.

The law says for shares purchased before 31 January 2018 which are long-term capital assets (that is, held for over 12 months), you have an option of substituting the price as of 31 January 2018 instead of the purchase price. Let us say the price on 31 January 2018 is ₹1,200.

Now the figures change as below:

   purchase price (deemed)   ₹1,20,000
   sale price   ₹1,50,000

Voila! The capital gain has been reduced to ₹30,000 now instead of ₹50,000.

The rate of tax being 10%, your tax will be ₹3,000. If you have sold no other shares during the year, there will be no tax; the exemption of ₹1,00,000 will take care of that.

Please keep these in mind:

1. As explained earlier, the concessional treatment will be available only if the STT has been paid on the transaction.
2. This special treatment is available to equity shares and some special assets alone.

Let us now consider taxability where income is not considered a capital gain but as a business income.

A. *Income from intraday trading.* Income from intraday trading is considered as a speculative business income. If you buy in the morning and sell in the afternoon or if you sell in the morning and buy it back in the evening, the income is considered a speculative business income.
B. *Income from futures and options (F & O).* F & O may be speculative instruments from the point of view of readers of this book; however, tax laws do not consider them speculative because some people use F & O for hedging. So they may be legitimate, non-speculative transactions (though, I suspect, the lawmakers want to promote F & O, thus this special treatment).

Income from the speculative and the non-speculative businesses is clubbed together and added to your income and charged to tax at the normal rate. Rate of tax depends upon your income slab and can vary from 0% to 30%. The only difference between the income from a speculative business and the income from a non-speculative business is that losses arising out of the speculative business (to recall, intraday trading) cannot be set off against the income arising out of the non-speculative business (that is, F & O). In short, they discourage intraday trading but not F & O.

Tax on Dividends

Dividends received from an Indian company are tax-free. The company is required to pay a dividend distribution tax before it pays you a dividend. As far as an investor is concerned, whatever he gets from his investments as dividend is exempt from tax.

However, in the case of a resident individual/HUF/firm, the dividend shall be chargeable to tax at 10% if the aggregate amount of the dividend received from a domestic company during the year exceeds ₹10,00,000. Thus, if you receive ₹12 lakhs as dividends, after deducting the exemption of ₹10 lakhs, the remaining 2 lakhs will be put to tax at 10%, and the total tax will be ₹20,000.

Note that dividends received from foreign companies are taxable.

Tax Is an Important Variable to Consider

Having understood the taxability of investment income, let us delve deeper into it. This book is about long-term investment and discourages speculation and short-term investments. Our investment periods are 5, 10, 20, or 30 years—or even a lifetime. So not many of your transactions will fall under taxation for trading and for short-term capital gains. Only a few would come in the category of short-term capital gains; for example, you buy a stock only to discover later that your fundamental assumptions were wrong, so you need to sell them. In my investing life of more than 30 years, I have not earned a single rupee from either speculative or non-speculative trading. I hope you also emulate my example.

Dividends are a welcome source of income, and the best part is, it comes tax-free. However, the dividend payout ratio of good companies is low. Whatever you get is tax-free, but you get little.

Let us talk about the tax we all are concerned with: tax on long-term capital gains. Tax rate is 10%. This 10% tax is payable when you sell your shares. If you are following the investment philosophy explained in this book, you will sell your shares after holding them for many, many years. The liability arises at the exit point. It means as your capital continues to appreciate, you pay *no* tax. You can watch your investment turn into a ten-bagger or a multi-bagger. Without paying a cipher penny as tax. Only when you sell it will the liability be attracted. If you understand the time value of money, the liability paid ten years from now has very little money value now. Your effective rate of taxation thus comes to a ridiculously low figure.

A short-term investor pays a high tax. First, the rate of tax to a short-term investor can range from 15% to 30%, depending upon whether he is a speculator or a short-term investor. Second, the tax is required to be paid in advance or during the year in which he earns it. Thus, his outflow is higher, and it's earlier. This reduces the funds available to him for compounding, reducing the overall return.

STT is also a major dent on the corpus of a short-term investor. The short-termer trades frequently, and he pays higher STT since the STT is to be paid on every contract note. The long-term investor buys far too infrequently and sells even less infrequently. Thus, he saves a lot from STT. STT is to be paid upfront on every transaction, and thus it reduces the investible funds, resulting in lower compounding. One often-ignored component is the brokerage paid on transactions. The brokerage curve runs parallel to the STT curve, and the more frequently you trade, the more money you make for your broker. When you trade frequently, you deserve a letter of appreciation from two sets of people you toil for: the government and your broker.

CHAPTER 24

Market Timing Does Not Work

"The average investor's return is significantly lower than market indices due primarily to market timing."

                                   Daniel Kahneman

When I tune into business channels, it amuses me to find experts debating on the best time to enter the market or a specific stock and the best time to exit. There are few topics in investing more controversial than market timing. There are many analysts out there willing to predict the time to buy for you, for a small fee.

Market timing does not work. Even if it may sometimes, timing the market is not a worthwhile exercise for an intelligent investor. The market moves up and down in cycles, and if one understands the general direction of the market, it can help him decide about long-term investing policy, but it cannot offer any help concerning the perfect time to buy or sell his investments. Noble Prize–winning economist Paul Samuelson says an investor who thinks he can move in and out of the market at the right time and who keeps jumping from one scrip to another does not do better than the passive investor, who puts 60% of his monies in the stock market and the remaining in the bond market.

Investors continue to believe countless websites and experts who claim they know that the time has come to buy a scrip. It does not work. Shuffling your portfolio again and again, hoping to make superior returns out of market timing, creates superior returns—not for you, but for your broker. If your market timing adviser is your broker too, every time you churn your portfolio, it must put a smile on his face and the commission in his bank account.

Studies after studies have proved that you cannot gain superior returns by timing the market. A recent research by the Centre for Retirement Research at Boston College showed that even professional money managers mess it up when they try to time the market. The researchers looked at target-date funds, which are designed to reduce risk as investors age by changing the portfolio's asset allocation. The target-date funds shift to less-risky stocks closer to the maturity date and would move towards the 'glide path'. But when target-date fund managers see an opportunity to time the market, some will temporarily deviate from the glide path. Their expertise is why we pay them the big bucks; they're the people who should be able to identify a short-term opportunity to profit.

The researchers found that target-date funds that deviated from the glide path underperformed their peers by 14.1 basis points each year when returns were weighted by age of fund. By trying to time the market and seize opportunities, they lost money.

Now that underperformance wasn't too severe: If you invested for thirty years in two funds, one of which underperformed the other by 0.141 percentage points annually, you'd see a total difference of about 3.8% in their returns. But the difference was statistically significant, and it shows that even the professionals lose when they try to time the market. It may be worse when retail investors try to time the market. As per the DALBAR's 2016 Quantitative Analysis of Investor Behaviour study, investors who try to time the market lost money even when the index rose. The data showed that when the investors reacted to the news and gossip, they ended up making impulsive decisions and lost money. It observed that the average investor has not stayed invested for a long enough period to reap the rewards that the market can offer more disciplined investors.

Investors behave irrationally, making the market pricing also irrational. Any theory to predict the market price however scientific-looking must fail. The market movement is not one way. Even if the long-term trend may be positive, the short term may be erratic, the prices going up some days and falling down on the others. It is easy to lose the sense of direction. If you time the market and sell off just before the next fall, it may rise again three days later. Market timing is thus nothing more than an exercise in futility. Trends happen, and trends reverse. Trends may last for three days and reverse, or they may reverse the next day. The best thing is to ignore the trends. The trend may be a trader's best friend, but the investor should stay away from it.

There is a big contradiction in market timing. You try to predict the market movement and want to buy or sell before others do it. You want to lead and see others follow, only then can you make money. This presupposes you are smarter than the market, so smart you can even predict the total of irrational behaviour of all the varied forces that make up the market.

If you can predict the market movements, value investors will have been losers. When the market is rising at an expected rate (e.g. in a massive bull phase), value investors lose out to momentum players. In a secular bull trend, you often hear the opinion that value investing is dead. Value investing does not die; it comes back with a vengeance when the market becomes jittery again.

Value investors are looked at with awe in a falling market. The fall hurts them the least. Since they are long-term investors, they don't sell and book loss. They continue to hold through the loss phase; the investment recovers when the bad days are over. Momentum players square off the losses and go out of business or become bear operators.

I have a theory on market timings, and it has worked for me. When you have a strong urge to sell, think of buying. Likewise, when you have a strong impulse to buy, it must be time to sell. I seldom sell, however strong that urge may be, unless there is a fundamental reason to sell; however, I evaluate the scrip to buy when the mind is telling me to sell.

Investors often become victims of apophenia. They look for patterns which are not there and try to find confirmation to their pre-existing notion. The solution is to recognise noise as noise and to learn to filter out noise. Long-term fundamentals do not change overnight. The event may not affect the long-term assumptions of a stock. Even if it does, if you show patience and analyse all facts before you take decisions, you are not likely to err. My personal solution to the problem is, watch less CNBC and Zee Business news, especially the programmes where they give you intraday-trading ideas.

The probability of making profits using intraday trading is the same as that of making profits in a game of poker or at a casino. Day traders carry out dozens or some of them hundreds of transactions every day. To record those transactions and to calculate the profits earned (which is too small compared to the size of transactions) is a humongous task. As a chartered accountant processing the tax returns, I often come across piles of contract notes of clients carrying huge transactions. I have yet to find a single case where handsome gains were made from these activities. Being active does not generate wealth; not doing anything does.

Remember that intuition, common sense, and luck may make timing work for you—at least on some occasions. Just know the dangers, the statistics, and the experiences of all those who have tried and failed. Do not time the market. Develop a bottom-up approach. If a share is good at the current price, buy it, no matter what the trend is.

Is It a Good Time to Buy?

I keep getting this question from many investors. The answer is yes; it is a good time. But yesterday was a good time too, and tomorrow will be a good time too. The stock you buy might change, but there are stocks available at any market conditions. Buy with a margin of safety. A margin of safety depends upon the intrinsic value of the stock you are buying and the price you are paying for it. As long as there is a sufficient gap between the two, it is the right time to buy, the direction of the overall market notwithstanding. When the bulls take charge of the market and drive everything to dizzying heights, the gap might vanish from all your target investments; that is not the time to buy. That situation of irrational exuberance arises occasionally. That is the only time when you can say it is not a good time to buy. Ironically, most people go out shopping at that very time. The stock market is the only place where people make the mistake of buying high and selling low (in panic, that is).

CHAPTER 25

Assessing Quality of Management

"Good management is the art of making problems so interesting and their solutions so constructive that everyone wants to get to work and deal with them."

– Paul Hawken.

Let me emphasise that the quality of management matters. Since you are investing for a long-term investment, you should not trust a management that is unscrupulous, non-transparent, incompetent, or short-sighted. The basic feature of corporate structure is the separation of ownership and management. As a shareholder, you are a part-owner of the company. You trust your money to the management, who must use it judiciously and create wealth for you. If the management is unscrupulous, it may destroy your wealth. If the management is not trustworthy, the quarterly and annual results lose their credibility. All the analytical tools that you are taught to use in this book will lose their reliability if the management has no credibility.

Bad management are known to compensate themselves disproportionately, even to the detriment of shareholders. Indian shareholders have suffered in the hands of bad management, and the scams have recurred every few years. Harshad Mehta, in the 1990s, connived with greedy management and banks and jacked up the share price of target companies. When the bubble burst, the banks had lost ₹4,000 crores, and the investors also lost crores of rupees. Ten years later, Ketan Parekh would collaborate with corrupt management and do circular trading to pump up the share prices. A decade later, Ramalinga Raju would cook the books of accounts of Satyam, causing a loss of ₹15,000 crores to shareholders. The unbroken record of cheating has continued in present times, with companies like Gitanjali Gems fudging accounts. These are extreme examples; management of hundreds of companies resort to questionable practices almost regularly.

Warren Buffett laid great importance to the quality of management. He understood the importance of a trusted management for passive investors like him. He once said, 'Over time, the skill with which a company's managers allocate capital has an enormous impact on the enterprise's value.'

At another time, he said, 'It's hard to overemphasise the importance of who is CEO of a company.'

When asked about his key criteria in identifying good companies, he said, 'Charlie and I look for companies that have able and trustworthy management.'

So much emphasis on quality of management by the greatest investor in the world. He understood that, in the first place, the business model had to be good and the company should have some kind of economic moat to keep competition at bay. They will lose this advantage if the quality of management is questionable. He puts it so aptly: 'You need two things—a moat around the castle and you need a knight in the castle who is trying to widen the moat around the castle.' Buffett knew it all too well that economic moat needs to be guarded by the king in the castle. If he is a weak king, the moat will not hold up against the enemies. In fact, a strong management itself is a moat.

A big question is how a small investor can assess the quality of management. In the olden days, when information was difficult to access, investors like Philip Fisher would travel and spend time in and around the company and try to get as much information as he could gather. We are living in a world where information is available at the click of a mouse. Every step that every human being and every corporation takes gets recorded. Information has become available like never before to someone keen to get it. The cost of gathering information has also come down to near zero. This has proved to be a great leveller. An informed investor with a capital of just ₹1 lakhs has access to the same information that a large institutional investor has.

A good starting point is always the annual reports of the companies. Warren Buffett reads every page of annual reports of companies he is invested in. I always imagine Warren Buffett sitting on his desk, reading under a table lamp, with a heap of annual reports and cans of Cherry Coke.

Following are the factors to look at for determining the quality of management:

1. Are acquisitions by management value creators or value destroyers? Are the acquisitions in the area where the company has the core competence, or is just done for the sake of spreading the empire by an overambitious management with excess liquidity? Will the new acquisition create synergy or destroy it? Is it growth for growth's sake or real value creation?

2. Do acquisitions widen the moat or destroy the moat? Is the company able to strengthen its position because of the acquisitions, creating wealth for shareholders? Or did the acquisitions make holes in the moat?
3. Does the company pay a fair price for the acquisitions? A value investor looks for a management which is also a value investor. It looks for acquisitions with a margin of safety. In the recessionary phase of every trade cycles, many companies get injured and are available at attractive pricing; a shrewd management looks for such opportunities.
4. Is the management willing to take long-term decisions, which may cause hardship in the short run but are great value creators for shareholders over a long period, or is the management more interested in pleasing the market and analysts quarter on quarter?
5. Is the management transparent and straightforward? Does it call a spade a spade, or does it show a rosy picture always? It is not uncommon for some managements to give a guidance that because of poor macros, or for whatever reasons, the profits of the next quarter or year will be impacted. It is not uncommon for such management to continue to post a great picture until the doomsday. Harsh words of the former are appreciated more than the pleasant expressions of the latter.
6. Does the company have a history of project cost or time overrun? Does the company stick to the implementation schedule (announced in the annual report)? Is delay or is discipline the norm?
7. Does the company have an appropriate amount of debt looking into the nature of its business and capital adequacy? What is the average cost of debt? (Bad managements are forced to borrow at a high rate of interest; great managements have access to cheap funds.) Does the management use short-term funds for long-term funding requirements? (This may cause liquidity problems when the funds are recalled.) What is the credit rating of the company in the debt market?

8. What is the dividend policy of the company? Does the management reward the shareholders adequately but, at the same time, make sure that enough money is retained in the business for the ongoing growth?

9. What is the management compensation policy? What kind of remuneration does the management pay to itself? Is it commensurate with the size of business and profits? Is the compensation linked to performance? Will the management be willing to cut its compensation in the event of lower profits of the company? Does the management allocate the compensation judiciously to all stakeholders or just cares for its own compensation? Buffett puts this very aptly in one of his letters to the shareholders: 'It has become fashionable at public companies to describe almost every compensation plan as aligning the interests of management with those of shareholders. In our book, alignment means being a partner in both directions, not just on the upside. Many "alignment" plans flunk this basic test, being artful forms of "heads I win, tails you lose".'

10. How are the minority shareholders treated? Are the investors' grievances resolved to their satisfaction? (A simple test of this is to raise a grievance if you are already a shareholder and see how management resolves it.)

11. Is the management proactive in changing the business and technological environment? Does it adopt new cutting-edge technologies to keep itself abreast of the competition? If a new technology disrupts the business model, what is the preparedness of the company in handling it?

12. What is the background of the promoters? Have they been hauled up by the regulatory authorities in the past for any offence or violation?

13. What kind of transactions does the company carry out with companies belonging to directors or their relatives? Related party transactions is a very important area to look into to detect unscrupulous managements. Funds are often siphoned off using companies and firms belonging to relatives. The law makes

disclosure of such transactions mandatory. You may recall the recent case of Videocon Industries. A loan of ₹3,250 crores was extended by ICICI Bank (and consortium) to Videocon Industries. It was alleged that after obtaining the loan, Videocon chairman, Venugopal Dhoot, invested ₹64 crores in NuPower Renewables, a firm owned by Deepak Kochhar, husband of Chanda Kochhar, MD, CEO of ICICI Bank. Later, Dhoot's company, Supreme Energy, took over NuPower, which was transferred to Dhoot's associate Mahesh Chandra Pugalia. Pugalia took over the company and later transferred his entire stake to Deepak Kochar's company, Pinnacle Energy, for only ₹9 lakhs. The ultimate effect of this series of transactions was to transfer ₹64 crores to Kochar. Unscrupulous members of management are known to create a chain of transactions in a way to hide the trail.

14. Is the management overtly concerned with share prices? Some managements are more interested in share prices rather than the actual operations of business. Any management that involves itself in the day-to-day price management of its own scrip must be looked at with scepticism. The job of the management is to manage the business, not the share prices. Good share prices follow good management practices. A strong stock market performance in the short run does not mean good quality management; nor does a weak performance mean bad management. It is expected that, in the long run, the stock market will pay the right premium for the management quality; however, keep in mind that stock prices consist of countless variables. More often than not, the price is likely to be off balance. The job of the management is to manage the company and not the stock market.

15. What is the management's stake in the equity? There are enough empirical evidence to prove that the management which has no stake in the equity of a company is reckless and often irresponsible. That is the reason intelligent investors shy away from companies where the promoters' stake is low. It is not unusual for promoters to sell off their entire stake and still sit

on the board of the company, directing the affairs of the business as owners. This is a dangerous situation. To paraphrase Nassim Talib, unless you have the skin in the game, you are not to be trusted. The recent case of the Singh brothers running Religare and Fortis long after selling off their stake is an example of 'no skin in the game'.

To cut it short, the investor should look at management that have a long-term track record of growth and profitability and go about doing their job with great honesty and integrity. There is no compromise on that. You will trust your money with them for years.

Let's hear more from the Oracle of Omaha, Warren Buffett, on this: 'Our experience has been that the manager of an already high-cost operation frequently is uncommonly resourceful in finding new ways to add to overhead, while the manager of a tightly run operation usually continues to find additional methods to curtail costs, even when his costs are already well below those of his competitors.' Buffett seems to emphasise on the quality of management in every letter to the shareholders and rightly so, as he realises that it is the most important input in investment decision-making. In the 1991 letter to the shareholders, he says, 'With superior management, a company may maintain its status as a low-cost operator for a much longer time, but even then unceasingly faces the possibility of competitive attack. And a business, unlike a franchise, can be killed by poor management.'

He advises investors to understand how the management treats the shareholders. 'You want to figure out how well that they treat their owners,' he says. 'Read the proxy statements, see what they think of—see how they treat themselves versus how they treat the shareholders. The poor managers also turn out to be the ones that really don't think that much about the shareholders, too. The two often go hand in hand.'

A strong management is the backbone of a successful company. It is like the captain of a ship, assigned with sailing the ship through all kinds of weather. The management represents the shareholders and must act in the best interest of the shareholders. The primary task of management is to create wealth for the shareholders. It is obvious that unless the management is adequately compensated for doing what they are supposed to do, they will have no incentive to produce wealth for shareholders. That is to say, unless the interest of the management is aligned with that of the shareholders, not much value creation is likely to happen.

CHAPTER 26

How Much to Diversify Your Portfolio?

"Always keep your portfolio and your risk at your own individual comfortable sleeping point."

-**Mario Gabelli**

When you carry only one stock in your portfolio, you've put all your eggs in one basket. Any fall in price of the scrip will hit you. If your software export company is quoted at ₹100 and the auditor of the company qualifies the financial statements, as a knee-jerk reaction, your scrip falls to ₹80. One remark has wiped off 20% of your capital. The solution is to diversify. However, not all risks can be mitigated by diversification.

While diversification may help you mitigate the specific risk, it does not mitigate the market risk. The specific risk is peculiar to a company or a small group of companies. Workers' unrest leading to the closure of the Tuticorin plant of Sterlite Industries is an example of a specific risk. The good news is that the specific risk is diversifiable. Statistics say just by owning 2 stocks, you have eliminated the specific risk of owning 1 stock by 46%; 4 stocks will reduce your risk by 72%; 16 stocks by 93%; and 500 stocks by 99%.

It does not matter if the above statistics are accurate or not; however, they bring out an important principle. As you move from 1 stock to 2, you reduce the risk. Moving up with every stock added to your portfolio, the specific risk reduces, but beyond a number, around 20 stocks, the gain is not substantial. Thus, while owning 500 stocks will nearly eliminate your specific risk, it will not be a prudent thing to do. Let us see why.

While buying 2 stocks instead of 1 has reduced your risk by 46%, it has also reduced the reward ratio to that extent. Taking the example further, if a sudden improvement in the results of your stock causes the price to rise by ₹20, your gains on a ₹100 stock will be 20%. However, if you have diversified into another company and are now holding 1 share of the other company that's, let us say, priced again at ₹100, a rise of ₹20 in the price of your first stock will now translate into a 10% gain in your portfolio instead of 20%.

Diversification is desirable as long as the mitigation of risk arising out of diversification outweighs the dilution in appreciation that may happen because of diversification. A number between 10 and 20, depending upon your risk appetite and the sectors and the company you invest in, should be an optimum diversification. The tendency of most investors is to diversify so much that their portfolio looks like a miniature model of the whole market, a poor strategy. Worse, when diversification is in inferior-quality stocks, the basket only has rotten apples and will underperform even the indices and may be called 'diworsification'.

Diversification does not mitigate market risk. Market risk is the possibility of a loss occurring to an investor which is caused by the performance of the overall market. Market risk is the systematic risk in the sense that it affects the entire system. Sources of market risk include recessions, political turmoil, changes in interest rates, natural disasters, and terrorist attacks. This risk cannot be eliminated though it can be hedged against.

Templeton versus Buffett

The successful investor Sir John Templeton says, 'Diversify. In stocks and bonds, as in much else, there is safety in numbers.' Equally successful investor Warren Buffett takes the opposite view and says, 'Wide diversification is only required when investors do not understand what they are doing.'

Buffett quoted Mark Twain: 'Behold, the fool saith, "Put not all thine eggs in the one basket"—which is but a matter of saying, "Scatter your money and your attention"; but the wise man saith, "Put all your eggs in the one basket and—WATCH THAT BASKET."'

Other successful investors like George Soros, William J. O'Neil, and Bernard Baruch are also known to recommend a concentrated position.

Charlie Munger says, 'This worshipping at the altar of diversification, I think that is really crazy.' Munger discovered that if we can find companies with great economics that continue to grow year on year, creating an additional margin of safety on the go, we must concentrate on them. That way, we may reduce the number of companies to ten. 'You should remember that good ideas are rare,' he would say. 'When the odds are greatly in your favour, bet heavily.'

So what's the right approach? Buffett himself recommends that passive investors who do not have the time or inclination to research the stocks will be better off by investing in indices. An index is nothing but a bundle of shares, so investing in indices means a broad diversification.

This may look like a contradiction, but it is not. If you can understand the business so well, you can trust all your eggs in that basket. You may do that, but if you do not, spread them in different baskets. Investors like Warren Buffett have the acumen and resources to know a business inside out and can afford less diversification, but for retail investors, what we discussed earlier sounds logical, diversifying in about 20 stocks.

Diversify less, and you must have the acumen to watch that basket carefully. One rotten egg, and the valuation is severely impaired. A one-star performer may bring about fantastic returns on your investment. This approach is more suitable to larger investors, who have resources to attend to each of the conference calls of companies they own and can keep track of every single piece of information concerning those companies.

If you diversify too broadly, as explained above, you are becoming something similar to the index, and your chance of beating the index is bleak. If you diversify too much, it becomes impossible to keep track of the updates pertaining to each of the stocks you own, and you end up becoming a passive investor, a mirror of the index fund. Diversification to the extent of around 20 companies is ideal. You may track each company. Reading 20 financial statements every year and as many results every quarter is no big deal and is easily doable.

My strategy is to buy about 20 stocks in unrelated sectors. When one sector (let us say technology) is on the rise, the speculators would often square up their holdings in another sector which seems slow (let us call it FMCG) and pour it over the momentum. This fuels a further rise in the technology sector, causing a fall in FMCG. When the reversal of trend happens, the money will flow out of technology and get into some another sector that is rising. Diversification across sectors provides a balance against this sectoral bias. Since we invest in a few securities, the number of companies we invest in must be evenly distributed across sectors, though sometimes we may find two or three companies in a particular sector which are attractive investments.

To sum up the discussion, diversification is a matter of individual choice. More knowledgeable investors may diversify less. An average investor should diversify sufficiently, say 20 stocks, to mitigate the effect of a couple of bad investments.

CHAPTER 27

Financial Crisis Equals Opportunities

"At some point, there will be some other financial crisis. It's in the nature of a capitalist system."

Lee Hsien Loong

India's post-independence progress has been non-linear. Some years have been years of great progress; some have led to an economic crisis. A quick review of economic policies will be in the fitness of things. We inherited from the British a system that was inefficient. The Partition of India displaced over 14 million people along religious lines, creating an overwhelming refugee crisis in the newly constituted nations of India and Pakistan. Two million people were killed on both sides of the border. On its birth, the nation faced poverty, hunger, communal hatred, and the resource crunch.

In this scenario, a socialist model of development was thought appropriate by Prime Minister Jawaharlal Nehru. Nehru was impressed by the Russian (USSR) model of growth and created a blend of the free-market model and the Russian model. The government nationalised various industries and banks and carried major land reforms. Vinoba Bhave and Jaiprakash Narayan worked for redistribution of land so that actual tillers could get the land. Industries were regulated under a licence-quota Raj; every commodity was scarce. Production cost was high. Industries were inefficient and complacent, thanks to protectionism offered by the state. It was impossible to import anything; you had to go through a complex, frustrating procedure.

During this period, two prime ministers, Nehru and Shastri, died. India faced two wars—one with China in 1962, another with Pakistan in 1965. We faced two droughts in 1965 and 1966. The situation was so grave that India had to seek charity from other countries to feed its teeming millions.

The global recession of 1970s created economic stagnation and chronic shortages. Corrupt and inefficient state policies left people disillusioned with state socialism.

Control, scarcity, and licence-quota Raj created a vicious circle of low productivity. The demand–supply imbalance created a system that was corrupt. Black markets flourished. It used to take ten years for the Bajaj scooter to be delivered! When I was in primary school, my father had booked a scooter for me which was expected to be delivered when after my graduation. In the black market, the Bajaj scooter would sell at double the showroom price. In 1987 when I started my practice, I paid ₹35,000 (a big sum of money 30 years back) as 'on money' to 'buy' a telephone connection.

Income tax laws were complicated; the maximum rate of tax was 97.5%! A doctor who was in maximum tax slab would be taxed ₹9,750 out of ₹10,000 that he would have earned from an operation, leaving ₹250 for him. Tax evasion was the norm.

Since there was a severe shortage of commodities, food grains were distributed through the public distribution system at a subsidised price. Most of the commodities would find their way into the open market to be sold at double the price. Commodities had to be imported to meet the country's requirements, leading to severe foreign exchange shortage.

The worst economic crisis erupted in the 1980s. In 1985 India had balance-of-payments problems as imports swelled, leaving the country in a twin deficit. The Indian trade balance was in deficit at a time when the government was running on a large fiscal deficit. By the end of 1990, in the run-up to the Gulf War, the situation became so serious that the Indian foreign exchange reserves could barely finance three weeks' worth of imports, while the government came close to defaulting on its financial obligations. By July that year, the low reserves had led to a sharp devaluation of the rupee, which exacerbated the twin-deficit problem.

This led the Indian government to airlift national gold reserves as a pledge to a large conditional bailout from the International Monetary Fund (IMF) and World Bank in exchange for a loan to cover balance of payment debts.

The crisis led to the liberalisation of the Indian economy, as this was one condition stipulated in the World Bank loan, requiring India to open itself up to participation from foreign entities in its industries, including state-owned enterprises.

Government took an emergency loan of $2.2 billion from the International Monetary Fund by pledging 67 tons of India's gold reserves as collateral security. The Reserve Bank of India had to airlift 47 t of gold to the Bank of England and 20 t of gold to the Union Bank of Switzerland to raise $600 million. National sentiment was one of outrage, and there was a public outcry when it was learnt that the government had pledged the country's entire gold reserve against the loan. It was later revealed that the van transporting the gold to the airport broke down en route and panic followed. A chartered plane ferried the precious cargo to London between 21 May and 31 May 1991, jolting the country out of an economic slumber. The Chandra Shekhar government collapsed a few months after having allowed the airlift. The move helped tide over the balance-of-payment crisis and kick-started P. V. Narasimha Rao's economic reform process.

P. V. Narasimha Rao took over as prime minister in June and roped in Manmohan Singh as finance minister. Together they ushered in various reforms known as the liberalisation of the economy. Eighteen years after the incident, in 2009, India bought 200 t of gold from IMF, which was three times the amount India pawned to IMF in 1991, proving that the economic reforms had worked wonders.

India has not looked back since then. India is the world's sixth largest economy by nominal GDP and the third largest by purchasing power parity (PPP). After the 1991 economic liberalisation, India achieved 6–7% average GDP growth annually. In FY 2015 and 2018, India's economy became the world's fastest-growing major economy, surpassing China.

The long-term growth perspective of the Indian economy is positive due to its young population, corresponding low dependency ratio, healthy savings and investment rates, and increasing integration into the global economy.

India has one of the fastest-growing service sectors in the world with an annual growth rate above 9% since 2001, which contributes to 57% of the GDP. India has become a major exporter of IT services, business process outsourcing services, and software services with $154 billion revenue in FY 2017. The IT industry continues to be the largest private-sector employer in India. India is the third largest start-up hub in the world. The Indian automobile industry is one of the largest in the world. India is the fastest growing e-commerce market in the world.

On 8 November 2016, Prime Minister Modi caused a major disruption in the economy by demonetising 86% of the currency at that point. It caused chaos, and the economy came to a standstill. Demonetisation dragged the rate of growth down, and the economy suffered for at least two quarters. It is difficult to find out any useful purpose that demonetisation served.

The next landmark change was GST. GST is a comprehensive indirect tax levy on manufacture, sale, and consumption of goods and services. It replaced all indirect taxes such as service tax and VAT levied by different states with a single tax, eliminating the cascading effect of taxes on production and distribution price of goods and services. GST is one of the most important tax reforms to have taken place in post-independence India. However, we are still struggling with the initial glitches and teething troubles. While GST collection is growing as compliance improves, it has not yet come to the break-even level, though it has to move way up the scale.

The weakening of the rupee has in recent times made imports expensive; petroleum prices have hit the roof, and the heat is being felt by all. This may pave the way for electric vehicles and may make the government create the infrastructure for electric vehicles faster. The government may be forced to renew its thrust on public transport and the alternative mode of transports.

The purpose of giving this chequered history of India's development is to show that there have been moments of crisis but the country is resilient enough to not only bounce back but stand taller than before. Every crisis has brought about a new reform. India's history of reforms is through the crisis.

Though one of the fastest-growing economies in the world, we are not without our share of problems. There is a wide disparity between the income of the rich and the poor. The richest 1% of the country's population holds 58% of the total wealth of the country. The concentration of wealth in their hands will continue to increase because as much as three-quarters of total income generated belongs to this 1% of the population; the poorest half of the population saw their income grow by only 1% last year. The major challenge of the government is to ensure a fairer distribution of the cake. But there is a positive side of this too. Wealth is concentrated where it grows fast. That wealth needs to be shared to impact the community, and it becomes the responsibility of those who create it to share the fruits of development with the have-nots.

This sharing may come from taxes they pay, jobs they generate, and the development that their capital can bring about in the economy. The government needs to work with the people with resources so that without disturbing the basic capitalistic model, we can maximise the welfare of the population at large.

India is facing its worst economic crisis. Non-performing assets (NPAs) of the banking sector is high. Most banks are suffering from the consequences of bad loans given in the past. Chanda Kochhar, who was till recently respected as the pioneer of retail banking revolution in India, had to step down on allegations of impropriety and vested interest. Axis Bank and Yes Bank faced the wrath of RBI on account of questionable quality of their assets. LIC had to bail out IDBI Bank. PNB is yet to recover from the aftermath of failed loans given to Nirav Modi and Mehul Choksi. Dena Bank, Vijaya Bank, and Bank of Baroda are being merged to save them from extinction.

India continues to be high on the corruption index; a precondition to improving the quality of life of the citizens is to give them a corruption-free environment. Though we have made considerable progress in 'ease of doing business', we are low on the scale compared to the developed world. Instances of religious intolerance, racism, and atrocities on women and on the weaker section of society continue to put the country to shame.

Should all these deter you from investing? It should not. I look at every such crisis as an opportunity. Every crisis in the country has resulted in measures that have reformed the process and made us strong. India continues to grow from strength to strength. Short-term hiccups will come and disrupt us from the growth trajectory, but only temporarily. The remedial measures will put us back on track with a stronger force. India is one of the best growth stories of our times. Asian tigers have peaked. It is the time for the elephant to dance.

Look at every crisis as an opportunity. GST was a temporary setback. Many companies came out with dismal performance in the aftermath of GST implementation. While speculators sold, investors saw that as an opportunity to buy. When samples of Maggi were found to contain worms, Nestlé shares plummeted by 30%. People thought it was the end of the road for the company. The event made the company improve its products and the government streamline its policy regarding packaged food; the company bounced back in less than a year and is growing stronger.

When the market is writing off the banking sector as bad, it is not distinguishing between good banks and bad banks. It is overreacting to the crisis. Isn't that a great opportunity for you? India will continue to grow in the foreseeable future; it is unstoppable now. Short-term contrary signals will throw an opportunity to buy. Grab them.

Steven Pinker, the author of *Enlightenment Now: The Case for Reason, Science, Humanism, and Progress,* uses statistics to argue that health, prosperity, safety, peace, and happiness are on the rise, both in the West and worldwide. It is a fallacy to think the world is becoming a worse place to live.

A commonly public perception holds that the world is in terrible shape. Pinker argues that life has been getting better for most people. He sets out 15 different measures of human well-being to support this argument, with the most obvious being the uncontroversial fact that people live longer and healthier lives on average than ever before.

Pinker argues that economic inequality 'is not itself a dimension of human well-being' and cites a study that finds inequality is not linked to unhappiness, at least in poorer societies. He also points out that the world is becoming more equal and states that even within unequal areas, the poor are still getting wealth and are enjoying technological innovations. For example, it is clear to Pinker that an innovation that makes the poor slightly richer and the rich massively richer is a positive rather than a negative achievement. In contrast, critics hold that enhancing social mobility and combating 'inequality because of unfairness' are important legitimate ends in and of themselves, beyond any effects of reducing poverty.

It is just that we have become more vocal and more critical of people and politicians. Free speech and social media have given us the power to express every bit of anger and resentment. We broadcast that at the speed of thought thanks to the power of the cell phone, which has made every human being on earth able to connect with the rest of humanity on a real-time basis. Few people would tweet good news. Good news does not carry much news value. Even if someone tweets or posts it, it may not get enough likes or upvotes to make it visible. The ugly, the bad, and the sensational spreads fast, and some unpaid representatives of Facebook and WhatsApp feel duty-bound to 'educate' all their contacts of such happenings.

Remember, the world is becoming a better place, life expectancy is rising, the general standard of living is improving, the world is getting more educated, healthcare was never so good, and India is a part of this improving world. Let sceptics talk crisis. You stay invested.

CHAPTER 28

Top Stock Market Myths

"Never make predictions, especially about the future."

Casey Stengel

The stock market has more than its fair share of myths and misconceptions. People with varied backgrounds enter the market, a few with a clear idea about how the market operates. People who win a lottery ticket or have received a large bequeathal or some windfall head towards Dalal Street to make their money grow further. The fool parts with his money too soon, and he is left with a bitter experience about the market and is ready to spread the market myths. Let us debunk the stock market myths.

1. **You Have to Be a Genius to Make Money on the Stock Market**

    People who lose money on the stock market believe they do not have the requisite level of intelligence to make money. Professional money managers are also happy to spread this myth. Unless you have a PhD in finance and unless you have a training in handling complex mathematical equations, the stock market is not for you, they advice. Your money will grow better with them, they claim.

    This is far from being true. Investment is nothing but common sense. You don't have to be an economist to invest; just being smart enough not to make stupid mistakes will suffice. What investment requires in abundance is discipline, and if you lack that, you fail as an investor. Let me reiterate: you don't have to be a genius to succeed in the stock market. You need the right discipline, the right attitude, and should know how to control your emotions and stay focused on long-term goals.

2. **You Need a Lot of Money to Be in the Market**

    A popular misconception is that the stock market is for rich people and you need a lot of money to enter the market. This myth is responsible for domestic savings not being channelled into the market. The stock market could change the fate of many who can raise their station in life and realise their financial dreams. I hope to see more people from the middle and lower-middle strata of society to invest. This can be a better poverty alleviation programme than the government sponsored plans and can uplift the masses and the economy to a faster growth track.

The stock market could be a panacea to the financial woes of individuals and the economy. I wish every citizen who has a bank account also has a demat account.

One aim of writing this book is to bring home the point that entry to the stock market is easy and cheap. It costs almost nothing to open a trading account. You can buy stocks for as low as ₹500, and you can buy them as and when you have the money.

3. Investing Is a Time-Consuming Process

You have perhaps watched a friend (let's call him Mr Speculator) glued to the screen the whole day, with his blood pressure mimicking the price chart of stocks on his screen. He must have his breakfast before the market opens and cannot have his lunch (perhaps a *vada pav* or a Bombay sandwich since that is what you can eat with one hand while operating the computer with the other) till 3.30 p.m., when the market closes for the day. He seems to be in a war zone, switching stocks on his screens, buying and selling at a frantic pace.

Looking at him, you conclude that the stock market is not your cup of tea and that if the way he does things is what it's like to be in the stock market, then it's better that it is not your cup of tea.

The investment we are advocating is a different world. Mr Speculator buys and sells dozens of scrips in a day; he may buy the same scrip again half an hour after selling it. He may sell something he does not own, intending to square up the transaction before the close of the market.

You as an investor will buy the same number of scrips during your entire lifetime that Mr Speculator buys during a day—maybe 20, 30, or 50 scrips at the max. You don't have to watch the screen or CNBC every day. The less you watch, the better it will be for your financial health. If you can presume that the market has closed down for the next five years after you have made your purchases, you will be better off. Your research (unlike that of Mr Speculator) is a real research and is restricted to the companies you own or the companies on your wish list. It may look boring to an onlooker. True investment is boring and unglamorous. There is more money to be made by inactivity rather than activity.

4. **Pay a Professional Instead of Invest on Your Own**

This is another myth professionals are happy to perpetuate. This whole book is about the DIY way, about doing better than the professionals. It has been proven repeatedly by research and empirical evidence that amateurs beat the professionals in investing. Have the mindset of an investor, and invest on your own. The entry and exit load, administrative expenses, company policies, and limitations on the category and type of investment that a fund can buy makes professional investment too restrictive and less profitable than the systematic amateur investor.

5. **For Higher Returns, You Must Take More Risk**

This comes straight from the economic theories. It sounds rational that the higher rewards will come only if you will take higher risks. This belief propels people into speculation as a quick road to success; on the other end of the spectrum are people who are content with bank deposits because they think investing in equity is risky, and they cannot afford to take risks.

Both extremes are misconstrued. I have explained elsewhere, and let me reiterate, equity is the safest investment class as a long-term investment. The longer you hold it, the safer it becomes. When you hold equity long enough, the risk–reward ratio axis of equity intersects that of bonds (which people presume to be the safest), and beyond that point, equity is safer than bonds. The keyword is *long-term*. Long-term investors are defensive players. The first thing they think of is protecting their capital. They know that rule number 1 is not to lose money.

6. **History Repeats Itself**

People look for patterns; they like to believe past trends will recur. A stock that has risen will fall, and because it has fallen, it will rise again. All these hypotheses are with no basis, and believing them is an exercise in futility. Trends are often nothing more than pseudo correlations.

Even when a trend has a basis, past trends do not guarantee a projected outcome. If a stock rises for three days in a row, it does not mean it will rise on the fourth day too or that since it has risen for three days, it should fall on the fourth day (known in the market as three-day running streak). It is the equivalent of saying that since three consecutive outcomes of throwing a coin has been a head, the fourth one has to be a head again (or the fourth one has to be a tail). The coin has no memory, nor does the market have any.

If it has gone down low, it can't go lower—this is another aspect of this history myth. To explain how fallacious it can be, let us consider Vakrangee Ltd, a software company. On 21 December 2017, the company declared a 1 : 1 bonus. The shares were trading at ₹380; the price rose to a high of ₹515 on 25 January 2018 and fell from the peak. It fell to ₹202 on 7 February 2018 and had a small bounce back. Many investors (technicians, traders, speculators included) would have said, 'It has gone low, it can't go lower.' And there was a fresh interest in the script, taking the price to ₹280 on 20 March. It was an uptrend. Going by the principles of technical analysis, it was a welcome move; however, the rally could not sustain, and it fell again. The current price of Vakrangee stock is ₹22! If you had paid ₹515 on 25 January 2018 to buy a share, your money has vanished, and the price as of November 15 is ₹22. How much lower can it go from here? Well, my answer is, you may lose ₹22 at the max on this share, because share price cannot go below zero.

Consider Kwality Ltd, a food-processing company whose shares fell from ₹160 in March 2017 to ₹7.50 on 15 November 2018 (having the name Kwality does not make it a quality stock). Or consider a stock which was once the darling of all operators in the stock exchange: Suzlon Energy. The company was said to revolutionise power generation and distribution by manufacturing and selling wind turbines and was said to be the largest producer of such turbines in the world. The profits are all gone with the wind, and the present market price is ₹5.70. Crores of rupees of the wealth of investors have vanished into thin air.

I am giving you these examples to caution you against buying on tips, buying without sufficient research, and buying without enquiring into the quality of management. Good companies will come back. Bad companies won't.

If history repeats itself in the stock market, it is randomness. The market does not bother about what the price was yesterday or the day before. The price is determined by the interaction of forces of demand and supply, which are influenced by a host of factors—some rational, some irrational. When the irrational factors outweigh the rational ones, the price moves away from value, though in the long run it comes back to touch the value line often. Do not bother about history repeating or not repeating itself. Buy when there is a favourable mispricing and sell when the price is realised or when the mispricing takes price above the valuations. Or if you have selected the stocks that grow to create an additional margin of safety, you may hold them forever.

7. **Buy Low, Sell High**

This is fantastic advice, easy to understand. But can you apply this in practice? Can you know how low is low and how high is high? As discussed above, no low is low, and it can go further down till it reaches a ridiculously low figure. Trying to catch the bottom of a falling share is like catching a falling knife. A falling knife can quickly rebound in what's known as a whipsaw, or the stock may lose all of its value. Buying low is wishful thinking; it may not happen in practice. If you sell high, the price may go higher, and you may feel the pinch of the 'loss of profit'.

The solution is to buy a quality stock at an attractive price, ignoring the market direction, and to have trust in your investment method. Review the assumptions periodically, and monitor your holdings.

You cannot time the market. There is one exception to this: there are times of gross irrational exuberances when the prices are driven to either dizzying heights or ridiculously low bottoms. That is the time you should sell or buy. Most successful investors remain invested when the crisis falls on the market and sell off substantial holdings and sit on cash when the market reaches a crazy high. This is the exact opposite of what speculators do. They panic and sell at the bottom, and they buy frantically at the top. 'Buy low, sell high' is observed more in its breach.

8. It Has Touched a Lifetime High; It Can't Go Further Up

This misconception does not let people grow rich in the stock market. Shares have unlimited potentials of growth. If you have invested in a company that grows, you have to sit back and relax and watch your company make money for you. The sky is the limit as to how high your stocks can grow.

Let us consider the example of Eicher Motors, the company that makes Eicher trucks and Royal Enfield motorcycles. The following is the price chart of the company on the last day of financial years.

Table 4. Eicher Motors Price Chart

Date	Price
31-03-1996	53.3
31-03-1997	21.5
31-03-1998	13.2
31-03-1999	17
31-03-2000	37.95
31-03-2001	22.1
31-03-2002	70.1
31-03-2003	84.7
31-03-2004	221.3
31-03-2005	315.2
31-03-2006	311.9
31-03-2007	270.75
31-03-2008	275
31-03-2009	205
31-03-2010	800.9
31-03-2011	1247.45
31-03-2012	2283.95

31-03-2013	2958.4
31-03-2014	6201.25
31-03-2015	15191.6
31-03-2016	20035
31-03-2017	26068
31-03-2018	31188.6
31-10-2018	23241.8

If you had bought the 1,000 shares at ₹13.20 in 1998, you would have paid ₹13,200. You would have been tempted to sell it in 2000 at ₹38, making a clean profit of ₹25 per share; 200% profit on your investment in two years is an amazing return. If you've had patience and held on, you would have become disappointed the next year as it fell to ₹22. If you hadn't had the mindset of a long-term investor, you would have sold it in panic for ₹22. Presuming that you were smart enough not to sell, and held on to it, I am sure few would have gone beyond the year 2004, when it was trading at ₹221, 17 times your initial investments in just 6 years.

Let me presume you had read this book back then and knew this company was growing at a spectacular rate and that you needed to stop thinking of exiting this company. If you did that, your share would have touched ₹31,188 per share. Even after the recent market crash, the share trades at ₹23,241. Your ₹13,200 investment 18 years back is now ₹23.24 crores. A whopping 1,76,000% return! Not a bad deal, I must say.

I missed this investment though I was tracking it for so long. But you don't have to regret having missed some multi-baggers. You don't need all multi-baggers in your portfolio. Just a few is enough for you to beat the market. 'You don't have to kiss all the girls,' says Peter Lynch.

My investment of ₹100 per share in CRISIL in 2005 has grown to ₹1,500 (after falling off from ₹2,000). That is 1,500% return in 13 years. Show me any other investment that can give this kind of return. If you have one multi-bagger such as this in your portfolio, it may make good the lower return you might have earned in 10 other stocks.

9. It Is Only ₹4 a Share; It Can't Go Down from Here

New investors who do not understand the nuances of the market feel that since they are beginners with less money to invest, they should buy stocks that are selling cheap so they can buy more shares out of the same money. Human thinking is far from rational. We are happier buying 1,000 shares of a company selling at ₹4 a share rather than buying a solid-growth stock selling at ₹4,000 each. The common thinking is that a ₹4 stock may not fall. It's already too low. But if it rises, it will rise faster compared to a ₹4,000 stock. I have heard investors say many times that 'high-priced' stocks are for institutions and large investors and 'low-priced' stocks are for people like us.

There was a time when this was true to a limited extent. When shares were sold in physical forms, the stock exchange used to specify the minimum order quantity. It was known as the market lot. You had to purchase in the multiple of the market lot. This made some shares beyond the reach of small investors, and they would stick to stocks which were selling cheap. The legacy thinking continues, though there is no market lot any longer and you can now buy just one share. I often buy shares worth ₹1,000 in companies I think could be my potential future investments so I can track them. If you own even one share, you are not likely to lose track of that company. What is out of sight gets out of mind.

It is folly to call a ₹4 stock cheap and a ₹4,000 stock expensive. A stock is cheap or expensive vis-à-vis its value. A ₹4,000 stock may be undervalued; a ₹4 stock may be overvalued. When the market falls, an undervalued ₹4,000 stock is likely to fall less, say 20% or 30%, but a ₹4 stock may come down to zero even when the market is not falling. It may have come down to ₹4 because the company may be heading towards bankruptcy. If it falls, your entire capital gets wiped off. If a stock goes to zero, it does not matter if you bought it for ₹4 or ₹40 or ₹4,000, your loss is exactly same: 100%.

There is another problem with a ₹4 stock, which we have discussed in the chapter of penny stocks. Since this liquidity of such stocks is low, there may not be any buyers when you want to sell them.

I know of investors out there who claim to have made 10,000% profits by buying a stock at ₹3 and selling it at ₹300. What they won't tell you is that one out of 100 stocks rose from ₹3 to ₹300, while most other stocks they own have no buyers.

These shares rise fast and fall faster, and the rise is momentum driven with no change in fundamentals. Our advice is to stay away from them unless you find a margin of safety in them.

10. I Will Sell It When I Break-Even

I have seen this happen to most of us. If I buy something at ₹100 and it falls to ₹70, I wait till it goes back to ₹100 again, and if it goes back to ₹100 and I sell it, I feel I have done a great job. Cognitive psychologists call this phenomenon 'loss version'. If you sell at ₹70, losing ₹30 hurts you more than the happiness that a gain of ₹30 will bring to you. Loss aversion implies that you lose more satisfaction from a ₹100 loss than the satisfaction you get from a ₹100 gain. This irrational behaviour is well documented in behavioural economics.

What should be the right approach? If it falls after you buy it, revisit your notes and the assumptions you relied on for making the buy decision in the first place. Are the assumptions still valid, or have you made a fundamental mistake? Is there a change in circumstances that has led to the fall, something you could not have expected earlier or not known earlier? Is the fall not related to any fundamental factors but to market irrationality?

If a change in fundamentals has eroded the intrinsic value of the stock, causing a permanent loss to its value, it is futile to wait for the price to come back to ₹100. Blame it on luck or whatever and get out of the stock. Stock might never see ₹100 again, and if at all it comes back to that again, it may take so long that the cost to wait may be more than the appreciation. Loss aversion ignores the time value of money. When you sell a stock languishing at ₹70 at ₹100 after six years, you are happy to have broken-even. You don't realise that during the six-year period, if invested the right way, your money would have doubled.

If the fall is for reasons other than the fundamentals of the company and the intrinsic value of the stock is intact, it is time to buy more at ₹70. I follow a golden rule. If a stock has fallen and I am tempted to wait for the break-even price, I put myself to a test: am I willing to buy more at ₹70? If the answer to this is no, I do not want to hold the share for a single day. If the answer to the question is in the affirmative, I will not only hold it but will put all my available money to buy more of the same stock.

Remember an important rule: stock price has no memory; it does not care for who you are and at what price you bought a share. A stock does not know you own it. The stock market has no compassion; it does not care if you took a loan to buy a share at ₹100 and now the price is ₹70. You buy at the prevailing price, and you sell at the prevailing price. The *market* is what the dictionary defines it to be: a place to buy and sell.

11. If It Has Gone Up after I Bought It, I Am Right

This is behavioural economics irrationality, and even professionals fall prey to this myth. If you buy a share and it rises after that, you feel it like a confirmation by the market of your buying decision. If it falls after you buy it, you suspect your own decision. If you are a day trader or a speculator looking for a quick gain, an immediate rise after you buy may be a cause of cheers for you. To an investor who is buying a stock to hold it for ten years, does it matter? Short-term volatility and price fluctuations are not for you; the market might swing in either direction. Remember, it is thanks to volatility and mispricing that you bought that investment. Market price at any point in time results from the equilibrium between the forces of demand and supply. The market does not take into consideration the fact that you had bought 100 shares of a company at ₹100 last month during the trade-off between the forces of demand and supply.

CHAPTER 29

Putting It All Together

"The art of investment has one characteristic that is not generally appreciated. A creditable, if unspectacular, result can be achieved by the lay investor with a minimum of effort and capability; but to improve this easily attainable standard requires much application and more than a trace of wisdom."

Benjamin Graham

How Do I Identify the Companies to Buy?

This book encourages you to do your own research to identify the companies you should invest in. I am sharing here how I do it. It might help you form your own method.

I am clear about my circle of competence. I understand certain industries and do not understand certain industries and business models. I rule the latter out as being out of my domain, however attractive they may look from the reading of their balance sheets. To put it in other words, I do not have the competence to read the financial statements of the companies whose business model I do not understand. I do not buy software companies because I do not understand the complexities of their business. Perhaps I have missed many ten-baggers because I filtered software out. Yes, I missed Wipro and TCS and Infosys; I saw them grow manifold in just a few years, but I avoided Satyam and Infibeam and scores of other companies with 'technology' as their middle name which have been blacklisted by the regulators. As for missing the opportunity in not investing in Wipro and TCS, well, there are many alternatives in sectors I understand. I would be happy making money in the industries I understand and do not repent having missed the bus in industries I do not understand.

When I am evaluating a business, I prefer to stay with the one easy to understand. Instead of buying a company that makes calcium sulphate dihydrate or sodium tetraborate decahydrate sulphur, I would rather buy a company that makes the best biscuits in the country. If I can understand what calcium sulphate dihydrate is used for or the intricacies of that business, I might evaluate that, but until I do that, biscuits is a safe option. I understand human hunger well and also know which company makes better biscuits than others.

While I am keen to study the quality of management, and that is a very important constituent of my investing decisions, I like to look at a business as one that 'any idiot can run'. This is the 'litmus test' of the business and its economic moat. If an idiot can run a business, it has a strong economic moat, because someday some idiot will! It only means that the business model must be simple to understand and that if the present management is no longer running it, it should be such that it can still run.

I look for companies which are debt-free. I have explained earlier that debt may be good for a company, as a certain amount of debt may be used as a leverage to improve the profitability of the company. However, my strict filter removes companies that have a debt beyond basic limits. I look at the figure of interest paid in the profit-and-loss account of the company as a starting point of my analysis, and if I find this figure to be large compared to the net profits of the company, I reject the company outright. Zero debt is the starting point of my investigation into companies that I want to buy.

I do not buy companies that have not made uninterrupted profits for the last ten years. I may miss out on many great start-ups, but as discussed above, there are no regrets on missing out on some companies. The ocean of investment is vast enough, and I would rather play it safe than venture into finding a future winner out of start-ups, many of which would fail.

If institutions do not own a company, I am interested. When a company is owned by institutions, the company already has sufficient visibility. In companies where institutional holding has reached the maximum permissible cap, further institutional investment is not possible. New institutions can buy only when old ones sell. I prefer a company which has either not been noticed by institutions or where the institutional holding is low. If this company performs well, expect more money to come from institutional players, which will make the price appreciate. I am interested in stocks that professional investors have abandoned in the past and would not buy them again. These 'fallen heroes' can deliver great returns when the institutions come back to buy them in the future. Before I invest, I like to investigate into the reasons the shares were sold by the institutions in the first place to find out if it was for a fundamental reason or if it was a momentum-driven move. Comparison between the market price and the intrinsic value is something I never lose sight of.

People prefer to invest in high-growth industries. I look for a profitable company in a low-growth industry. If a company can grow year to year in an industry that is a low-growth, that company must be efficient. The inner strength and efficiency of the company makes it grow despite the sluggish space it operates in. This company is more likely to survive the economic downturn than a growing company in a growth sector. When the industry this company belongs to picks up momentum, this company must become a star performer.

The economic moat is the most important factor to look at, and I do not buy a company that does not have a strong economic moat. The moat should be high, and there must be a method to protect the moat from attack from competitors.

I like to see the trend of holding by company management. This information is available at the stock exchange website. If they are buying and upping their holdings periodically, it is a great factor in favour of investing. Company management are closest to the actual operations. If they buy, that is a great scuttlebutt for you to consider. Though a sale by an insider may be for a wide variety of reasons (a director selling part of his holdings to invest in his own start-up), I consider it to be a normal market sale unless there is a concerted sale by many of the directors, which needs to be looked into.

There are companies where management has near-zero investment. They keep selling their investment when they know the price has gone beyond valuation and continue to draw a salary with no skin in the game. SEBI requires a listed company to have a minimum 25% public holding, but there is no stipulation of the minimum holding by promoters. Companies with zero management stakes are likely to be reckless and speculative in their dealings.

I do not buy companies whose management has pledged a substantial part of their holdings. If the share price should fall for any reason, the lending institution will sell the shares to meet the margin requirements. Forced sale of large management shares will cause the price to crash.

If a company is buying back its own shares, I consider it to be a great positive. The company knows the best use of its money, and if it knows its money cannot be put to a good use within the company, it likes to reward the shareholders by returning money to them by buying out their shares.

If the picture of the president or the CEO of a company is printed on the cover of a leading business magazine and his interview is to be found in many business papers, I am sceptical of that company. If that is the leading company in a leading sector and every analyst is recommending it, it is out of my investment list. If you hear every Tom, Dick, and Harry speak about a stock, the idea has already peaked. It is time to sell it rather than buy. Hot sectors do not remain hot forever; a change in technology make many of them out of favour.

Anyone remember Moser Baer, the biggest manufacturer of CDs in India? The company was trading at ₹313 at its peak price a few years back. CDs meanwhile became obsolete and got replaced by better storage media. The current price of the company is ₹1.20.

Compare this to ITC, the cigarette company, which operates in a tough market segment with negative growth prospects. The company has learnt to diversify and de-risk itself by spreading its wings in different sectors, such as fast-moving consumer goods (comprising food, personal care, apparel, education and stationery products, incense sticks, and safety matches), hotels, paperboards and speciality papers, packaging, agri-business, and information technology. Though the cigarette business contributes over 80% of the profits of the company, 80% of the capital is invested in non-tobacco businesses. If the government policies make cigarette unviable, or in the event the company is required to close down the cigarette business, it has many other activities to fall back on. That most investors think of a cigarette when they think of ITC is an advantage to a long-term investor as the company continues to create value in many other sectors.

I stay away from a company that grows at 50% per annum. In a competitive market we have in present times, it is impossible to maintain that pace over a long time. Projecting long-term value based on such a high growth rate might make you err. If you have bought a stock at a fair value based on a reasonable rate of growth and the company grows at a high rate, that could be a windfall to you. It will create a further margin of safety for you, but keep in mind that such superprofits may not last forever and it will regress to mean soon.

I make full use of the Internet to do my research. Google records everything. It forgets nothing. It deletes nothing. (They delete now, if you go out to delete your personal search history, but it won't delete much. Things remain stored on the World Wide Web forever.) It is a repository recording every footstep of every person who walks this planet in real time, and it records everything that every company does during its lifetime. You may trace everything good or bad about the company done anytime in the past. Google Trends may show you how much a certain product has been searched online. Amazon reviews may give you insight into the customers' minds. There are websites that provide platforms to consumers to air their grievances against companies. A visit to such sites may give you far better clues than any market research can do. And it may give you an edge over professional stock market analysts.

Action Points

If you are looking for glamour, this book cannot help you. We teach how to make money the scientific way.

The value stocks may not give you an immediate payoff. Their growth is incremental, and they grow over a period. If 'Buy today, sell tomorrow' or 'Win all, lose all' is your attitude to investing, you have come to the wrong road. We do not sell lottery tickets here; we explain how to get rich the slow and sure way. This approach is the opposite of a lottery ticket.

I promise loads of money, but it requires a commitment on your part to instil in yourself the discipline and the patience. Read and reread this book till you develop these traits. If you want to read more, you may read the books given in the Selected Bibliography. However, if you do not want to read further, this book is sufficient to guide you in every respect. You may also subscribe (for free) to my blog at www.tsrawal.com/blog, which will help you refresh yourself on the key concepts. Value investing is a philosophy for life. Infinite wealth accrues to those who remain committed to it for life.

We human beings are loss-averse. A loss is more painful than a gain is pleasurable. When you win big and you lose big, you are happy when you win but not as happy as you are sad when you lose. The intelligent investor invests with a margin of safety in a business he understands and waits for the market to discover the mispricing; he does not lose his capital. It makes this approach least stressful. You don't have to check your portfolio when you are trekking in the Himalayas.

Most investors fail because of lack of a benchmark. When they buy, they don't know if they are paying the right price. They end up buying at an exorbitant price since they have no base value to compare their stocks to. Such excesses happen when they sell too. Since they do not have any benchmark price, when the market falls, they sell in panic, often at the worst price. Value investing gives you that benchmark. If you are a mathematical person, you may calculate the intrinsic value. Most investors, however, do not calculate a precise value and are content with the fact that they have a margin of safety in the price they are paying. Either way, you have the benchmark, the value, whether calculated or not, as the guide. You will not buy at a price which is above that, and you will not sell at a price below that. As said before, it is simple but not easy. Develop the attitude of a successful investor explained in this book and meet me after ten years. You will thank me for having changed your life.

Waiting for the stock to shine to its glory is a long and painful journey. Some stocks may languish for so long and may frustrate you. As a new investor, if you are sufficiently diversified, in two to three years, you may reach the tipping point from which there is no looking back. Investors don't have the guidance (such as offered by this book) or patience to stay invested that long. Hence, long-term investors continue to be a in a minority.

Value investors are less, but most of the successful investors are value investors. If you want to succeed in investments, value investing is the only way.

I hope to reach out to many of you through this book and wish to create many successful investors in India. It is the mission I am working on. If you find a struggling investor or a losing investor or anyone you wish should succeed in his life, do him a favour: gift him a copy of this book. He will thank you forever.

Value investing is for everyone, whatever your background. The simple approach is to find stocks that are out of favour by the market or are languishing for some temporary reason or, for whatever reason, have been ignored by the market. We often take a contrarian stand. We are seen buying when others are selling. We are seen buying apples when others are buying oranges. But it is not reckless contrarian buying. We never lose track of the fact that a share is worth buying only if it's being sold below its intrinsic value.

In a world ruled by speculation, unscientific technical analysis, and herd mentality, this is the only method that has worked. You may follow any variant: value or growth investing. No other method of investment has worked consistently, without fail, in all situations.

If there are so few long-term investors, what do others do?

Many of them are news-traders. They have a favourite adage: 'Buy the rumour. Sell the news.' News-traders build a buy position during the period leading to the news. You find a great deal of volatility during this period; the price is constantly affected by the conflicting rumours, often being spread by the interested parties. They use all kinds of data and behavioural studies to predict whether the price will rise or fall on the official news. The news (e.g. quarterly results) is like the examination result to tell you if you have passed or failed.

Some others are the technical traders who swear by the trend. Fundamentals don't matter to them. They just know a trend is a trend is a trend. If the chart says the price will be up tomorrow, they buy it. A majority of them are momentum players.

Then there are some who believe in the efficient market hypothesis. They believe the market is fully priced and reflect the perfect price based on all available information. This is the darling model of academics.

In a market driven by these diverse unscientific forces, the systematic long-term investor always wins. Ample researches and empirical evidences have proved this beyond any doubt. As long as markets continue to be inefficient, success as a long-term value investor is guaranteed. As long as you buy for ₹0.50 something that is worth ₹1, you will increase your chances of success.

Markets are far from rational, and so long as Mr Market remains manic depressive, value investors will continue to beat the market. Markets will remain irrational; mispricing will keep happening. Price and value will regularly diverge.

I belong to that camp of value investing which does not like to find a precise intrinsic value. Three decades of exposure to the world of accounting and finance has made me sceptical of valuation and quantification process. I look for an 'effective valuation', which gives me confidence of the presence of a reasonable to a high margin of safety. I do not want a precise number.

That does not deter me from practising long-term investing. As you gain experience in the method explained in this book, you will develop the mental resources to understand if an investment is cheap compared to its value. Understanding the financial statements and basic ratios explained in this book should be enough to get you going. If you want to study further, reading a book on fundamentals of accounting will help you more than a book on advanced valuation techniques.

This brings us to the point of the circle of competence. Trying to value a business outside your circle of competence may prove dangerous. Do not tread in an area you do not understand. If you try to be an expert in everything, you will be an expert in nothing. Develop specialised knowledge.

If you are eager to buy a stock in a sector you don't understand, expand your knowledge base to bring that industry within your circle of competence. Read, read, read.

Please do not read books that teach you momentum and technical trading. Worst is the investor who tries to blend two divergent investment methods.

Intelligent investing requires patience. Buying great companies is important, but more important is buying them at an attractive price. Because of the presence of too many momentum players, emotions, rumours, and news will continue to drive prices high or low. Like a tiger waiting to pounce upon its prey, you must wait patiently till the opportunity arises. You don't have to swing at every ball. Wait till you have the ball on the sweet spot and hit it hard. Mark my words. Every stock gives you an opportunity to buy it at a fair price if you stay patient.

When you invest for the long run following our method, you will be swimming against the current. You will be a loner. But trust me, you will be the winner. If a stock is recommended a as buy by hundreds of analysts, it is time to sell, not to buy. When hundreds of people are buying it, you might be the last one to buy it before the fall. When hundreds of analysts predict a fall, it may be a time to buy. Buy when there is blood in the market, and you will emerge the winner.

Trust your broker but not his recommendations. Ignore the tips. Ignore the experts on TV. Nobody can decide for you other than yourself. If you do not want to do the hard work, buy the index fund. It will do better than funds managed by experts.

Develop your search method based on key financial ratios. A great deal of data is available at the website of NSE, BSE, and SEBI. Financial websites like the *Economic Times, Moneycontrol.com, LiveMint* are sources of great information. Brokers like Motilal Oswal, ICICIDirect, HDFC securities, Kotak Securities publish research reports on their sites. I like to read those reports to get data about companies. I ignore their recommendations and use my judgement to draw my own conclusions. Make Google your friend. Spend a few minutes learning the syntax to get the right information from Google search.

Review your judgements periodically. Find out if your assumptions are still valid. If they have ceased to be valid, does it call for action?

Do not time the market. Every time is a great time to buy if you find a mismatch between value and price. Market timing does not work for anyone. It won't work for you.

Before you buy an investment, make a list of the factors you have considered arriving at your decision. This will serve two purposes. First, it will free your memory of the clutter of excessive information. Second, it will act as a reference point for you to come back to when reviewing your investment decision in the future.

Make boring your friend. People like speculation; they love the stocks that steal the limelight. They like the winners. As I write this, I find every analyst recommending Page Industries, the makers of Jockey inner wear and garments. Tune to any business channel or read any analysis report, and you'll find a buy recommendations of the stock, which is trading at a P/E ratio of 76, and a price-to-book-value ratio of 35. Unless I am an industry insider (remember circle of competence), I know this is not the time to buy this scrip. Look for quality stocks not on the radar of analysts. Look for trouble: labour unrest, litigations, demand–supply mismatch, companies affected by crude oil price surge, companies struggling to migrate to the GST regime, mergers, spin-offs, and all the boring situations that others are not interested in tracking. Look for companies that have gone down because sectoral sentiments are down. Recent meltdown in banks and non-banking financial companies has pulled every finance company, good or bad, down. Don't you see an opportunity there? Sectoral sentiments is an excellent place to search for contrarian stocks.

If you buy a stock based on its growth, keep in mind that if a company is sprinting at a high pace, the pace may not sustain forever. The future rate of growth will depend upon the strength of the franchise. If the economic moat is not strong enough, competition will kill the growth rate, and you will see a regression to the means. Buy future growth with caution. Be conservative in valuation.

Diversify, but do not diworsify. Underdiversification means higher risk; overdiversification leads to the lowering of overall profitability. Decide to what extent you should diversify. My preference is about 20 securities. You may decide your own. The rule is, if you have a strong understanding of the companies you buy, less diversification will give higher profitability. Decide your scale from 5 to 50. Below five makes it risky for all investors, and if you diversify beyond 50, you will be better off buying the index fund.

Have a defined default investment strategy in place. Write your default strategy based on the parameters we discussed in this book. Include identification and selection criteria, risk management, review process, and valuation criteria in your investment strategy. Treat yourself as the owner of the business even if you are buying only 1 ₹500 share out of the total capitalisation of ₹5,000 crores.

AFTERWORD

This is my dream project. During my long career in finance, one universal feature I have discerned among most people is the lack of financial intelligence. You may shine in your line of work and make it big, yet unless you are good in the art of saving and investing your money, you are likely to dissipate the resources of your hard-earned labour. Managing money is more challenging than making money. Challenging, not in terms of IQ but of the psyche, the patience, and the discipline that makes you a successful investor.

In a world full of speculators and day traders, finding a true mentor is difficult. I count on this book to mentor you to your road to successful investing. I have seen the magic of compounding work for people who adopted the approach offered in this book, and it has generated astonishing wealth for them.

I wish a mass investment revolution to take place in India. I am committed to that mission. Stock market investing is a perfect means to channel domestic savings into the production channel. It creates as much wealth for the economy as it does for the investor.

You may follow my blog at www.tsrawal.com/blog, where I will continue to educate you. You may follow me on social media. Just search for my name and connect. If you ask me questions that concern investors in general, I will be happy to answer them.

Happy investing!

SELECT BIBLIOGRAPHY

I have benefited by reading classic books on investing, and my investing philosophy has been formed by these books I've read over the years. I have taken from these books what works for me as an Indian long-term investor.

Extraordinary Popular Delusions and the Madness of Crowds (1841) by Charles Mackay

First published in 1841, *Extraordinary Popular Delusions and the Madness of Crowds* is often cited as the best book ever written about market psychology. It includes Charles Mackay's account of the three infamous financial manias: John Law's Mississippi scheme, the South Sea Bubble, and Tulipomania.

For modern-day investors still reeling from the dot-com crash, the moral of the popular manias scarcely needs spelling out. When the next stock market bubble comes along, as it will, you are advised to recall the plight of some unfortunates on these pages and avoid getting dragged under the wheels of the careering bandwagon yourself.

The Intelligent Investor (1949) by Benjamin Graham

Benjamin Graham is the father of value investing. Two of his books, *Security Analysis* and *The Intelligent Investor*, are the most important source materials for anyone interested in learning value investing. The greatest tribute to *The Intelligent Investor* comes from Warren Buffett: 'By far the best book on investing ever written.'

The greatest investment adviser of the twentieth century, Benjamin Graham, taught and inspired people worldwide. Graham's philosophy of value investing has made *The Intelligent Investor* the stock market bible ever since its original publication in 1949.

Common Stocks and Uncommon Profits (1958) by Philip Fisher

Widely respected and admired, Philip Fisher is among the most influential investors of all time. His investment philosophies, introduced almost forty years ago, are not only studied and applied by today's financiers and investors but are also regarded by many as gospel. Warren Buffett describes his own investing style as 85% Benjamin Graham and 15% Phil Fisher. Before I read Fisher, I was unambiguous about how long *long term* means. A great book.

A Random Walk Down Wall Street (1973) by Burton G. Malkiel

With its life cycle guide to investing, *A Random Walk Down Wall Street* matches the needs of investors at any age bracket. Burton G. Malkiel shows how to analyse the potential returns not only for stocks and bonds but also for the full range of investment opportunities, from money market accounts and real estate investment trusts to insurance, home ownership, and tangible assets, like gold and collectibles.

Competitive Advantage: Creating and Sustaining Superior Performance (1985) by Michael E. Porter

Competitive Advantage introduces a whole new way of understanding what a firm does. Porter's groundbreaking concept of the value chain disaggregates a company into 'activities', or the discrete functions or processes that represent the elemental building blocks of competitive advantage.

Now an essential part of international business thinking, *Competitive Advantage* takes strategy from broad vision to an internally consistent configuration of activities. Its powerful framework provides the tools to understand the drivers of cost and a company's relative cost position. Porter's value chain enables managers to isolate the underlying sources of buyer value that will command a premium price and the reasons why one product or service substitutes for another. He shows how competitive advantage lies not only in activities themselves but in the way activities relate to each other, to supplier activities, and to customer activities. *Competitive Advantage* also provides for the first time the tools to strategically segment an industry and rigorously assess the competitive logic of diversification.

One Up on Wall Street (1989) and *Beating the Street* (1994) by Peter Lynch

Legendary money manager Peter Lynch explains his own strategies for investing and offers advice for how to pick stocks and mutual funds to assemble a successful investment portfolio.

An important key to investing, Lynch says, is to remember that stocks are not lottery tickets. There's a company behind every stock and a reason companies—and their stocks—perform the way they do. In this book, Peter Lynch shows you how you can become an expert in a company and how you can build a profitable investment portfolio based on your own experience and insights and on straightforward do-it-yourself research.

In *Beating the Street,* Lynch for the first time explains how to devise a mutual fund strategy, shows his step-by-step strategies for picking stock, and describes how the individual investor can improve his or her investment performance to rival that of experts.

There's no reason the individual investor can't match wits with the experts, and this book will show you how.

Margin of Safety: Risk-Averse Value Investing Strategies for the Thoughtful Investor (1991) by Seth A. Klarman

Taking its title from Benjamin Graham's often-repeated admonition to invest always with a margin of safety, Klarman's *Margin of Safety* explains the philosophy of value investing and perhaps the logic behind it, showing why it succeeds while other approaches fail. The blueprint that Klarman offers, if followed, offers the investor the strong possibility of investment success with limited risk.

Margin of Safety shows you not just how to invest but how to think about investing—to understand the rationale behind the rules to appreciate why they work when they work and why they don't when they don't.

Stocks for the Long Run (1994) by Jeremy Siegel

This book provides a portrait of the stock market with the strategies, tools, and techniques investors need to maintain their focus and achieve meaningful stock returns over time. Siegel draws on extensive research over the past two centuries to argue not only that equities surpass all other financial assets in returns but also that stock returns are safer and more predictable in the face of the effects of inflation.

The New Buffettology: The Proven Techniques for Investing Successfully in Changing Markets That Have Made Warren Buffett the World's Most Famous Investor (1997) by Mary Buffett, David Clark

The New Buffettology is the first guide to Warren Buffett's selective contrarian investment strategy for exploiting down stocks—a strategy that has made him the nation's second richest person. Designed to teach investors how to decipher and use financial information the way Buffett himself does, this book guides investors through opportunity-rich bear markets, walking them step by step through the equations and formulae Buffett uses to determine what to buy, what to sell, and when. Authors Mary Buffett and David Clark explore Buffett's recent investments, proving repeatedly that his strategy has earned enormous profits at a time no one expects them to—and with almost zero risk to his capital.

The Warren Buffett Way: Investment Strategies of the World's Greatest Investor (1997) by Robert G. Hagstrom, Peter S. Lynch

The Warren Buffett Way offers investors their first in-depth look at the innovative investment and business strategies behind the spectacular success of the living legend Warren E. Buffett. Tracing Warren Buffett's career from the beginning, Robert G. Hagstrom Jr. tells us how, starting with an initial investment of only $100, Buffett built a business empire worth $19.4 billion. It offers a close-up look at Buffett's successful investment theories and strategies and identifies the businesses Buffett now finds most attractive (and which ones he avoids) based on the author's ten-year monitoring of Buffett's numerous shrewd investments and ventures.

The Essays of Warren Buffett: Lessons for Corporate America (2001) by Warren Buffett and Lawrence Cunningham

The definitive work concerning Warren Buffett and intelligent investment philosophy, this is a collection of Buffett's letters to the shareholders of Berkshire Hathaway written over the past few decades that together furnish a valuable informal education. The letters distil in plain words all the basic principles of sound business practices.

The Motley Fool Investment Guide: How the Fool Beats Wall Street's Wise Men and How You Can Too (2001) by David Gardner, Tom Gardner

The Motley Fool Investment Guide, with clear and witty explanations, deciphers all the new information, from evaluating individual stocks to creating a diverse investment portfolio.

The Little Book of Common Sense Investing: The Only Way to Guarantee Your Fair Share of Stock Market Returns (2007) by John C. Bogle

Filled with in-depth insights and practical advice, *The Little Book of Common Sense Investing* shows how to incorporate proven investment strategy into your portfolio. It will also change the way you think about investing. Successful investing is not easy. (It requires discipline and patience.) But it is simple, for it's all about common sense.

The Art of Value Investing: How the World's Best Investors Beat the Market (2013) by John Heins, Whitney Tilson

Based on interviews with the world's most successful value investors, *The Art of Value Investing*, by John Heins and Whitney Tilson, offers a comprehensive set of answers to the questions every equity money manager should have thought through before holding himself or herself out as a worthy steward of other people's money. What market inefficiencies will I try to exploit? How will I generate ideas? What will be my geographic focus? What analytical edge will I hope to have? What valuation methodologies will I use? What time horizon will I typically employ? How many stocks will I own? How specifically will I decide to buy or sell? Will I hedge, and how? How will I keep my emotions from getting the best of me?

The authors interview many experts—including Julian Robertson, Seth Klarman, Leon Cooperman, David Einhorn, Bill Ackman, Joel Greenblatt, Marty Whitman, Mason Hawkins, Jean-Marie Eveillard, Bill Nygren, and Bruce Berkowitz—to answer these questions.

The Education of a Value Investor: My Transformative Quest for Wealth, Wisdom, and Enlightenment **(2014) by Guy Spier**

What happens when a young Wall Street investment banker spends a small fortune to have lunch with Warren Buffett? He becomes a real value investor. In this fascinating inside story, Guy Spier details his career from Harvard MBA to a value investor. Along the way, he learnt some powerful lessons, which include: why the right mentors and partners are critical to long-term success on Wall Street, why top-notch education can sometimes impede your success, that real learning doesn't begin until you are on your own, and how the best lessons from Warren Buffett have less to do with investing and more to do with being true to yourself.

Warren Buffett's Ground Rules: Words of Wisdom from the Partnership Letters of the World's Greatest Investor **(2016) by Jeremy C. Miller**

Using the letters Warren Buffett wrote to his partners between 1956 and 1970, a veteran financial adviser presents the renowned guru's ground rules for investing—guidelines that remain relevant today.

The letters spotlight Buffett's contrarian diversification strategy, his almost religious celebration of compounding interest, his preference for conservative rather than conventional decision-making, and his goal and tactics for bettering market results by at least 10% annually. Showing Buffett's intellectual rigour, they provide a framework to the craft of investing that had not existed before: Buffett built upon the quantitative contributions made by his famous teacher, Benjamin Graham, showing how they could be applied and improved.

Tao of Charlie Munger: A Compilation of Quotes from Berkshire Hathaway's Vice Chairman on Life, Business, and the Pursuit of Wealth (2017) **by David Clark**

This book contains words of wisdom from Charlie Munger—Warren Buffett's long-time business partner and the visionary vice chairman of Berkshire Hathaway—collected and interpreted with an eye towards investing by David Clark, co-author of the best-selling Buffettology series.

This collection—culled from interviews, speeches, and questions and answers at the Berkshire Hathaway and Wesco annual meetings—offers insights into Munger's amazing financial success and life philosophies.

Enlightenment Now: The Case for Reason, Science, Humanism, and Progress (2018) **by Steven Pinker**

In seventy-five graphs, Pinker shows that life, health, prosperity, safety, peace, knowledge, and happiness are on the rise, not just in the West, but worldwide. This progress is not the result of some cosmic force. It is a gift of the Enlightenment: the conviction that reason and science can enhance human flourishing.

Far from being a naive hope, the Enlightenment, we now know, has worked. But more than ever, it needs a vigorous defence. *Enlightenment Now* makes the case for reason, science, and humanism: the ideals we need to confront our problems and continue our progress.

<<<<>>>>

www.ingramcontent.com/pod-product-compliance
Lightning Source LLC
Chambersburg PA
CBHW020726180526
45163CB00001B/119